THE SEMEN BOOK

D1478344

The Semen Book

Vivien Marx

FREE ASSOCIATION BOOKS / LONDON / NEW YORK

First published 2001 by
FREE ASSOCIATION BOOKS
57 Warren Street
London W1T 5NR

Copyright © Vivien Marx 2001

ISBN 1 85343 501 5 pbk

A CIP catalogue record for this book is available from the British Library

10	09	08	07	06	05	04	03	02	01
10	9	8	7	6	5	4	3	2	1

Designed and produced for Free Association Books Ltd by
Chase Publishing Services, Fortescue, Sidmouth EX10 9QG
Printed in the European Union by WS Bookwell, Finland

Dedicated to men and the women who share life,
love or friendship with them.

Contents

Acknowledgments

Size matters. When writing a book. And so thanks are in order when dealing with a project of these dimensions. First and foremost I would like to thank the men who answered my questions on the phone, in chats, via e-mail or in personal conversation in a patient and honest fashion. To protect their privacy, I have only used first names, sometimes changed at their request.

Without the help and insight of many experts, my quest would have gone nowhere. In particular I would like to thank Dr. Lisa Tenover, Dr. Marie-Claire Orgebin-Crist, Dr. Arnold Belker, Dr. Roger Short, Prof. Eberhard Nieschlag, Dr. Geoffrey Waites, Dr. Alvin Paulsen, Dr. Larry Johnson, Dr. Barry Hinton, Dr. Richard Clark, Dr. Roman Pryzak, Dr. Gladys Friedler, Dr. Sheldon Segal, Dr. Luigi Mastroianni, Dr. Paul F.A. Van Look, Dr. Jon Pryor, Dr. David Karabinus, Dr. Deborah Anderson, Dr. David Page, Gerald Schatten, Dr. Ron Weber, Dr. Kathy Ensrud, Uschi Radermacher, Dr. Steve Rozen, Dr. Haydar Karatepe, Dr. Dirk Propping, Dr. E. Genis, Dirk Hetzel, Dr. Andreas Zober, Dr. Fritz Schuckmann, Prof. Walter Krause and Dr. Carrie Marin Bevins.

I would like to thank the MIT Knight Science Journalism Fellowships for permitting a rewarding and productive stay at MIT – Boyce Rensberger, Victor McElheny and the selection committee, the Knight Foundation and the MIT Science, Technology and Society program, the ever thoughtful Martha Henry, Trish Fleming, Helen Samuels and Ann Chaney as well as my co-Fellows and of course, Carol, the ever-cheerful librarian in Barker Library. Thanks also to the Science Writing Fellowship Program at the Marine Biological Laboratory in Woods Hole; Pam Clapp-Hinkle, Dr. Bob Goldman, Dr. Rex Chisholm, Dr. Bob Palazzo and their great staff, as well as the students, faculty and staff of the MBL Frontiers in Reproduction and Embryology courses in the year 2000. Thanks also to the Society for the Study of Reproduction and the American Society of Andrology. Thank you, Writers' Room of Boston, for advice, interest and for offering a place for the words to settle.

And then there is a committee of people who gave me the personal strength, support and encouragement to complete a book on a seemingly odd topic. I am indebted to them, particularly: Albert, Thomas, Ina, Detlev, Graham, Lynne, Heiner, Gisela, Regula, Arlene, Roger, Naomi, Barry, and Zoë, who never doubted.

Introduction

A good man is hard to find.
A hard man is good to find.

In the Age of Viagra, this women's bathroom wall scribble seems totally outdated. If a man feels like having sex, his body agrees and he finds a consenting partner, the case is settled. If a man feels like sex but his body does not agree, yet he has a consenting partner, he pops a blue pill and then again, usually, the case is settled. End of story. So men have a choice. Until now, choice for many men may have involved choosing between strawberry- and chocolate-flavored condoms. But Viagra is not just any recreational choice. It is a choice of medication. And there are more selections coming around the corner; drugs, accessories and sexual performance enhancers of many kinds. Before quickly embracing any such products, a moment of thought may be worthwhile. The body deserves as much respect as a beloved four-wheel drive. You don't just pour any substance into the tank of your SUV.

Pull it out, jack it up, hammer it in – from a superficial engineering vantage point, the male body and the male genitalia in particular are no longer a riddle. The mechanics, tension, pressure, friction and lubrication issues are manageable. But you can't really tweak a system if you do not understand it well. Real engineers like to know how their gadgets and machines work. Oddly enough, myths, legends and outright ignorance seem to have very long lives when it comes down to thinking about the hows and whys of making men come. Locker rooms still harbor amazing legends about many aspects of sex. "Masturbation will make your hand fall off or make your babies deformed," or "The liquid coming out of your penis is bone marrow" are statements boys and men have heard and continue to hear.

"I have two girlfriends," began one man. "And what I would like to know is, will I be running out of semen at some point?" It was a succinct question about a biological aspect of his lovelife. When I embarked on the research for this book talking with medical experts around the world, they confirmed that this quantitative worry is indeed very common among men. The experts have a clear answer. As long as the testicles and other male organs, like the prostate gland, are healthy, any man – including the aforementioned man with the hectic lovelife – will be able to spend his semen with two or more women without endangering his health.

Former US President Bill Clinton's affair with Monica Lewinsky certainly brought semen onto dresses and into the news. But instead of benefiting a bit from the limelight, semen dropped right off center stage and scads of misinformation about this male bodily fluid seem to remain. The science of the male reproductive system is a field not well established in medicine, science or in the public consciousness.

Try asking for the men's health section in a public library – it just may not even exist. Ask for the andrology section at the bookstore of a reputable medical school and the response may well be blank stares. Only in the last 10–15 years have researchers begun to study the male in earnest. And the field is still almost hidden from sight.

Doctors in the US and around the world state that their male patients – whether they come in for a general check-up or for more particular reasons – are appallingly unfamiliar with their bodies. What is known is that if placed at the right time and in the right place, semen can lead to pregnancy. In some cases it can transmit AIDS. So it seems apparent that if you choose to avoid a pregnancy or seek to avoid an HIV infection, you shield your mucous membranes. Often, that is where the semen and sperm story ends. But that is just a small part of it all. Few men ask their doctor, or father for that matter, what the penis spurts. It is, for most, some liquid of unknown origin that flows more freely at some times than at others.

When not in use nor endangered by a soccer ball or other low-flying objects, the penis is not exactly at the center of public attention. The approximately 50 men I interviewed often used engineering terms when talking about their private parts and had a rather matter-of-fact attitude towards their genitalia. In the course of conversation, it seemed that despite plenty of Viagra hype, there were many questions on their minds but no one to talk to. Somehow male sexual health seems to get the short end of the stick.

Unlike gynecology, the science of the male, andrology, is a young discipline and is currently generating some amazing new insights as well as many new and puzzling questions. This book summarizes some of the newest research in this field – evolutionary biology of sex; wellness and sperm quality; fertility; potency and contraception; molecular biology of the most manly of chromosomes, the Y; penis and testes well-being; genitals and the world of sports; the zoology of male-ness, and offers some practical details on what happens when you let your trousers down for an exam in the doctor's office. The information is framed to be practical and helpful and not just a summary of pure, dry science. Male sexual physiology may well be a kind of rocket science, but dry it is not.

This knowledge can be entertaining and useful by allowing you to enhance the way you use God's gifts to man in more ways than you perhaps previously thought. And if there should come a time when serious issues call for a doctor's appointment, you will approach that situation with fewer basic questions and can cut to the chase faster. Experts estimate that in at least 40–50% of cases of involuntarily childless couples it is the man who is infertile. There are researchers who predict a rapid increase in male infertility. In virtual forums on the Web as well as brick and mortar neighborhoods it seems as if so many people are TTC, or trying to conceive. Men in these situations will want to face medical exams knowledgeably and courageously. Knowing more means getting puzzled less.

Looking at the scientific literature it becomes apparent that pretty much everything a man eats, drinks, smokes, or ingests may well affect his semen and much of what he does can impact on potency. In addition, in recent years, some scientific studies conclude that environmental factors may have a troubling effect. The tabloid press sometimes calls it "eco-castration", an alarmist term. Some chemicals definitely have an impact on sperm quality, and no man can really afford to ignore these types of below-the-belt impacts.

Of course you may want to keep this knowledge to yourself and be stronger for it. But amusing, odd or informative factoids can also always be shared with a willing partner, particularly in these days of tobacco-less afterglow-talk when deciding who gets to sleep on the wet spot.

1 The Physiology of Orgasm

There was a young man of Kent
Whose kirp in the middle was bent.
To save himself trouble
He put it in double,
And instead of coming, he went.

(Limerick found in a medical textbook.)

Orgasm and Ejaculation

"Jerk it off", "milk it", "spank the monkey", "shoot a load" – slang diction-aries contain a bounty of words and phrases for male orgasm and its sidekick, ejaculation. As one man states in the Hite Report, "During orgasm, I lose control totally. It starts from my toes like a tidal wave until I ejaculate."

"Incredible." "Pure bliss." "The greatest invention." "It absolutely blows my mind." This is the way some men describe the feeling that accompanies ejaculation. Pretty clever of Mother Nature to invent something so sweet in order to achieve her goal of propelling sperm out into the world to find a nice egg to fertilize. Although some women ejaculate, male and female physiolo-gies are so vastly different, it is hard and perhaps misleading to compare the male and female orgasm. They are in classes of their own. This book will mainly be about men but will certainly include aspects about women when the context is right. In speaking to men and both male and female experts, I certainly got the impression that male orgasm is less talked about than the female counterpart.

In 1979, anthropologist Donald Symons wrote: "Unlike the unicorn, which is specially interesting precisely because it does not exist, or extrasensory perception, which probably does not exist but is interesting because of the possibility that it might, or the male orgasm, which exists with monotonous regularity and for the most part is interesting only to the people directly involved in one, the female orgasm definitely exists and yet inspires interest, debate, polemics, ideology, technical manuals, and scientific and popular literature solely because it is so often absent." Then along came Viagra and, thanks to people like Bob Dole, all of a sudden the supposedly uninteresting male orgasm became a popular topic of discussion. In restaurants, on park benches and in that ultimate democratic forum, the lines at the Registry of Motor Vehicles, it became OK and fun to talk about erection.

When Viagra hit the market in April of 1998 it also became evident that male orgasm was not exactly occurring in as regular a rhythm as one may assume or as was desired. An estimated 30 million men in the US suffer from some form of impotence or – in medicalese – erectile dysfunction. And all the guffawing jokes surrounding the blue pill seem to indicate that erection and the male orgasm are not exactly Symons' monotonous, natural occurrences.

They certainly are not completely understood – not by a long shot. Andrologists, medical and biology specialists in all things male, who work in a young research field still struggling for recognition can attest to that. They focus their attention on the testes, the prostate, the penis and the man attached to theses specialized and fascinating organs. They know the few answered questions surrounding male sexual physiology and are intrigued by the many that remain unanswered.

For example, why does each ejaculate contain 300 million sperm? There is no consensus on the answer.

Even though Viagra has given the penis and its favorite pastime a shot at the limelight, the sizeable progress in this field to date is not exactly the subject of public debate. Whether or not Viagra will "free the American male libido in the same way the Pill did," as *Penthouse* publisher Bob Guccione puts it, remains to be seen. The contraceptive pill was certainly not the last word on pregnancy or sexual liberation. The V-word has propelled the penis into the news but has not has not really managed to keep it there. As the *New England Journal of Medicine* stated in an editorial, "Among the components of sexual function and satisfaction in men – desire, erectile function, orgasmic function, ejaculation, and fertility – decreased erectile function is not only the most common but also the most distressing and threatening." According to Lisa Tenover, an andrologist at the Wesley Woods Hospital and Emory University as well as President of the American Society of Andrology, "Viagra has made an impact on the issue of men acknowledging the problem of sexual dysfunction." But she and many other colleagues say it is no cure-all and certainly not the answer to every question.

Many intriguing findings, fierce debates, pointed disagreements and complex puzzles surrounding male sexual physiology populate specialist journals and conferences that all have much relevance for health and sexual well-being. Oddly, this knowledge does not seem to trickle down to where it could be pretty useful – everyday life. According to urologist Dudley Seth Danoff, the genitals and male sexuality in general are still taboo subjects, and "the penis remains closeted behind a curtain of prudishness." Why on earth keep such an intriguing member of society in a closet? This is not just some kind of theoretical, political-socio-economic musing on the role of the penis in society. There is a pretty sensible medical reason for this question. Doctors across the US, in Japan, in Denmark or Germany all tell the same sad tale: when men come to see them for advice, in the vast majority of cases the men have little clue as to how their bodies work. This global pattern piqued my interest and I set out to discover some of what there is to know.

Coming

A 23-year-old man sees no point to my questions: "What is there to say about it, I just simply come." "Man, sex is one of my favorite subjects," a 27-year-old man tells me. "Coming is a big deal but I don't talk about it much," he continued. In an answer to sex researcher Shere Hite, one man wrote: "I love the feel of my cream splashing all over my body, or shooting on the floor, wall, blankets, etc.". Many women I interviewed stated that their boyfriends and husbands enjoyed talking about sex very much but skirted ejaculation. Experts have quite a bit to say on the subject. As sex researcher Alfred Kinsey wrote, "There is only one other phenomenon, namely sneezing, which is physiologically close in its summation and explosive discharge of tension. Sneezing is, however a localized event, while sexual orgasm involves the whole of the reacting body."

Orgasms only last a few seconds and beside the head trip, the feeling gyrates throughout the genitals and other parts of the body. During orgasm and ejaculation there are many coinciding events that are hard to separate from one another. If you do want to go into sexual overtime in any way, knowing the various phases which can be influenced in different ways can be helpful.

In sexual situations erections are all in a man's head. A thought, a touch or a particular sight stimulates the nervous system, and blood flow to the penis increases and stays there. During an erection, blood flow is six to ten times the normal state of affairs. The penis, or more precisely the three cylindrical pillars of erectile tissue, two called corpus cavernosa and one called corpus spongiosum, become engorged with blood. At night this happens repeatedly – anywhere from one to five times while the penis' owner is asleep. As Irwin Goldstein, a Boston University urologist, points out, these nocturnal events are "battery-recharging mechanisms" for the penis, bringing in blood flow and thus oxygen which re-energizes the organ. The morning erection is possibly a remnant of last night's battery recharge. "I'd rather have a hard-on than be hard-up," reads one bumper sticker on the car in front of me on the highway. That makes more sense than a lot of other things you see on the highway.

Erection Control

A morning erection can be even more puzzling than the quiz on the back of the cereal box. There is no way to judge a penis by his looks. An erection may have erotic intent, or may not. Basing sexual activity on a morning erection, however, may lead to disappointment. Erections not based on erotic stimulation – like the morning erection – can disappear faster than you can say "corpus cavernosum".

Erection and ejaculation result from the interaction of the psyche along with nerves, hormones and blood vessels. As in sports, there is indeed a difference between wanting to do something and being able to do it. Even if a man concentrates on his pelvic muscles and his penis, even if he is one of the most influential politicians or venture capitalists on the planet, the penis cannot be forced or willed to adhere to orders because the nerves involved belong to the autonomic nervous system. According to George Benson, a urologist at the University of Texas Medical School at Houston, "The innervation of the penis and its vasculature is complex and controversial."

"Sometimes erections happen definitely at the wrong time," says Michael, 32. "At the beach I sure wish I had my dick under control. Women have an easier time to hide it when they are turned on." Sex therapist Bernie Zilbergeld points out that men often have erections when sex is not first and foremost in their thoughts. "Teenage boys for example have erections in class," he writes, "when they are trying to concentrate on the classroom material, and on many other occasions. I played football in high school and invariably had an erection when 'The Star Spangled Banner' was played before each game. Did that mean that I wanted to make love to the flag, to someone in the band, to one of the cheerleaders? I guarantee that sex was farthest from my mind at the time."

Erection Mechanics

In a flaccid penis, however contradictory it may sound, the muscles surrounding the blood vessels are contracted and blood flow to the penis is at a basic low. For an erection, pelvic nerves send impulses which relax the muscles around the blood vessels, the arteries dilate and blood can flow to the penis at a higher rate than normal, where it lingers for a while letting the penis grow to the tumescent sizes dreams are made of. But the elasticity is not endless. "Infinite elasticity," states andrologist Abraham Morgentaler, "would result in enormous penises that would be completely useless. It is the limited stretch of the sheath around the corpora that confirs rigidity to the penis."

Researchers have found different types of erections for which different parts of the spinal cord set the tone. Reflexogenic erections result from direct genital stimulation which sends signals to the "erection-generating center" of the spinal cord and can occur even after certain types of spinal cord injuries. As Irwin Goldstein points out, doctors used to think spinal cord injuries always led to impotence, a "mistaken view." When the brain is essentially not directly connected to this point on the spinal cord, erections can occur more frequently. Psychogenic erections due to a stimulating thought or a picture, hit the erection center of the spinal cord in a different way, via the brain. Nocturnal erections and emissions are, as one respected andrologist honestly admits, "not thoroughly understood." There are usually three to five erection events – each one about 20–30 minutes long – which occur during the so-called rapid eye movement (REM) phase of sleep.

During waking hours, if sexual arousal is maintained, blood flows to the penis, muscle tension in the arms and legs increases, blood pressure rises, breathing quickens, the skin of the scrotal sack thickens and contracts, the testes increase in size – in some cases up to 50% – and they move upward. As sex play continues, muscle tension continues and so does penis rigidity as blood flow to the penis reaches a maximum level. Erection is not caused by muscles – it is entirely a blood flow event.

As sexual excitement continues, a milky fluid oozes from the bulborethral glands and lubricates the urethra to reduce friction when the semen passes through. If this is orgasm number one of that night, this fluid will most probably not contain sperm. If it is one of the next orgasms down the line, then sperm may very well be in it – an important fact if you are keen on contraception. And if a man is HIV positive, recent studies have revealed that HIV can also be found in this 'pre-cum'.

Ejaculation itself encompasses a number of almost simultaneous steps. Nerves running to the testes, the vas deferens, ductus deferens, the epididymes, the prostate and the seminal vesicles produce rhythmic muscular contractions. The contractions in the "bridge of sighs", as one sex handbook calls the pelvic muscles between the scrotum and the anus, take center stage. Other players are the muscles of the colon and the urethra. "Ejaculation is a total-body response, not just something that happens to the crotch," writes Bernie Zilbergeld. Muscular contractions and spasms may occur in the legs, stomach, arms and back. E.J. Haeberle, a German sex researcher, notes: "This experience creates the most intense physical pleasure that humans are capable of."

During ejaculation, the bladder neck closes and semen and its precious cargo, sperm, is sent on its way. Semen is spurted into the urethra deep inside the prostate. This partially contributes to the pleasure in male orgasm, especially after a phase of abstinence when there is a bit more semen. "Pressure seems to build up like in a pressure cooker but it's a nice kind of pressure," describes 34-year-old Stefan. Sperm cover a long distance in a very short time – from the epididymis to the ejaculatory duct in front of the bladder which leads to the urethra. "It is like a marathon in two to five seconds," comments andrologist Abraham Morgentaler.

Shortly prior to orgasm, a man's movements become more uncontrolled and rapid. During the climax itself, as the Danish physician Frede Bro-Rasmussen describes it, "one can observe heavy sweating and sometimes various sounds and grunts." The lust accompanying the grunts is often centered on and around the penis, the testicles and the prostate. During sexual stimulation there is a point of no return for men. Let the cell phone ring its little head off, the baby can squeal and squeal, the TV might implode, but at that point nothing can interrupt the ejaculatory event.

It is a remarkable just-in-time process. All secretions that need to be together are forwarded just at the right time. The sperm leave their storage site called the epididymis and travel up, with the seminal vesicles and the prostate contracting and adding their juices. When the seminal vesicles contract and contribute the bulk of semen, the sperm are propelled out. The entire batch – which can contain 300 million sperm – is expelled at about 10 miles per hour subjecting the sperm to incredible shearing forces. The first portion of the ejaculate contains the most sperm and the second is mainly fluid from the seminal vesicles. If you really like numbers, here are some more: blood pressure can reach 30–100 systolic and 20–50 diastolic above the normal, heart rate increases to 110–180 beats per minute and respiration may be as high as 40 breaths per minute. Ejaculate is propelled out with the help of muscles which contract at 0.8 second intervals. The orgasm itself lasts between 3 and 10 seconds, and in exceptional cases longer than 15 seconds.

Lions

Intriguingly, the male genital system has two sets of muscles which are players in ejaculation. There is an internal and an external urinary sphincter. The internal muscle closes during ejaculation so semen is propelled out throught the urethra and not inwards into the bladder. Why have two sets of muscles? As one andrologist points out, it is essentially like wearing a belt and suspenders. One idea to explain the layout is that man the animal needs it this way. Lions, for example, can squirt their urine quite spectacularly, for distances of up to 30 feet. What they do is essentially build up pressure between these two sets of muscles and then fire away.

Men have told me that as boys they held competitive peeing matches to see who could send urine the furthest. But man has yet to topple the lion's record. Lions need no training; they just know how to do this well. Whether or not men can train for this type of sport is not known. At any rate, men have the muscle set-up for the task. Theoretically then, they could use them to propel urine further or squirt semen further or more forcefully.

When is a Man a Man? At First Ejaculation?

"Now I have to be careful, now I am a man, and I can get someone pregnant," explains Andrew, 30, commenting on his thoughts when he ejaculated semen for the first time at age eleven. Ejaculation and orgasm do not necessarily coincide. Some men report feeling the two as separate events. There are also "dry orgasms." "I was maybe only ten. I gave it a good rub and then had an orgasm," says 39-year-old James. Even as infants, many boys experience hard-ons, as anyone who has changed nappies can attest. Danish physician Preben Hertoft mentions that nearly all boys are capable of having orgasms three to five years before they go through puberty. "We are talking about dry ones, of course, without any sperm, but their intensity does not seem to be any less," he states. And according to Haeberle, "Nearly all boys have experienced an orgasm before their fifth birthday." Among 10–13-year-olds the figure is close to 80%. Most of the men I interviewed said that they had experienced dry orgasms which were accompanied by just as intense a feeling as the ones they had later which were accompanied by ejaculation.

Writer Sven Holm describes a personal coming-of-age story. As an eleven-year-old he did not really enjoy physical education class, but then he discovered he loved to climb ropes. He became better and better at it, and much happier. "But nobody – not even I – really understood that sexuality fuelled these activities," he writes. "When I climbed up a rope I had an orgasm. It always happened when I was right at the top – there I was, at the top, probably with a blissful expression on my face."

He kept his secret, and climbed as much as his arms and legs would carry him. When he didn't make it to the gym, he climbed up streetlight poles – always with orgiastic pleasure. "But when orgasm began to be accompanied by semen there was a problem," he writes. The liquid running down his legs gave away his precious secret and he gave up climbing entirely.

Carl, 39, reports that as a little boy – he was maybe eight or nine – he experienced a dilemma. His mother used to lie next to him in bed when reading him his bedtime story. He liked it. But he had vague stirrings he later identified as sexual and was afraid his mother might notice. "I knew very well that this was something, although I was not sure what exactly, I had to avoid at all cost, and I felt very guilty," he says. For their bedtime story reading he put on extra layers of clothes over his pyjamas to avoid any kind of incident. His mother wondered why, but he simply claimed to be cold or invented other excuses.

Parents may not always realize how appeasing it might be to try talking about sexuality. Teenagers get very clear messages about unwanted pregnancies. In conservative families they tend to be told what shame they would bring on the whole family; in other families, teens are warned they will not be able to continue school and training and will be financially responsible for another person earlier than they had planned. And of course, sex is fraught with the danger of HIV infection. With girls, it seems there is a tendency to leave it at that, even though not all methods of sexual pleasure necessarily lead to pregnancy or HIV risks.

"Masturbation is very bad for your health, the liquid coming out is your bone marrow," was the message that 44-year-old Peter received from his mother when he was growing up. Some men recount the strangest parental explanations. And they don't make puberty any more fun. "In grade nine I heard some extremely bizarre tales," says Jordan, 16. "For example, if the length of your shot is not a few good feet, you will never have healthy kids; they will be retarded." He also wonders about the rumor involving a certain kind of soft drink that supposedly causes lower sperm counts. His man-to-man talk was handled by his mother. "I walked away believing I had understood the whole ordeal." There are parents and educators who give practical advice that is helpful and encouraging, although there may be no standard "right" for anyone.

Most men I spoke to admitted that much of their sex education had been gleaned from reading pornographic and men's magazines. Yves, 22, knew "everything", as he says, very early and was very frank about it. "In a crowded department store elevator [as a young boy] I asked a pregnant woman, 'Did Daddy put his dick into you?' It was very embarrassing." Alex, 25, says: "When I was 14 or 15 my father sat down with me for a formal talk about sexuality. But all he told me were the facts that I had learned in school two years earlier. And I made it clear that I was up to date. Somehow we reached a more delicate subject, the question whether it was possible for a man to urinate with an erect penis." Fathers hardly ever seem to mention involuntary erection or ejaculation.

The old, old days were different in that respect. Scholar Erasmus of Rotterdam wrote a book called *Colloquia familiaria* for his six-year-old godson to educate him in the ways of the world. The book contains detailed descriptions and essays about sexual desire, sexual pleasures, intercourse, conception, pregnancy, childbirth, marriage, divorce, prostitution and venereal diseases. It was published in 1522.

Wet Dreams

Many male adolescents experience nocturnal emissions or 'wet dreams' in their sleep. The name, unsurprisingly, derives from the fact that the emissions occur during an erotic dream. Some boys seem to take it as proof of their budding manliness; others consider it an odd bedwetting incident and are happy when it never returns. According to Alfred Kinsey, 83% of all males experience at least one nocturnal emission over a lifetime, usually between the ages of 15 and 20. A dictionary printed in 1907, stated that nocturnal ejaculations are caused by "sexual debauchery, too much rich food with little exercise, too much sleep, especially in the morning and under featherbeds, self-stimulation of the genitalia." Men were advised to avoid coffee, tea and hot spices, to eat very little for dinner, to follow a routine of brisk exercise and to sleep on a hard mattress in a cool room. People suffering from nocturnal emissions should harden themselves by occupying their mind and body with serious tasks and stay busy with practical things. Preoccupying the mind with sexual imagery was to be avoided and an advisory tidbit was: "Marriage often helps." Whether it is a conscious act or an involuntary part of a dream, a man's first ejaculation marks a new phase of his sexuality. Alex had his first dry orgasm when he was 12. "When I was 13 or 14, a boy in school teased me saying I was collecting semen in a jar. A few days later I actually discovered the first few drops of semen when I masturbated." Some men don't remember this first sexual experience, with first intercourse being the event more firmly lodged in their memory. Peter, 21, had his first sexual encounter at the age of 19. "Well, the first time was not exactly mind-blowing. These days it is far more intense."

Most men I spoke to admitted that they did not talk to male friends about their sexuality, but some did, on occasion, speak to female friends. Quite often they mentioned they found it "hard to find the right words." One man in his early forties told me: "We are just plain screwed up. Maybe that is why so many men are so bad in bed. We should talk about this stuff." Some women mentioned they found it strange that urine and semen are discharged through the same passage in men. None of the men I interviewed said that they had ever really thought about this.

Nearly all men experience a kind of resting phase after an orgasm. Further ejaculation is only possible after a while, even if the penis stays erect. During puberty, this phase between ejaculations is pretty short but it gets a bit longer as men leave their teens. After ejaculation, blood pressure and pulse return to normal, the testes return to their usual spot, the penis grows flaccid and the blood can flow out. So how soon is soon enough for orgasm number two? Experts on male sexuality – Herb Goldberg, for example – criticize traditional male conditioning that seems to say men have to perform sexually as if they were machines. That is a good way for a guy to alienate himself from his own sexuality.

Different Strokes for Different Folks: Ejaculation Types
Too Fast: Premature Ejaculation

Premature ejaculation is one of the most frequent complaints men have about their ejaculaory capacity. Very often, men keep it a secret. In 1948, sex researchers Alfred Kinsey and colleagues reported that 75% of all men questioned ejaculated two minutes after penetration; many reported coming after 20 seconds. Shere Hite stated that every fifth man reported coming after one minute of penetration, a "Wham, bam, thank you ma'am" kind of timeframe. Sometimes coming fast has been learned. John, 36, explains, "We had these circle jerks in high school. A bunch of us would stand around in a remote end of a park and masturbate. Whoever came first, would be the winner."

Essentially, there seems to be no ideal amount of time after which it is fine to come. The pop group Frankie Goes To Hollywood's old hit "Relax" with the hook "Relax – when you want to go to it, relax – when you want to come" was explicit enough to get it banned on British radio. When to come is a question of taste and negotiation. Some partners will like quickies, always, sometimes, or never. Animals offer no clear role models. In bison, genital contact is brief with immediate ejaculation, other animals like the rhinoceros have extended periods of copulation. If you do want to train your abilities to stave off a few more minutes or several dozens of minutes, experts recommend working the PCs, the pubococcygeus muscles. There is no exercise machine in the gym for these muscles – you can work them anywhere. The best way to locate it is to recall situations during which you are on the highway and have to pee but cannot or do not want to pull over. If you start off by holding a contraction of these muscles for a few seconds you can graduate to sets of contractions with varying speeds and for varying lengths of time. To avoid coming too quickly, some men report using a squeeze technique while others apply a mind over body method and concentrate on some abstract issue or sports scores while thrusting. But there is a fine line to wander – getting too bummed out about how your favorite team played may lead to your penis feeling similarly.

Coming too fast – is it the foreskin's fault, or rather lack thereof? Depite the ongoing controversy about the pros and cons of male circumcision, therapists agree the lack of a foreskin is not to blame for premature ejaculation. Is it natural to come fast? Is it an evolutionary advantage? An animal that gets right to the point is certainly less prone to attacks by enemies. True. But then again how many enemies are there in a classic bedroom? The animal kingdom delivers plenty of examples of both quickies and protracted copulations. There is little conclusive evidence on whether our human ancestors chose quickies over longies. So it looks like it is every man for himself out there on the savannah.

Too Long: Prolonged Ejaculation

Some men report that it takes them too long to ejaculate. This can be related to epilepsy medication or to treatment for some psychiatric conditions or for high blood pressure. If a man is afraid of fathering a child or of hurting a partner, he may unconsciously hold his body, penis and testes back.

Although hard to imagine, some erections do last too long. Clinically, this is rather vaguely defined. "I met a guy at a conference and soon he was telling me all about his Viagra-induced four-hour erection. Man, who can stay lubricated that long?," asks Joe, in his early forties. A prolonged erection may last several hours and usually does not require treatment, but priapism, an erection lasting longer than four hours, can be damaging since it starves penile tissue of oxygen. If an erection seems to be lasting too long and is unpleasant or painful, see a doctor immediately. Penile tissue may become irreversibly damaged. The term "priapism" is derived from the Greek fertility god Priapus who is depicted as a man with a huge erect penis. This condition is definitely no macho joke but an emergency requiring immediate medical attention.

Too Retro: Retrograde Ejaculation

With age, the penis and testes may change in their range of actitivity, but overall they tend to serve their owners well. In many cases, the prostate seems to take a different course. This organ located below the bladder contributes 10–30% of semen. Prostate infections are both common and painful, and as a man ages, the prostate has a tendency to continue to grow. Since the urethra is embedded in it, this growth can lead to urinating problems. This condition, also called benign prostate hyperplasia (BPH), is treatable with medication, watchful waiting or in some cases an operation will be needed. When it comes to prostate cancer, operations are often, but not always, unavoidable and early detection is the key to survival for this most prevalent type of cancer in men.

These days, nerve sparing surgery allows for the preservation of nerves involved in orgasm, particularly with smaller tumors. This technique may not be possible in the removal of larger tumors. If an operation in the pelvis is unavoidable, retrograde ejaculation can result. What happens is that nerves are damaged and during ejaculation the bladder neck does not close. Instead of semen being fired outward out of the penis, ejaculation becomes an internal event, with semen travelling inward landing in the bladder. It is then excreted in the urine, leading to a slight foaminess in the toilet bowl. Although it may sound strange, it is not painful. Urologist James Gilbaugh reports that some couples find it preferable because it is less "messy."

Penile versus Prostate Orgasm

In a cafe adjacent to a library I meet a male acquaintance who is intrigued by my current book project. "So what is something men don't know?," he asks unbelievingly. I proceed to tell him that some men I spoke to report a marked difference – in intensity of feeling and overall sensation – between a penile orgasm and one arising from prostate stimulation. My friend said he had never heard of a prostate orgasm. "Oh, it is just sooo different, but sort of like chocolate and vanilla, two delicious flavors of the same thing," Billy, 26, had told me in an interview. Whichever flavor you desire, urologists agree that the prostate benefits from the exercise that ejaculation brings. Being good to your penis, in this sense, means doing your prostate some good as well.

Condoms

"I can't say I really love them," says Jay, 26. "But I use them." Younger men raised in the age of AIDS are accustomed to the classic latex. Some older men, who were sexually active before the dawn of AIDS, seem to have a rather strong dislike for condoms. One man stated he could not get a hard-on with a condom on. When you risk contracting a disease for which treatment has a truckload of side effects and a cure has yet to be found, there seems to be little room for whining. Some sex handbooks actually recommend using two or three on top of each other with lubricant on each layer because of the sensual stimulation that offers.

The Evolution of Orgasm, Sperm Competition and Post-Coital Snooziness

"When a worthy man is in the company of women his member grows, becomes strong vigorous and hard; he is slow to ejaculate and, after the spasm caused by emission of semen, he is prompt at re-erection," writes Cheikh Nefzaoui in *The Perfumed Garden*, an Arab treatise on sex dating back 500 years. "Prompt" is a relative term. Many women seem capable of multiple orgasms, so is it normal for men to have, say, half a dozen orgasms a night? Teenagers may very well be nodding at this figure and other men may have their doubts. Since sex is not an Olympic discipline, the question would be whether a man with a stressful job, a mortgage, wife and children requires a weekly seriously double-digit orgasm count to say he is a man? In his book *Superpotency*, urologist Dudley Seth Danoff describes a "superpotent man" as a man with "penis awareness." "Any man whose self-image hinges on things like how often he scores and how great his performance is," Danoff writes, "will probably *not* meet the standards of true penis power. To be a superpotent man, you must view sex as a pleasure, not a sporting event." A penis should perform in accordance with personal standards and "not some imaginary yardstick." When it comes to multiple orgasms, Nature has shaped women and men differently and is not dictating numbers or standards, but it is intriguing to ponder why some facets have evolved the way they have.

As anthopologist Helen Fisher notes, the human male has the largest penis of all primates relative to body size. In her view, this has evolved because women have favored men with penises like that. "It seems that the largeness of this male anatomical part has no practical function other than for sex," she writes, "and undoubtedly it evolved in size long ago because women liked men with large penises." With the word "large," by the way, she is referring to the so-called normal girth and length of the male penis.

The debate about the evolution of female and male sexual strategies has been long and full of strife. According to anthropologist Sarah Blaffer Hrdy, many studies that stress the male quest for a variety of females, or tomes that deal with the burden of competition between males for mates, just deliver "the biological infrastructure for the double standard." "Men are prone to roam, women prone to home," and many other snappy rhymes seem to offer the rationale behind each gender's supposed strategy. But recent studies, particularly studies of sperm and sperm competition, are revealing that the rhyme may be based on myth rather than fact.

Culture, class, nationality, race, religion, laws, traditions, taboos, individual choice and personal idiosyncracies govern our behavior. In and out of the bedroom. And while life in the office cubicle is not much like the life our ancestors led, we nevertheless remain animals shaped by an evolutionary past. As Lynn Margulis and Dorian Sagan state in their book *The Evolution of Sex*, "Biologically, sex is part of the rich repertoire of life." But the origin of sex has "long perplexed." For a long time it lent itself to myth-making, but that has been abandoned. "We now realize, thanks to the insights of Darwinian evolution, that the sexual differences that loom so large in the daily lives of men and women did not arise at some specific time in the history of the human species." And it began, according to Margulis and Sagan, when microbes dominated the planet. "The story of sex starts with an account of the earliest life on Earth. The private activities of early cells are involved even today in courtship among human beings."

This does not imply that "Honey, I am feeling amoebic today," is the basis for twenty-first-century pillow-talk. What these thoughts do say is that it behoves us to look at the biological underpinnings of what we do and why we do it. One former male roommate of mine once explained he was not biologically wired to wipe the hairs out of the sink after shaving. After all, males were wired to hunt and tend to big-picture issues. Too much biology in an explanation, especially when given a self-serving spin, makes my hair stand on end.

"Sex," states sociobiologist E.O. Wilson, is "in every sense a consuming biological activity." And, he says, sex is an antisocial force in evolution – there is a conflict of interest. "The male will profit more if he can inseminate additional females, even at the risk of losing that portion of inclusive fitness invested in the offspring of his first mate. Conversely, the female will profit if she can retain the full-time aid of the male, regardless of the genetic cost imposed on him by denying him extra mates." Everyone seeks to have their genes live on in the next generation and different reproductive strategies apply.

MIT evolutionary psychologist Steven Pinker points out that men have – relative to their body size – smaller testicles than chimps but bigger ones than gorillas and gibbons. Studies in zoology have revealed that the more competition there is for mates, the larger the testicles are in the male animals. Pinker concludes the human male testicle size suggests that "ancestral women were not wantonly promiscuous but were not always monogamous either." Hence, competition for mates is present but not severe in humans. Pinker points out that the human mating system may not be like any other animal's, "But that does not mean it escapes the laws governing mating systems, which have been documented in hundreds of species." If a man sleeps with 50 women, writes Pinker, he has possibly sired 50 children, whereas a woman who has slept with 50 men may not have more descendants than if she slept with one. "Thus," Pinker argues, "men should seek quantity in sexual partners; women quality." Robin Baker, retired biologist of the University of Manchester, contends that the "greater urgency of males and their relative indiscrimination sometimes translates into enormous levels of reproductive success." And he gives the example of a human male credited with the most offspring – an ex-emperor of Morocco who reportedly sired 888 children.

New York Times science writer Natalie Angier criticizes evolutionary psychology which, as she states, goes to extremes "to argue in favor of the yawning chasm that separates the innate desires of women and men." Angier points out that the challenge for men is that this "random shooting of a gun" may not be such a successful reproductive strategy. A woman's ovulation is concealed, so "each episode of fleeting sex has a remarkably small probability of yielding a baby." Among, in Angier's words, the "cardinal principles" of the evolutionary psychologist "is that men are by nature more polygamous than women are, and much more accepting of casual, even anonymous sex." Evolutionary psychologists see the discordance between the sexes based on the male's – relative to the female's – stronger sex drive.

Are men innately more promiscuous? Roger Short of the Royal Women's Hospital at the University of Melbourne and a well-known authority in the field of reproductive medicine agrees that the relative size of the testis and, in addition, sperm shape are "infallible predictors of the mating system." Judging by these criteria, he says, men were not designed to be promiscuous. According to Timothy Birkhead, behavioral ecologist at the University of Sheffield, there has been a gender bias in biology that held fast to the idea that sexual selection is a male-dominated process. As it turns out, both males and females of various species are promiscuous. Both genders are applying many strategies to obtain, as Birkhead writes, "the best genetic deal they can get." It is true, he says, that "the reproductive potential of males far outstrips that of females." But that does not get them their way all the time as females counter-adapt to this male adaptation. Both sexes are in a state of "dynamic flux," he explains, "each evolving, now in response to adaptations in the other." One intriguing aspect in all of this is the role of sperm competition. There is more about sperm and competition in Chapter 5, but here are some first remarks.

Unlike animals in the wild, in the doldrums of most human daily lives, the competition level in, say, a classic bedroom – except for the occasional incident of the other lover hiding under the bed or in the closet – is rather low. Immediately following intercourse, women rarely get up to mate with another male in the next room. But continuing this theoretical scenario and setting morals aside, it would certainly be in the man's biological interest to stay the night, to make sure she does not do so. As part of his reproductive strategy, post-coitally he should be wide awake and clear as a bell to watch her behavior. He usually isn't.

Biologist Robin Baker is certain that sperm competition dictates human sexual behavior and he writes, "Our bodies simply uses our brains to manipulate us into behaving in a way dictated by our programming." The acting central force is sperm warfare. "Whenever a woman's body contains sperm from two (or more) different men at the same time, the sperm from those men compete for the 'prize' of fertilising her egg." Male behavior is, in his view, geared towards preventing this kind of warfare and a woman's goal is to "outmanoevre her partner and other males." Birkhead does not doubt the idea of sperm competition in animals which he has studied for over twenty years, but questions Baker's evidence in humans. Due to a lack of evidence, Baker's ideas are currently not mainstream biology.

But perhaps these considerations can be applied to another aspect of male sexual behavior. Greek philosopher Aristotle described the exhaustion that follows semen emission as "quite conspicuous, which suggests that the body is being deprived of the final product formed out of the nourishment." After orgasm, men and women could not be more different. Basically, she wants to chat and cuddle, he wants to chill out and snooze. OK, this is a totally, politically incorrect over-exaggeration, but it is the gist of it.

Men describe their feelings after orgasm as "satisfied, peaceful and sleepy." The refractory phase, as is it called in the male, is, as one andrologist states matter-of-factly, "a period during which further sexual stimulation does not produce subsequent orgasm." A study by the University of Rome and St. Bartholomew's Hospital in London showed that Viagra does shorten the refractory period "in the prescence of a continuous erotic stimulus," but the period itself still remains. In rat cerebrospinal fluid, sexual activity changes the concentration of certain amino acids – inhibitory neurotransmitters – but experts are not clear on the biochemical nature of this event. In 1966, Masters and Johnson already found that unlike males, females do not necessarily experience a refractory period following orgasm during which they are resistant to sexual stimulation. Some researchers – to pick an extreme view – have pointed out that women's ability for multiple orgasm is evidence that they are unable "ever to reach complete sexual satiation in the presence of the most intense, repetitive experiences."

So does the refractory period then deliver proof of ultimate male satiation? That may seem like a politically correct way to settle mattress-level spats, but it does not seem to make enough Darwinian sense. What is the refractory phase? It is a pronounced physiological event unlikely to be just learned behavior. Men of various age groups differ in their experience of it. Pre-adolescent boys are markedly dissimilar from men, as Kinsey and his colleagues already reported in 1948. They recorded orgasms in boys of many ages, from five months to adolescence, and found that except for ejaculation, the orgasms in boys are comparable to those of sexually mature males. "The most remarkable aspect of the pre-adolescent population is its capacity to achieve repeated orgasm in limited periods of time," they write. "This capacity definitely exceeds the ability of teen-age boys, who, in turn, are much more capable than older males." The refractory period can last only 30 seconds in Syrian hamsters, several minutes in some rats and can last for hours or even days in other species. So the human male and his post-ejaculatory drowsiness is no exception to the animal rule.

The refractory period, says andrologist Morgentaler, has not been studied in great depth in humans and he postulates that "it seems likely that it is related in part to overcoming the release of adrenaline that occurs with ejaculation." He explains that changes within the sexual centers of the brain occur and they must be "reset" before full sexual behavior can be produced. But women also have the same adrenaline rush without the snooziness afterward. So why has it evolved?

Perhaps a human male can be a post-coital snoozer because the woman has decided in this clearly defined situation not to subject his sperm in her body to competition with another man's sperm. He can relax. Courtship and sexual behavior seem to entail foolhardy exposure out on an open plain or savannah – particularly if natural enemies are nearby waiting for a meal. Then again, after the deed is done and the sperm is deposited, perhaps the male is, in nature's view, well, expendable. But we humans neither reside on the open plain nor is the male regularly devoured after sex. Today's man is usually involved in caretaking of the young. So is post-coital napping just another way to get him to stay?

With ejaculation, a man's seminal vesicles and personal sperm banks are depleted. So even if he ejaculates soon he could probably not sire offspring and the energy expenditure would be wasted. So the snooze may simply be a way to deter that from happening. Why the refractory period? "That's a good question," said andrologist Larry Johnson of Texas A & M University when I asked him. "But I sure don't know the answer to that one." Other andrologists reacted similarly.

A puzzle to some may be a tool for others. Some articles in women's magazines mention post-coital sleepiness and advise women to seize the weakness of the moment and try to talk about contentious issues in the relationship just then. Sometimes I really wonder about the opportunism of my gender-mates. Nature is – for some mysterious yet sensible reason – making men sleepy after ejaculation. And someone, some day, will explain why. So go ahead and snooze after orgasm. Just try to can the snoring.

2 What is Semen?

The Amount

Semen is one of nature's most impressive and mysterious cocktails. As one authoritative medical text chooses to state, "The male accessory glands contain a rather bewildering array of chemical constituents and we still remain rather ignorant of the specific physiologic function of many of the components."

A male ejaculate contains 2–6 milliliters, or about one teaspoon, of a cloudy-whitish-opalescent gel-like substance. Some men can produce an ejaculate of up to about 10 milliliters in volume, but at no matter which amount, at first it is more of a clot that then liquefies after about 20 minutes. Of the ejaculate, 50–70% arises from the seminal vesicles, 10–30% from the prostate and about 10% from both epididymes. Sperm make up only about 1% of the semen volume. So having a vasectomy does not markedly decrease the total amount of semen. In interviews some men mentioned they would like to be able to control how much semen they ejaculate. While sex therapists do offer advice on ejaculatory control, there seem to be no obvious ways to tailor the amount of semen ejaculated – perhaps because the entire event is not readily controllable by conscious effort.

Men are not touched by such a marked event as the cessation of menstruation in women, but there is a comparable phase that medical researchers call climacterium virile, andropause, viropause or male menopause. As Jed Diamond says in his book on the subject, this event is "a more gradual affair." He points out that the US lags behind European countries in studying this assortment of physiological changes in men. Testosterone levels decrease slightly with age, and in particular the amount of semen ejaculated as well as the force with which it is expelled also decreases.

Surprisingly perhaps, men do not have identical ejaculates, nor does one man always have the same type of ejaculate. Researchers and clinicians report that semen quality differs depending upon whether it arose during masturbation or intercourse. Biologist Robin Baker states that men can actually subconsciously alter their semen composition according to the situation. For example, in his view, during normal intercourse a man ejaculates more sperm because he knows this is all about getting an egg fertilized. There are plenty of researchers who find Baker's hypotheses unbelievable. But it is true that there are individual differences between men when it comes to semen volumes

21

and seasonal changes in semen quality do exist. Also, the time intervening since the last ejaculation makes a difference.

"If I Masturbate Too Much, Will I Run Out of Semen?"

Some men told me of a saying: "3,000 shots, that's all you got." That seems to be a legend with an extremely long half-life. Jordan, 16, says, "I have heard that if you masturbate too much your babies will be deformed." This kind of advice is a sure way to keep a boy's anxiety level high and his hands out of his pants. But the tall tales are certainly not based on fact – the literature and the experts I consulted are in agreement on this issue. At one point during puberty the male testes begin producing sperm. And that production capacity or quality is not changed by frequent ejaculation. This store has essentially no supplier delivery problems. Restocking is an ongoing process. If by any chance you find that your semen volume is decreasing over an extended period of time, then you should consult a physician.

Odor

Medical jargon is not exactly known for its poetic expressions. Yet in medical publications semen odor is described as resembling the scent of chestnut blossoms. It is an odor with a long tradition and part of what makes a man smell sexy. In "cultured man", wrote Theodor Van de Velde, a famous doctor who penned marriage manuals in the 1920s, there is a direct relationship between the sense of smell and sensuality. Authors Patrick Süskind, Charles Baudelaire and Emile Zola have written extensively about this connection. According to physiologists this powerful link may very well be due to the fact that the sense of smell is connected with the more archaic parts of the brain. Many facets of the olfactory pathway are directly linked to the proper functioning of the sexual endocrine system. As D. Michael Stoddart, zoologist at the University of Tasmania and author of *The Scented Ape: the Biology and Culture of Human Odor* points out, "Human males do not react to pheromones in the way that male dogs do for example to the odour of a bitch in heat, but the ancient linkage, however remains quite intact. The nose has a powerful part to play in sexual reproduction … ."

In one of the most erotic sections of the Bible, in "The Song of Solomon", a "well-beloved" is described as being "a Bag of Myrrh." As the poem runs, "My beloved is unto me as a cluster of henna flowers in the vineyards of En-gedi." According to Stoddart, henna was in widespread use through Egypt and the Middle East when the poem was written. He writes that the "author presumably did not recognize consciously the significance of henna … The perfume of the flowers, when crushed and smelled closely to the nose, has a semenlike odour that transcends any floral note." Berberry, lime and the aforementioned chestnut blossoms all smell this way. So the perfume that scented the lover in question may well have been accompanied by a related scent of genital origins.

On another location of the literary scale, French author the Marquis de Sade, purportedly influenced by the scent of chestnut candles, wrote a short story called "La Fleur de Châtaignier." In the text, a young girl embarrasses a young priest she is visiting with her mother. She inquires about the odor in the air that she claims to remember but cannot quite recall its context.

When I asked Axel, 25, what he thought about his semen's odor he said, "It smells a bit too clinical, but that is OK." One man told sex researcher Shere Hite, "It gets cold and sticky and smells like Ajax. Hate it." According to Van de Velde, the scent can vary individually as much as the chestnut blossom scent varies from tree to tree and season to season. He reports being told that the semen of the same man may smell "pungent" after psychologically taxing events and "spicy" after physical exertion.

Doctors who handle semen routinely do not seem particularly fond of doing the odor test and Theodor Van de Velde already noted that doctors avoid this test because this leads "to more or less of a feeling of disgust". Men do seem to be disgusted by the smell of other men's semen, but even this type of reaction can apparently be held in check in special situations such as porn movie theaters and peep show cabins.

When I asked women, they stated they liked the smell of their man in general, his sweat, his aftershave, but did not differentiate according to bodily secretions. Van de Velde writes of one "very talented and sophisticated woman" who ended a relationship with a man when she discovered "she could not stand the smell of his semen."

Color

"Universal white," was the rather jocular term used in the embryology post-graduate course which I audited at the Marine Biological Laboratory in Woods Hole. Lab experiments there involved sperm from a vast array of species from sea urchins to mice. White or off-white seems to be nature's color of choice for semen and that includes men's semen.

Semen can take on a yellowish tinge due to pigments from the seminal vesicles and age may influence the coloring as well. Shorter intervals between sexual encounters lead to a more translucent semen – the cloudiness correlates with the amount of sperm in the ejaculate. Reddish coloring in the semen may mean it contains traces of blood and should be reported to a physician.

Biography of a Sperm

"The mature spermatozoon is an elaborate, highly specialized cell," write Martin Johnson and Barry Everitt of the University of Cambridge. As befits such a cell, it has a mighty specialized biography. As the andrologist Abraham Morgentaler notes, "The life story of a sperm would make for an excellent adventure novel. There is everything required for a good read – romance, pathos, teamwork, daunting obstacles and external forces, success against tremendous odds."

Since one milliliter of ejaculate can contain 20–40 million sperm or more, one orgasm can send the impressively large group of, say, 200 million sperm on their way. A woman's output of one egg per month seems to pale as old-fashioned handicraft in comparison with the high-level output of one testicle: about 1,000 sperm per second per testicle. One might be tempted to debate whether quantity is better than quality but then again that issue may not lead anywhere interesting. Suffice it to say that sperm and egg have evolved differently and are each in their own league.

Sperm production numbers impress and puzzle scientists. The famous biologist Sir Julian Huxley already wondered in the 1930s why nature was so curiously lavish with sperm. And today that still remains a question without an easy answer. Norman Hecht of the University of Pennsylvania opened his talk at an andrology conference by asking, "Why do men have so many sperm?," and delivered the answer: "Because none of them want to stop and ask for directions." The room full of andrologists had a good laugh, even though, in andrology circles, this is a bit of an old joke. The andrologists I encountered, men and women, have a great sense of humor. Perhaps this is because their research, while involved as any other biological and medical discipline, is connected to an intimate part of everyday life.

The testicles, more particularly the spaghetti-like seminiferous tubules which make up the testis, are the sperm production site. As Roger Short of the Department of Perinatal Medicine at the Royal Women's Hospital of the University of Melbourne states, the testis is "the witness of the mating system, the site of mutation and the engine of desire." Quite the power-pack. All mammals have two egg-shaped organs containing these seminiferous tubules. In rodents and ungulates, such as bulls, the testes reach 1% or more of the body weight. Human testicles do not quite reach these dimensions. According to *The Physiology of Reproduction*, the largest testes in relation to body weight are found in an animal not exactly known as nature's macho-man – it is the Australian marsupial *Tarsipes spenceri*. The animal has testes that can reach 5% of its body weight. Humans are different from head to testis, with size variations from man to man, and studies have even covered the differences between ethnic groups. As men age, their testes' size decreases slightly.

If rolled out, the coiled seminiferous tubules in each testes would reach 360 meters in length. Within these tubules lie stem cells called spermatogonia – the parents of all sperm in a man's body. For each developmental stage, sperm carry different names. The spermatogonia maintain themselves and give rise to spermatocytes which develop further – through the process of cell division called meiosis – into spermatids. The round spermatids then need to undergo, as one textbook states, "a remarkable and complicated transformation" that leads to the elongated sperm with a tail. Throughout their development, sperm have a kind of physiological babysitter called the Sertoli cell. These cells are in physical and functional contact with the sperm they produce.

Sperm production is no fly-by-night operation. While the human testes produce around 200 million sperm per day, spermatogenesis takes around 60–70 days. Sperm development is a 24-hour, no vacation and no personal days off, sweatshop kind of job completed in accordance with a complex hormonal choreography. If you were to peek at the seminiferous tubules in a cross-section you would see columns of developing sperm: on the outer edge are the 'beginners' and the more 'advanced' sperm are closer towards the center.

Just like a good wine, sperm take time. All in all, and if you include the maturation process, it takes about 90 days from start to finish to create one sperm. In the film *Everything You Always Wanted to Know about Sex*, Woody Allen plays a sperm unwilling to go out into the world. Who knows, maybe that sperm had not matured enough. When they leave the testes, sperm cannot swim and are unable to fertilize an egg of their own accord.

Maturation does not occur in the testes but in the epididymis, another intricately coiled structure right next to the testis, and these coils would be six meters long if unfolded. As the sperm pass through the particular microenvironment of the epididymis, they acquire all of the abilities of an 'adult' sperm. As Barry Hinton of the University of Virginia points out, during this phase they are also carefully shielded from harmful substances that the body may contain. "It is the responsibility" of this organ, he writes, "to ensure that the conditions for sperm maturation are kept optimal." Sperm that develop in the left testicle travel to the left epididymis and remain in the left "system" until their call to duty, and this holds true for the sperm arising from the right testicle. The epididymis is the male body's sperm storage site. New cells arising from the spermatogonia arrive at a constant pace. As andrologist Abraham Morgentaler jokes, "It is like moving up an elevator; once at the penthouse, it is time to step out into the party."

This party can be ejaculation. But, as so often happens with parties, sometimes they get rained out or cancelled for other reasons. Up until about the tenth or eleventh day of abstinence the concentration of sperm continues to rise and then the body decides that they need to be replaced by fresher goods. The sperm die and are flushed out of the body along with urine and are replaced by the incoming newly produced sperm.

During their development, sperm become defined structures with a head, a mid-piece and a tail as well as a special kind of cap that fits snugly like a condom. This cap, or acrosome, contains a load of fireworks. The enzymes it packages are key to getting the sperm close to the egg. Complex biochemical reactions that are not all thoroughly understood need to occur when sperm actually does meet egg. And when the genetic material from both converge, new life can be formed … or not. Even if the sperm gets a date, spontaneous abortion is not uncommon in both humans and animals. For some reason the body performs a process that no fervent debate can halt: abortion. Hence, the sperm is a bit of a day-trader where life is all about risk-taking and lottery-playing. Sometimes, but not always, fertilization leads to a love child.

Fertilization itself is a complex blend of male and female. A sperm has to jump through many hoops to get to the egg which is surrounded by several protective layers, making her pretty picky. During sex, sperm enter a woman's body and then use their swimming skills acquired during maturation in the epididymis to get moving. But just being able to move is not enough to be able to fertilize an egg. As Ryuzo Yanagimachi of the University of Hawaii puts it, "In species in which the semen is deposited in the vagina at coitus, the spermatozoa must negotiate the highly folded, mucus-filled cervix before entering the uterus." The journey is long and arduous and most sperm simply poop out on the way. Once upon a time it was thought that sperm just race to the site where all the action is and wait for the egg to saunter by. As it turns out, the ascent of sperm to the uterus is facilitated primarily by uterine contractions. When the sperm reaches the egg and fertilization can occur, the sperm throws itself into the job head-first. More about all that excitement in a later chapter.

Knowing the Ropes

Since sperm are complex, biochemically puzzling structures it is not easy to understand why they do what they do. Computer-assisted imaging allows researchers to track their trajectories. This kind of examination is crucial, for example, when performing in-vitro fertilization, a technique that brings egg and sperm together in a test tube. Doctors seek to pick the most mobile sperm as they seem most capable of fertilizing an egg. But just being mobile is not enough. Being in the female reproductive tract triggers a not completely understood process called capacitation which involves changes on the surface of the sperm and in its metabolism. In addition, sperm undergo another little reshuffling of the membranes of their head part which is termed the acrosome reaction and which aids the passage of sperm to the egg. In order to be in perfect working order sperm need to be cool, a few degrees below body temperature. But that might be a somewhat arbitrary standard, as fertility researcher and physician Sherman Silber at St. Luke's Hospital in St. Louis points out, "In a nudist colony, testicular temperature would be much lower … ." Essentially the temperature is affected by the air temperature around the scrotum. Comedian Dave Barry thinks that it is "an incredibly stupid design flaw" to have a man's privates "hanging right out in the open in an absurdly vulnerable manner." But having the testes outside the body makes them the ideal and cool spot for sperm.

In general, men are, if limited to their sperm production, a bit inconstant. In the course of a year, sperm production varies quite a bit. Richard Levine, a researcher at the National Institutes of Health, has looked at the factors involved in this variation. In countries with warmer summers, sperm production is affected and apparently correlates with lower birth rates in the spring. In Texas, in a study with men who work outdoors, sperm density is lower in the summer – and the same is true in the European cities Lille, Basel and Edinburgh. In addition, he also found lower numbers of motile sperm in the summertime ejaculate of men in Texas. In northern Europe the birth rate is higher in the springtime than in other seasons. But Levine believes this is associated with a higher frequency of sexual intercourse in the fall which masks the "natural" effect – the decrease in semen quality during the summer months.

Other Stuff in Semen

Besides the sperm that are ready for action, an ejaculate can contain immature sperm. Other cells from the urogenital tract may be found in semen, as well as red blood cells and many white blood cells which are part of the body's immune system.

Seminal fluid contains the secretions from the accessory sex glands such as the prostate gland, the seminal vesicles and bulborethral glands, making it a quite unusual body fluid. During ejaculation the various secretions are released in a sequential fashion with the first fraction high in sperm concentration and with a higher fructose level in the later fractions.

Compared to other body fluids seminal fluid is unusual due to its high level of potassium, zinc, citric acid, fructose, phosphorylcholine, spermine, amino acids, prostaglandins and a wide variety of enzymes.

The prostate produces 100 times more citric acid than other soft tissue.

Fructose is a major player in semen and is the sperm's energy source. Actually sperm seem to take sugar any way they can get it. The female cervical mucus is quite high in sugar content so the sperm essentially have two sources of sugar. As men age, apparently the fructose level in their semen drops. Semen is intricately associated with a man's physiology and according to sex therapist Barbara DeAngelis you can influence the taste of your semen. Drinking fruit juices can sweeten it. (More information on this subject in Chapter 3).

Other components of semen include hormone-like chemicals such as prostaglandins. They arise mainly in the seminal vesicles and are emitted during ejaculation. Their pharmacologic qualities have effects in both the male and female reproductive systems.

Molecules called polyamines can be found in semen as well as chemical compounds called amines, such as choline and phosphorylcholine. Cholesterol and lipids are also found in semen as well as very high levels of zinc. It appears to arise mainly from the prostate gland which has the highest concentration of zinc of any organ in the body. Semen contains many proteins grouped together under the name prostatic secretory proteins. There are, for example, prostatic specific antigen, prostatic acid phosphatase, aminopeptases and others. There is some debate as to the biologic role of prostate specific antigen but it is perhaps best known as a protein used as a marker for prostate problems.

Self-Made Man

A man is his own body's most knowledgeable buddy. After all, you spend a lot of time together. In everyday conversations between clothed people – for example, among colleagues at a water-cooler – it is not uncommon to see a man hands in pocket, rearranging his private parts in some way or just playing "pocket pool." While it may be fine behavior in sexual contexts, in public this seems a bit out of place. Unless of course it is a man's way of doing a testicular self-exam, fifteen times a day.

In general, it seems that women are more accustomed to the idea of regular self-exams. "Men are bad health consumers," says andrologist Abraham Morgentaler. "But that is slowly changing." For both men and women the whole idea is early detection of cancer, and in the case of men, testicular cancer. Even if you are tired of hearing it, prevention is key and does save lives.

The self-exam can also help to identify health conditions that may involve sexually transmitted diseases. Doctors recommend knowing your testicles well because you will then be able to sense changes more easily. A self-exam once a month is a good idea. You can always try different types of touch tests which can also be done with a partner. If you wish to know the exact moves, you can check with a physician, call a helpline, check with a health information center or look on the Web (some helpful sites are listed at the end of this book).

The oval organs in the scrotal sac below the penis are the testicles and they should feel like hard-boiled eggs without the shell. Feel around them gently in order to see if there are any lumps or bumps on the smooth surface of both testes. They should both feel about the same; the left testicle will hang a bit lower. Running up the back of each testis is a mini spaghetti-like coiled structure, the epididymis, which feels like a fleshy mound on the back of the testis. It is best to do the self-exam after a warm bath or shower since the scrotum around the testicles is relaxed then. Testes are usually about 40–45 millimeters long and 30–35 millimeters wide. The right and left one may differ in size but, in general, volume is considered to be somewhere between 12–30 milliliters, usually around 18.

Sometimes fluid collects around the testes either as a palpable mass or as a sort of extra coating on one testicle creating a so-called hydrocele. If they increase in size – some can grow larger than a grapefruit – they can be uncomfortable but are not necessarily troublemakers. Nevertheless, if you have the impression that you have a hydrocele, you should see a doctor. Part of the exam will be to shine a flashlight at the mass to see its consistency, to possibly extract fluid and/or to perform ultrasound as well as other tests. One doctor reports that a friend, quite alarmed, called saying he had three balls. He did the flashlight test and could reassure his friend that he need not worry about this seemingly unusual condition.

Some men develop a clumpy coil of veins above a testis. Physician Sarah Brewer describes it as feeling like a "like a warm tangle of worms." Most often this varicocele arises on the left side, when a valve problem may occur. On the right side of the body, the testicular vein empties into the body's major vein, the vena cava. On the left side, the testicular vein drains into the kidney's vein, a constellation which more frequently leads to valve issues. When the valve system between the two veins on the left fails, essentially the blood flows back down, causing the veinous coil not dissimilar to a varicose vein in the leg. The clump disappears when you lie down because the veins swell under higher pressure. Sometimes a varicocele will cause pain and will require medical attention. Some fertility specialists believe varicoceles may contribute to male infertility, others dismiss this possibility as hogwash. Whether varicocele treatment increases pregnancy rates is not quite clear.

In an exam, a doctor will feel all around the testes, and the fleshy structure behind and above the testis (the epididymis where sperm mature). If small grape-size balls form there, so-called spermatoceles, these are cysts that will probably have to be removed. At one end the epididymis leads to the testicles and the other end is its attachment – the spermatic cord which has a guitar-string-like feel to it. It travels up into different parts of the genital tract and is not easily accessible during a self-exam.

The Virtual Andrologist

It may not be easy to find an andrologist or get an appointment with one. Women can call a gynecologist for routine check-ups, but it is not the same with andrologists. It is considered downright unusual to go to an andrologist for a regular check-up. But let's say there is something about your genitals you wish to understand better. Erectile issues, premature ejaculation, pain in the testicles, fertility problems. Then you may feel that contacting an andrologist will help you. There may not be one in your area. Or you may choose to see a urologist instead. Both specialties deal with male genitals but from different vantage points and traditions. Urologists may not necessarily be involved with fertility issues but some are.

Medical fields are organized into broad disciplines. Obstetrics and gynecology is a major division; hospitals will have departments by those names, as will research institutes. "Andrology often goes across the traditional disciplines and would be a subdivision of some department," explains Lisa Tenover, President of the American Society of Andrology and practising andrologist at Emory University and the Wesley Woods Hospital. "Andrology might be part of endocrinology, it might be in urology or even in Ob/Gyn [obstetrics/gynecology], as a subdivision in the infertility section." Tenover and many colleagues state they would like to see a field called reproductive biology emerge, a multidisciplinary area that embraces andrology, Ob/Gyn, urology and others. Right now, says Roger Short of the Royal Women's Hospital at the University of Melbourne, andrology is not as recognized as gynecology. And that makes it harder for patients to find an expert. The most important issue is to find a doctor you feel you can trust and respect. And if they do or say something that makes you feel uncomfortable, you can get up and leave at any time.

Let's say you have an appointment with a recommended doctor. So what will he or she do? I contacted a few doctors to ask them about their examination methods. In Europe, a first visit does not necessarily entail letting your pants down; in the US it usually does. This also has to do with insurance companies who pay doctors mainly to examine and perform procedures. But that does not mean there is no talking.

"The first thing I do," says Abraham Morgentaler, director of the male infertility and impotence program and director of microsurgery at Beth Israel Deaconess Medical Center in Boston, who is both a urologist and an andrologist, "is listen." Usually a man will come to see him with his partner. Sometimes the man will have seen other doctors and will have had a semen analysis done, so they talk about that. Then Morgentaler asks the man's partner to leave. And the man lets down his pants. No changing into gowns or anything like that. Often, says Morgentaler, the men make some kind of remark such as, "I don't have much to work with, doc," and he usually takes a moment to assure them that everything looks fine, if, in his opinion, it does. How else does he make a man feel at ease? "Well, I am very matter of fact about it all, I project that I know what I am doing and that this is an everyday situation for me." Morgentaler has been practising medicine for twelve years and has done approximately 10,000 exams. "I always make sure I have warm hands," says Haydar Karatepe, an andrologist with a practice in Frankfurt, Germany. "I talk about what I plan to do and why – as I examine the penis and testicles," says Lisa Tenover. In her view it is not a disadvantage to be a female andrologist. Actually, in many situations such as with male patients with whom she will talk about hormonal therapies, she believes it may be easier for men to speak to a woman. "In general before or during the exam, I tell men what I am looking for, because it takes their minds off the physical contact," she explains. "And I also tell them what I find as I go along."

The men I interviewed thought this type of exam was extremely unpleasant and awkward. Actually, I could not find a man to come along with me or to make an appointment separately and then tell me what it was like. Having a stranger – either a man or a woman – examine the "plumbing," as many men call it, seems to be a tough pill to swallow. There is an aversion to being touched "down there."

The Penis

As the editors of *Men's Health* say, "Think of it as a Mercedes SL. Maybe you'll be nicer to it." Whether you think of it as an SL, the Maserati 3200 GT or the Lexus LS 430, an exam of the medical penile kind will be a check-up for an instrument that does you great service. During an exam a doctor will carefully examine the penis' skin surface to check for any irregularities, like lumps or lesions or scars. If you are uncircumcised the doctor will pull back the foreskin. The glans underneath will be examined. Penises come in different sizes and even shapes. For example, a rare condition is penile duplication, giving the owner not one but two favorite toys. Another condition called hypospadias is when the urethra does not extend the full length of the penis to the glans. A penis may be smallish and perhaps curved which can cause penetration problems. In the vast majority of cases surgery will correct these conditions without impairing fertility or the ability to have sex.

If there is a St. Nick, I am sure he and his coworkers get plenty of wish-lists starting with "I want a bigger penis." According to many doctors, penis size is first and foremost on men's minds when they are examined and they will usually ask whether they are the "right" or "normal" size at one point during the exam. As Roger Short and Malcolm Potts explain in their book *Ever Since Adam and Eve*, Lieutenant William Schonfield carried out one of the most detailed studies on the penis by studying 1,500 boys of various ethnic backgrounds in the 1940s. He found that the penis undergoes rapid elongation during puberty, reaching adult length by age 17 – with the mean adult length of an erect penis being 5.9 inches. The average penis, according to textbooks, is between 6.5 centimeters (2.5 inches) and 10 centimeters (4 inches in length) when flaccid and around 11–15 centimeters (4.4–6 inches) when erect, but can be as long as 12 inches. Short and Potts add, "We are indebted to a group of prostitutes in a Japanese brothel for publishing in a popular magazine the erect measure of their clientele." The mean length they found was 13.75 centimeters (5.4 inches).

Physicians are presented with many types of penile emergencies, including of course the infamous but extremely infrequent Bobbit-cut or the penis-jammed-in-the-zipper situation. Urologist James Gilbaugh states he has removed pencils, pens and hat pins from penises. The objects got stuck when men and boys experimented with their erections. In one case, a man had sustained skin damage to his penis after having inserted it into the tube of a vacuum cleaner.

The Testicles

The testicles are responsible for quite a bit of action in the male body considering they are the place where both sperm and testosterone are produced. The word "testes" is derived from the Latin root that means "witness". Holding the testes was the Roman way to take oath, which also explains the word "testimony" – and indeed the testes give witness to much about a man. A doctor will first seek to determine if a man has two testes. If a man only has one, he is not half a man and things can be just fine. If his other testicle did not descend to its proper place and is still in his body, that could be an issue requiring further medical attention.

A testis should have a firm consistency. If it is very soft, a doctor will consider possible hormone deficiencies, and if both testes are hard, or if one is very much harder than another, a doctor may suspect that more exams will be necessary as this could possibly, but not necessarily, indicate a tumor. A man and his wife once came to see Abraham Morgentaler and he found a rock-hard lump in one of the man's testicles. The patient said that it had been there for quite a while. The couple had come to see him because they were trying to conceive and had begun infertility testing, discovering that the man had no sperm in his ejaculate. Morgentaler talked to them about their fertility options and then said that he was afraid there might be a tumor that was also affecting the man's fertility. The man turned to his wife and said, "You see, that is exactly why I hate going to doctors." And his wife replied, "You idiot, that is exactly why you go to doctors." The conversation continued, mainly at the wife's insistence. Indeed the man did have a tumor which was removed as part of further treatment and he is now cured.

During the examination of the testes some doctors might compare the testis to a bunch of beads on a string, an orchidometer. This instrument, nicknamed "the urologist's rosary", helps to gage the volume of the testis which is usually around 18 milliliters but can vary from 12 to 30 milliliters. The orchidometer itself is a string of beads marked with numbers indicating volume in milliliters. In general doctors report that men are not exactly completely familiar with their own genitalia. For example, as Roger Short of the Royal Women's Hospital in Melbourne reports, he asked men and women to show what they thought was the normal human testicular size was using the orchidometer. "The women got the answers perfectly right," says Short, "and the men's estimates were all over the place." The testes are usually examined while the patient is standing. Obviously, retraction of the testicles is not a practical thing and as one medical text puts it, "cold and excitement to the patient are to be avoided" for just that reason. It is up to the doctor's talents to provide the right atmosphere for a patient to feel comfortable. The testicles may vary in size, even over the course of a single day and their size may also change with age.

The Prostate

Some doctors might say the famous, "turn around, bend over and cough," or a variation thereof; others may perform the rectal exam while the man is lying on his back, and others will ask a man to bend over just slightly. Examining the prostate gland means doing the digital rectal exam – having a doctor place a finger in the rectum. He or she will be wearing gloves and using lubrication, and should be gentle. The exam will allow him or her to feel the texture of the prostate gland which, when in its normal and healthy state, is firm but a bit rubbery. In one men's magazine this exam is called a "mega-hurt" and is ranked with some other "medical ordeals on the Richter scale of agony," such as getting your wisdom teeth removed and getting a rabies shot.

Abraham Morgentaler explains that he asks a man to turn around and bend over slightly with his elbows on a table. He asks the man if this kind of exam has ever been performed before and talks about it before performing the examination, and then talks the man through it. "I tell them what I will do, that they will feel a bit of pressure but nothing major." It does not assuage all fears. What he then does is place a gloved and lubricated finger at the anal verge, at the entrance to the anus. "Usually the anal sphincter is all tight, because the man essentially does not want the exam. But he will relax a bit and I move my finger gently inward and perform my exam." Lisa Tenover also chooses to have men bend over slightly while leaning their elbows on the table, a position which allows for the symmetry of the prostate to be assessed better. "If the man seems a little uneasy, as I do the exam, I comment on how long I have been doing this, for over 15 years, that I know this isn't his most favorite exam, but that the advantage I have is that my finger is smaller than most men's," says Tenover. "This usually makes them laugh and eases any tension they have." She has never had anyone complain or refuse. "I guess they realize how important it is." Afterwards, men say they are glad it is over, and often that it was not as bad as they thought it was going to be.

"I remember my first rectal exam," muses Abraham Morgentaler. "It was in medical school as part of a physical. The physician's assistant told me to turn around and bend over and without any warning did the exam. I felt so violated." Talking about the exam helps a man to prepare for it. And obviously Morgentaler's style is based on his own experience.

It is likely that some of the discomfort arises from embarrassment. During the exam, a man might very well feel the urge to urinate, or his penis might become erect. After all, the doctor is touching a man's G spot – for some, a moment to blush by; for others, no big deal. Tenover says this has occurred but not very often during her exams. "Unless the man brings up the topic or seems overly embarrassed, I never say anything about it. If you act professionally and treat it as a normal event, it really doesn't seem to be a problem." Haydar Karatepe says, "It all depends on the atmosphere in the doctor's office and how he relates to his own sexuality. If the doc is uptight, the patient will be too."

Other Exams

Depending on an individual's health situation, that might be the end of the exam or there may be more, such as blood tests to get an overview of a man's hormonal situation or Doppler ultrasound. With transrectal ultrasound, the prostate and the seminal vesicles can be imaged. (Additional information about these exams follows in Chapter 6.)

In some cases, semen analysis will be required. Which is when you have a job to do. Nurses generally do not giggle when handing over the little vial and pointing you to the room where you masturbate and ejaculate into the vial. Semen analysis only makes sense after a certain period of abstinence, some-where between 48 hours and seven days. Some of the facilities offered to men are in a rather sorry state. It might be a bathroom stall or a dedicated room. Usually a man is told he can take as much time as he likes. And when the deed is done and the vial filled with a teaspoon or so of semen, there is no time for a nap. Luckily you do not have to walk through a doctor's office with the container: you leave, a nurse comes in and picks it up to take it immediately to the lab. Semen needs to be studied when fresh.

If a man's hormone levels are to be evaluated, then other types of questions will involve the symptoms, which can be varied. Decreased libido, decreased overall endurance or osteoporosis many point in the direction of hormonal imbalances. Hormone levels, in particular testosterone, will change with age. "Men are more aware than ten years ago that it may happen," explains Lisa Tenover. At the same time they wish to believe it is not happening to them. Men do not seem to talk about bodily changes with their friends; perhaps, suggests Tenover, they do not wish to complain or cause concern, or "because of the cultural idea of men not being strong and physically not supposed to get sick is seen as a sign of weakness." Women are perhaps a bit more used to dealing with health issues because of gynecological and childbearing issues. "I think many men are aware of what is happening to their external bodies, but tend to ignore the changes they see," says Tenover.

In some practices a doctor may ask quite varied questions. (A list of possible questions is on p. 173.) Some will be medical: about current prescriptions, a medical history that includes the onset of puberty, voice change, beard growth and general medical history. Other questions – particularly if the doctor, like Haydar Karatepe, is also trained as a sex therapist – will be about sex life, sexual preferences, frequency of intercourse, professional or personal stress factors. "When I question patients, I often discover that men do not have a male friend with whom they can talk about sexual issues," explains Karatepe. A female friend is no true back-up; a man needs a male friend for this, he says. There are many reasons why erections are not happening when the conditions are seemingly right, or why ejaculation timing is off. And some of it may not be explainable in medical terms. Sometimes a vacation is all that is needed. But for the moments when it seems like something is amiss or you need to ask a few more questions, it is good to find a knowledgeable doctor whose manner you like.

3 The Potency of Potency

Potency Today

The penis "confers with the human intelligence and sometimes has intelligence of itself, and although the will of the man desires to stimulate it, it remains obstinate and takes its own course, and moving sometimes of itself without license or thought by the man, whether he be sleeping or waking, it does what it desires; and often the man is asleep and it is awake, and many times the man is awake and it is asleep; many times the man wishes it to practise and it does not wish it; many times it wishes it and the man forbids it. It seems therefore that this creature has often a life and intelligence separate from the man, and it would appear that the man is in the wrong in being ashamed to give it a name or to exhibit it, seeking rather constantly to cover and conceal what he ought to adorn and display with ceremony as a ministrant." The words of Leonardo da Vinci.

As Maggie Paley points out in her book about the penis, this has been a fashion-adorned body part. In both the Middle Ages and during the Renaissance, clothes that accentuated the penis were popular. In those days of men in tights, men would move their colorful money pouches to front and center to attract additional attention to the genitals. In the fifteenth century, so-called codpieces, padded pouches explicitly for the male genitals, became fashionable. Those old days seem rather more open on the topic of public genital adornment than today's world. Paley believes that men "might love codpieces, if someone revived them the right way." And they might offer just the right kind of individualization. They could be shaped like a police car, a pit bull, a submarine or even a submarine sandwich. The fashion industry has not yet taken up her suggestion. Tight jeans for men, particularly tight around the crotch, were the rage in the 1960s but that is one clothing item that has not resurfaced. "Man, they were so uncomfortable," explains one man I asked. "I don't want them to be back anytime soon."

As far as a penis having a mind of its own, many men I spoke to confirmed that idea in no uncertain terms. Rather than being a pre-programmed robot, the penis is a performer, affected by all the ups and downs of the artistic world. In essence, it seems that the penis' owner is judged and judges himself by the many aspects of this performance. In conversations with men and as evidenced in perhaps an exaggerated fashion via the pop culture barometer of men's magazines, one of life's priorities is about being as hard as possible as often as possible. And that is work, mainly of the physical kind. Learning about ways to "boost your performance" is in one case a workout regime involving those muscles and joints involved in sex. "Love muscle training" are exercises geared toward training abs, thighs and buttocks, as well as those handy Kegel exercises to train the PCs, the pubococcygeus muscles between the scrotum and the anus. But since the penis is not a muscle, that activity is work on the supporting actors in this movie and not the main character. Working out in moderation will surely enhance general as well as sexual well-being, but it is not the direct 3-step-no-frills method to 100% erectile success.

To cut to the chase, some people choose another route by popping a diamond-shaped blue pill. For most men, it is the surefire path to erection. It is also the medicated path to erection. Is it important how you reach a particular goal? As Gail Sheehy writes, "This chemical machismo has special appeal to a great many boomer men, performance-conscious in every way and obsessed with remaining ever young." But she points out that therapists are reporting that younger and younger men are complaining about potency problems and says the reason is probably not an increase in impotence but "inflated expectations."

As one man told sex researcher Shere Hite, "Masculinity is having a penis. Macho is trotting around like a rooster advertising it." And part of the macho-man image is being able to perfom at the drop of a zipper. As sex therapist Bernie Zilbergeld points out, "the sexual messages conveyed in our culture are the stuff of fantasy, of overheated imaginations run wild," what he terms "the fantasy model of sex." After quoting a scene from a Harold Robbins novel in which a man's penis springs out at a woman "like an angry lion from his cage," with ensuing penetration by "a giant of white hot steel" which eventually erupts with a "hot onrushing gusher of his semen," he explains that these kinds of texts are fun escapes but they basically lead to huge amounts of anxiety. "Penises in fantasyland come in only three sizes: large, extra large and so big you can't get them through the door." And they function "automatically and predictably, like a well-oiled machine." The challenge is, though, that you can never measure up to the fantasy-land view of sex. The absolute need to have erections, particularly when they are in the real world where not everything happens at the flip of a switch, causes problems. Zilbergeld tells men, "a real man is *not* someone who can live up to other people's standards and expectations."

At any age, the penis may just not perform when the owner wishes it to. These events are more common as men age. While the National Institutes of Health estimate that between 10 and 20 million men suffer from some form of impotence, experts believe the figure may even be much higher in reality. Not being able to get or keep an erection is still a taboo subject and perhaps a much more frequent occurrence than previously thought.

One of the worst ways to insult a man is to say he cannot get it up. A man does not have impotence, he is impotent. A telling phrase, since it seems to be describing the whole man. That is not just about sexual prowess; his entire virility is at stake. "I don't feel like a real man," admits Jack, 55, who has suffered erection problems time and again which have caused him, he says, much embarrassment.

Whence the embarrassment? Some people have quick answers. It's the advertising industry. Or Hollywood. There is certainly a call and pressure on both men and women to be picture-perfect, youthful, sexualized. Women do not have evidence of their sexual stimulation in the form of a visible erection, or lack thereof. The men I questioned all view situations in which they desire an erection but do not achieve one as their personal failure. "It was unbelievably embarrassing," said 44-year-old Michael. "There was this woman I was talking to in a bar. She was really keen. But once we were in bed – nothing happened. I talked myself out if it and pretended I was drunk. I wasn't really, but my prick was."

Occasional bouts of erectile moodiness are one thing, continuous situations involving erectile dysfunction are another. Over the years many products have been developed to be used in those cases. Penile implants, various types of injection therapies and suppositories. Sometimes surgery is the chosen treatment. And then there is Viagra (sildenafil citrate), an oral medication that is not a sexual stimulant but an erection provider. And it works by inhibiting a particular enzyme.

An erection may be triggered by a thought or a sight and that leads to the release of nitric oxide. This in turn leads to a cascade of events that causes increased blood flow to the penis. Another enzyme called guanylate cyclase is activated and that leads to a higher level of cyclic guanosine monophosphate or cGMP which is what gets blood flow into the penis to increase. As long as there is cGMP you've got an erection. Sexual stimulation causes it. Viagra makes it hang around if it does not do so naturally. Because erections are sort of a conversation between cGMP and another enzyme called PDE-5 (phosphodiesterase type 5) which is in a sense the antidote to cGMP. Viagra inhibits PDE-5 from playing its role as the anti-hero since breakdown of cGMP leads to the end of an erection. But you cannot simply take the pill, sit back and wait for an erection to be provided. "In the absence of sexual stimulation," as the manufacturer points out, the drug "has no effect." Viagra's side effects, minimal in most cases but important to know nonetheless, can include muscle pains, headaches, blurring of vision and seeing the world with a bluish tint. Men and their prescribing doctors also need to take the cardiovascular condition of the man into consideration. If you are on nitrate drugs, like nitroglycerine, you cannot use Viagra.

The drug took off like a rocket – $78 million worth of prescriptions in its first 48 hours on the market. And according to the company, around the globe, four tablets of Viagra are being dispensed a second. An opportunistic travel agent offers "Viagra Fantasy Trips": six Viagra pills for six nights in Bangkok. It has certainly made oral therapy for erectile dysfunction more popular. Since

Viagra's approval more so-called phosphodiesterase blockers are reaching pre-clinical trials. Other substances will soon be available for treatment, such as phentolamine and apomorphine.

In a study by Irwin Goldstein at Boston University, oral phentolamine, chemically phentolamine mesylate, also called Vasomax, was well tolerated and turned out to be efficacious for the treatment of erectile dysfunction. Minoxidil has been reported to increase blood flow to the penis when applied as a cream. It has been tested for the treatment of erectile dysfunction for example in men with spinal cord injuries and it yielded positive results. Other studies yielded more mixed results on the substance.

As sex therapist Bernie Zilbergeld has stated, drugs sound attractive to him and his colleagues, too. But achieving erections that way is not what sex therapists believe is true success. In many cases psychotherapy has a high success rate for the treatment of erectile problems. However, often many sessions over an extended period of time are required and that is too long a process for some men. But time is not the only problem. German sex researcher Volkmar Sigusch explains that a man who is willing to undergo psychotherapy, "has to be prepared to confront himself with previous painful experiences and short-comings, reflect on himself and deal with the rejection by others. That is not exactly a Sunday afternoon stroll in the park."

Sigusch crititizes the "medicalization of sexuality" that has occurred over the last ten years. Before that, the most popular treatments were more oriented toward psychological approaches and today pharmacological and surgical methods are more popular. "The one set of methods focuses just on the erections alone whereas the other only has the psyche at heart." Both, according to Sigusch, ignore the manifold cultural changes in recent years. Neither method works on its own. Patients live "in a culture that promises us that everything is possible and we as physicians are surprised when they come to us to be checked and rapidly repaired. These days men practically demand to retain all of their sexual functions up to a high age. Apart from that, from their first steps as little boys, men are conditioned into thinking that a true man is a man who can stand his own," states Sigusch.

Urologist and psychiatrist Leonore Tiefer of the Albert Einstein College of Medicine in New York points out that saying a man is impotent usually means much more than just the fact that his penis does not get erect. It is a "stigmatizing and stress inducing label" that reflects "a significant moment in the construct of male sexuality." She analyzes the allure of what she terms medicalized sexuality. "A medical explanation for erectile difficulties relieves men of blame and thus permits them to maintain some masculine self-esteem in the presence of impotence." And yet at the same time that very medicalization of male sexuality has many disadvantages. Besides the fact that medications may have unpredictable long-term consequences, this tendency to find medical answers obscures the fact that there may be social causes to a problem, too. Social demands are linked to a certain kind of male sexuality, one that is scripted in the sense that being a man entails sexual adequacy and hence "a rigid, reliable erection is necessary for full compliance with the script." But Tiefer would prefer changing this male sexual script simply because there is no such thing as perfect potency. "Men will remain vulnerable to the expansion of the clinical domain so long as masculinity rests heavily on a particular type of physical function." Chasing this non-existent perfect potency may line a few pockets, she points out, "but for most men it will only exchange one set of anxieties and limitations for another."

Sigusch criticizes what he calls the so-called "dissociation in medicine." When erections are manufactured medically or surgically, doctors also manage to artificially separate men from their libido and eroticism. "Men can function sexually without an inner desire and often without the psychophysical sensations that are unique for sexual experiences. Intercourse is then reduced to a purely one-dimensional physical act."

Some men will be choosing the medicated route to erection and have every right to do so, particularly if their erectile dysfunction is chronic. Other men might have doubts about whether or not popping a pill is right for them. And then there will be the more ideologized view of this. A British microbiologist at a lab where I was taking some classes passed me by one day wearing a T-shirt that read, "Viagra is for wimps." Of course, I asked him what the shirt meant to him and he just laughed, "It is just a joke, really, I am not serious about this." A few days later I saw him wearing another shirt. "Chicks hate me." Didn't ask him about that one.

At an AIDS awareness event, I met Yves, 22, and began talking to him about my book. We moved a bit away from the crowd and I asked him about the pressure to perform and whether he had ever had erection difficulties. "Of course," he smiled. "But that doesn't really matter. No use cranking and cranking if it is not having an effect. Sometimes it is nice to just cuddle." In a society that is geared toward achievement and success it does not seem easy to push aside some of those demands. Erections at the push of a button and orgasms on command sure seem more suitable for male robots than for men of flesh and blood.

How Important is Size?

"Ladies, look out – mine is really long!" reads a truck's bumper sticker. Yes, size matters. "It is the yardstick of my life," said one man in a poll about the importance of penis size. An odd yardstick at that. The magazine *Esquire* had a cover story a few years ago. The cover was a cute and doctored ruler and the blurb promised "the truth about male vanity." The ruler marked off the inches in a sequence that read, 1,2,4,5,7,10. Obviously, a penis ruler has to be a special kind of instrument. Nearly every man seems to desire some added inches or centimeters. There will always be women and men who prefer well-endowed men, as well as doctors who can perform the necessary plastic surgery and men who are totally happy with their 10-inch penis.

The normal length – if that term can be applied at all – is 6.5–10 centimeters (2.5–4 inches) non-erect, and 11–15 centimeters (4.4–6 inches) when erect. So whence the desire for a longer one? According to sex therapist Barry McCarthy this feeling of inferiority may result from when a boy compares his own penis to his father's. To a child a normal penis probably appears gigantic. And it is probably hard to fathom that one's own organ will ever grow to that size. Homosexual men have much more opportunity for comparisons than heterosexual men. Heterosexual men, though, admitted to me that they do sneak a peek in changing rooms or public toilets and very often feel less well-endowed than others.

Fashion magazines recommend trimming pubic hair to make the penis appear longer. In the era of Wonderbras it only seems appropriate that men try out the various means of enhancing and exaggerating their sexual attractiveness. As ever, the truth is revealed when textiles fall. "Men with longer penises," say 25-year-old Tom, "have more stamina in bed." Extensive studies – for example, by the pioneers of sexual research William Masters and Virginia Johnson – have shown that there is no connection between libido and penis length. But most men do not seem to believe that size does not automatically guarantee their partner's satisfaction. Then again sexual preferences are pretty much governed by just that, individualistic preferences. Some people may choose to have their penis enlarged such as through fat grafts from other parts of the body to increase girth or by surgically releasing a ligament called the suspensory ligament. Or they may choose to enlarge their testicles. In the latter procedure a silcone mould is inserted into the scrotum during an operation. At any rate "he" remains man's best friend even if the dimensions are not quite comparable to the stars in X-rated films or to fantasy measurements. Whether the penis is an X, XL or XXL, the tool is as interesting as what the owner does with it.

"I Want More!"

Wanting more in this context may mean more than length or girth. "Sometimes I really would like to have a lot of come," says Ralph, 26. There is no surefire way to influence either the consistency or the amount of semen of an ejaculate. Some men shoot for quality. Roman Pyrzak, an andrologist at the Fertility Institute in New Orleans, has the following anecdote: "One patient told me that he wanted to remain abstinent for a long time before giving his next sample, because the quality would be much better," the scientist smiles. "Sometimes men have strange ideas."

After a period of abstinence, the semen volume of an ejaculate will have increased slightly. Which is exactly why sperm banks request about two to three days of abstinence before delivering a sample. But sperm quality does not increase with time after that, nor does the amount continue to collect. Sperm just don't keep. And that's a bodily decision. After longer phases of abstinence, sperm begin to dissolve and are resorbed by the body. The older models are put away and the body replenishes the supply. Of course, tantric masters may very well find a biofeedback method to allow a man to consciously increase both the amount and the quality of his semen. That will certainly make headlines all over the world and would be of particular interest to doctors treating infertility. But so far there is no method of the sort out there.

There is slightly more information around on how to influence potency and fertility in a more general fashion. This is often shady territory populated by plenty of quacks. A critical consumer cannot really just follow unsubstantiated recommendations. So it is a good idea to talk over any kind of self-therapy with a doctor. Ingesting a supposed cure-all can have health-damaging effects or simply be a way of throwing your money out the window.

It may sound rather boring, but experts explain that sensible habits contribute to enhanced sexual performance. For example, non-smokers have fewer problems with erections than smokers. Excessive alcohol consumption does not go well with erections either, nor do most recreational drugs, although some people do say that alcohol or cocaine may make a man less inhibited. But illegal drugs cannot be a good quick fix particularly due to the mass of problems associated with them which include health problems such as physiological and psychological dependence. In parts of Germany legend has it that children fathered after a drunken bout will be mentally impaired. They are even given a name, "Rauschkinder" or "children of stupor." Scientifically, the legend may be a bit hard to prove. But lifestyle certainly impacts on many facets of potency. Bernard Jensen, author of Love, Sex and Nutrition, says sensibly: "We have to eat right, or our bodies will not work correctly." And that includes feeding the body and in particular all the players in the reproductive system, glands, organs, tissues. Extreme behavior of any kind can impact on a man's lovelife. Tired people are probably not the most brilliant lovers. Getting enough sleep, eating a balanced diet, getting enough exercise, all the recommendations that drone on in that well-known fashion do have a pro-penis effect.

"Sometimes older people come to me and ask for some advice in regard to some support," says one Swiss andrologist who states that men beat around the bush when talking about sexual issues. Risk factors for erectile dyfunction include diabetes, hypertension and smoking. There are some things he does not have a pill for. As men age, their testosterone levels change. This does not mean a man becomes any less of a man, only that the body changes and bodily changes of any kind are not usually mentioned by men to their friends, says Lisa Tenover of the Emory University who specializes in the male menopause. "When I tell them they are surprised that their hormones should change with age." But there is no golden hormone level that is true for all men. "It is possible that not every man will be clinically testosterone deficient with the same testosterone level," she explains. It may depend on what the individual's average testosterone level was when he was a young adult and the decrease from that level with age. Another factor is which bodily organ is most affected by declining testostcrone. "It may take more testosterone to impact muscle than to impact bone, and more to impact bone than to impact libido," adds Tenover. As urologist Dudley Seth Danoff points out, "You don't stop having sex because you get old, you get old because you stop having sex."

According to Eberhard Nieschlag of the German University of Münster, older men often need longer phases of stimulation to reach erection. Ejaculation may take longer as well, which is not something many women will yell and scream about. In quite a number of men, potency problems can have a "psychogenic" origin rather than a precise physiological cause. And these can be treated with great success. Erection difficulties may have a physical origin which is made worse by psychological factors. Experts state that erectile disturbances are usually not clearly defined by one precise cause, so sex therapy may truly help. As sex therapist Jed Diamond points out, "Men who hold their anger in, as well as men who are often angry at others, have more difficulties maintaining erections." Life, stressful as it often is, can leave its traces. Let-downs at work, arguments, family problems can all hit below the belt. Sexual rela tionships mirror other aspects of life. What if success in bed skips a beat? Sex therapists say talking can do the trick. If a man can admit why he thinks he is not having an erection, then a woman may not feel it is all "her" fault. And if a woman does not react with compassion or sympathy and storms out of the bedroom, well maybe the relationship was not all that hot after all.

Urologist Dudley Seth Danoff has dealt with patients who have a tough time with the contrast of success in their professional lives while experiencing supposed "failure" in the bedroom. One man who came for advice realized that the pressure he placed on himself stemmed from his father never having acknowledged his achievements which, in turn, had hurt his self-esteem. He approached therapy with as much perseverance as everything else in his life, and managed to reattain what Danoff calls Penis Power. This is not the answer for everyone nor the appropriate answer when physical issues are causing potency problems. As Danoff puts it, the bottom line is: "The penis wants to get hard." But if you try too hard, then things may backfire leading to what he calls the Penis Paradox: "The harder you try, the softer it gets." He recommends that a man leave work and other stressful elements of life at the bedroom door. You can burn off stress in other ways before you get between the sheets, or you can burn off stress in bed. By indulging in one of the most pleasant forms of stress – sex – anxiety can be turned into an energizer. Although these methods do not sound bad, a pill seems like a quicker fix. But there are pills and then there are pills.

Love Potions and Other Little Helpers

Small ads in magazines or flashy Websites promise that the earth will move for both you and your partner if you try the advertised love potion. "Enhanced sex," "Explosive sex," "The world's best kept secret," "Natural aphrodisiac," "100% natural and safe." Right. And you get to give $59.95 to someone making money with the placebo effect. Your own wishful thinking may be just as good a "pill" to give you an erection as some of those concoctions you can buy. You believe it is the remedy, your penis believes it and you are set. Science does not have all the aspects of the mind–body connection unravelled, but the mind is known to be a powerful healer. And a potent one.

One problem with those products is that it is likely that the US Food and Drug Administration (FDA) has not approved them. Chances are, there was no quality control in their manufacture. So there is little way for you to really know what is in the bottle. And if you are buying something exotic, like powdered rhino horn, then you might need to remember that is both cruel and illegal. After all, horn chasers are poachers. If phallic magic is called for, why not make it a symbolic gesture and hang a cucumber over your bed?

Since you often do not know the precise make-up of a love potion, the results can certainly endanger your health or possibly even cost you your life. Men and women have purportedly taken substances that were given to cattle to get them into heat. And paid the price with their life.

Cantharidin, otherwise known as Spanish fly, has long been known to be a sexual stimulant. The chemical is derived from insects called blister beetles. The so-called Spanish fly you can buy contains the substance but, as analyses have shown, apparently usually in negligible amounts. But the substance is also available illicitly and is definitely known to be toxic. Emergency physicians at Temple University School of Medicine treated four men and women who had taken Spanish fly. They had stomach aches, dark urine, nausea and internal bleeding.

Just because a substance is a herbal supplement of some kind does not mean things are automatically fine. There may be an effect, there may be none. The substance might be toxic. It is a good idea to check to see if studies have been done on the efficacy of a particular extract.

So-called poppers, chemically inorganic aliphatic nitrites, which are inhaled for the kick they apparently deliver, can cause unconsciousness or worse: for example, tissue hypoxia, a condition in which oxygen cannot reach body tissue. There are various products derived from toads and toad venom, bufotenine or bufadienolides, both illegal substances in the US. This product type, called the Love Stone in the West Indies, has been known to cause toxic reactions and heart failure.

In addition to these types of potions which should not be taken, there are plenty of so-called natural substances with purported aphrodisiacal qualities. In drug stores or pharmacies you might spot men's teas and drinks, which contain ginger, cinnamon, sarsaparilla, cardamom, ginseng and other ingredients. At my request some men tried them, saying they tasted OK but they could detect no aphrodisiacal quality to them.

These very ingredients are mentioned time and again throughout history as having aphrodisiacal qualities. Is the effect of the tea, or lack of it, all in a person's head? After all the head is a pretty potent love potion right in itself. Or perhaps the components might well have an effect but it was lost in the way

44 THE SEMEN BOOK

these ingredients were processed? Hard to tell. Everyone reacts differently to foods and food supplements. And then maybe legendary recipes may just well be legends with a teaspoon of superstition. According to the Food and Drug Administration, "the reputed sexual effects of so-called aphrodisiacs are based in folklore, not fact." In 1989, the agency declared that "there is no specific proof that any over-the-counter aphrodisiacs work to treat sexual dysfunction." OK, so there you have the authoritative word.

Over centuries alternative health concepts have developed in many cultures. It is enlightening to look at the history of some common practices. This is not an attempt to condone these substances or ideas. If spinach works for you as it obviously did for Popeye, then that is fine. No need for FDA approval on that one. A female version of Popeye, albeit a brutal version, was the Assyrian queen Semiramis, who subjugated many nations and tribes during her campaigns. She was also known for her considerable sexual appetite. When her armies were victorious, she chose the most handsome men in her army ranks and gave them love potions to put them in a state of ecstasy. Then she spent one day and the following night with them. The love hangover was less than pleasant for the men because they were subsequently executed, lest they spend their pleasures elsewhere.

According to the cultural historian Friedrich Lehmann, "A number of the love potions that have been used throughout history had positive effects, others at least contain some ingredients that could have the desired result. Without doubt some of them caused considerable harm." In his charming book, which came out in Germany in 1955 and was banned but later allowed, he pulled together anecdotes and recipes that were supposed to incite love, to curb it, to increase the capacity to make love or to maintain or renew fertility. The following passages draw on his work as well as others on the subject.

Drinking love potions has put an untimely end to the lives of men throughout history, such as the Roman poet Titus Lucretius (96–55 BCE) as well as Roman commander Lucius Licinius Lucullus (117–57 BCE). In some cases reactions were rather violent. Priests of the Peruvian sun god are said to have obtained a higher level of consciousness by chewing the fruit of the plant Datura but sometimes the ecstasy ended with their death from this extremely toxic plant. May these sad events suffice as warnings.

The Mayans developed the first beverage made of cocoa and it was alleged to be stimulating. Much later, the Aztecs continued this tradition and the Aztec emperor Montezuma, as legend has it, fortified himself with many cups of cocoa before entering his harem. Anthelme Brillat-Savarin, a writer and cook of various culinary delights who lived in the late eighteenth and early nineteenth century, describes a potion to "cheer up the downhearted" that essentially is based on a thick brew of hot chocolate. Eighteenth-century scientist Etienne Geoffreoy Saint-Hilaire recommended chocolate with cinnamon, cardamom, Peruvian bark and vanilla instead of amber as a reliable love tonic.

So-called nightshade plants (*Solanaceae*) have been used for various types of witches' ointments, modern poisons and anaesthetics. The alkaloids which the plants contain – atropine and scopolamine – will produce hallucinations and, in higher dosages, coma. Extracts from these plants have been used to treat sexual and reproductive disorders. Pythagoras (582–507 BCE), perhaps better known as a mathematician, mentioned the magical and medicinal use of mandrake (*Mandragora officinarium*). In Europe this plant enjoyed the same reputation as ginseng in Asia and has been known and used since earliest times to promote longevity and as an aphrodisiac.

Ginseng is used in Chinese medicine to treat various ailments such as fatigue. As Norman Gillis of Yale University Medical School points out, it may enhance nitric oxide production in various tissues such as the corpus cavernosum which may explain part of the aphrodisiacal action of ginseng root.

Many recipes thoughout history contain ingredients that are not exactly easy to get at your local butcher's. Testes. The Romans chose wolf testes, the Indians chose rams, other peoples chose bulls, stallions, roosters, stags, bucks, kangaroos, beaver. Along with other organ extracts such as from brain, liver and pancreas these recipes were applied as infertility treatments by Indian, Chinese, Persian and Egyptian doctors 3,000 to 4,000 years ago.

The Arab scholar Cheikh Nefzaoui, whose treatise *The Perfumed Garden* is believed to have been written in the early 16th century, describes recipes for a variety of situations. For premature ejaculation: "The man whose ejaculation is too precipitate must take nutmeg and incense mixed together with honey." In his chapter with prescriptions for "increasing the dimensions of small men and for making them splendid" he has a number of recommendations for a man "who wishes to make himself grand or fortify himself for the love." He should rub himself with tepid water, "until he gets red and extended by the blood flowing into him, in consequence of the heat; he must then anoint with a mixture of honey and ginger, rubbing in sedulously." Another remedy uses pepper, lavender, galanga (an Indian root) and musk, reduced to powder, sifted and mixed with honey and preserved ginger. The mixture is to be rubbed in. Another kind of mixture entails using "an ass's member" prepared with oil, either to be used for anointing or as a drink.

In the Middle Ages when it was believed that somebody's potency had been cursed, the man was advised to take aquilegia extract, or extract from the buttercup family. The tea supposedly cured all kinds of male problems.

There are numerous other love potion recipe traditions. In India, milk and sugar as well as pepper, liquorice, asparagus juice, barley, fennel, jasmine, anise, nutmeg and cloves were favored as ingredients for a lover's drink that would also lead to a longer life. In other recipes "pure, heated butter" in combination with sugar is recommended as a tonic, as well as liquorice, fennel and milk, after which a man will purportedly want more than one woman. Further indulgence was to be enhanced if you added sugar cane root, sesame seeds, Tuscan jasmine and egg yolks. In case you were suddenly surprised by an opportunity, an Indian wisdom is to mix milk, warm butter and egg yolk. It seems as if back then, no one had cholesterol problems. Indian master Vatsayana did point out that it was important never to use doubtful or unclean ingredients.

Arabian recipes contain similar ingredients. "Drink some camel's milk mixed with honey. That gives you so much power that some men never get any sleep at all." For the lactose-intolerant reader here is a non-dairy recipe: "Sip a glass full of thick honey together with twenty almonds and one hundred pine nuts."

Drawing on the idea, shown for example in the film *Like Water for Chocolate*, aphrodisiacal qualities may also stem from the way the potion is prepared. Friedrich Lehmann studied historical texts by physicians and found many foods and spices were often part of a physican's recommendations for love potions that needed to be prepared in special ways. In particular, he focused on Hippocrates (460–375 BCE), perhaps the most famous physician in pre-Christian times and author of important works on nutrition; the scientist Pedanius Discorides (20–79 CE), whose book *De Materia Medica* described the medical value of 600 plants; the Greek doctor Claudius Galen (*c.* 130–*c.*200 CE) who, among many volumes on human anatomy, also wrote a book on semen as well as a book about the "powers of food"; and the court physician of Emperors Ferdinand and Maximilian, Pietro Andrea Mattioli (1500–1577) who was also a botanist and did extensive studies on plants and their aphrodisiacal effects. Here are some of their findings:

Anise (*Pimpinella anisum*): According to Discorides it stimulates the desires of men. European and Asian cooking recipes praised anise as "stimulating the desires in men and women."

Curry: A mixture of spices that apparently does not only stimulate the palate and the tongue.

Dill (*Anethum graveoleus*): Reported to weaken potency.

Fennel (*Foeniculum vulgare*): According to Arabian recipes and in the Middle Ages in Germany it was thought that fennel increases the amount of semen.

Clove (*Eugenia caryophyllus*): According to Mattioli, "Two parts of ground cloves in milk increase the natural amount of sperm and weakens your morals."

Ginger (*Zingiber officinale*): Supposed to stimulate the nerves and blood vessels and it also has a long standing reputation in Asia and India as an aphrodisiac.

Calamus (*Acorus calamus*): Was called the Venus plant by the Romans.

Cardamom (*Elettaria cardamomum*): The pods are believed to be an aphrodisiac.

Garlic (*Allium sattivum*): According to Mattioli it stimulates the libido and potency.

Turmeric (*Curcuma longa*): Tastes hot, with the equivalent effect.

Linseed (*Linum usitatissimum*): Good for fertility.

Laurel, marjoram, horseradish, coriander, damiana, jasmine, nutmeg, paprika, parsley, pepper and safran all have a purported aphrodisiacal effect. As one text from the sixteenth century states, pepper delivers unchastity and lust.

Salt, however, always had a bad reputation in this context. There was supposedly no salt on the dinner table of the Greek gods who are said to have had lively and turbulent lovelives. During the Renaissance salt was believed harmful to a man's seed.

A thumbs up for mustard, thyme, and vanilla which were all considered aphrodisiacs, especially during the eighteenth century rococo period. Juniper, Worcester Sauce and cinnamon also had a good reputation and were all alleged to be stimulating.

On to the vegetable world. According to some traditions and beliefs some vegetables have a good reputation in the love department. Mattioli wrote that leek would increase the amount of sperm. An old German recipe states that "elder knights of Venus" who wished to be loved by their young wives should consume a salad of fried or boiled onions prepared with oil, vinegar, pepper and salt. Carrots, wrote Mattioli, create a desire for other food and marital duties. A similar effect was ascribed to radishes by the Egyptians.

In the older Arabian cultures and in the Middle Ages, celery was considered lusty and traditional verses and songs apparently contain many such references. Among the mushrooms, morels and truffles enjoy a centuries' old reputation as aphrodisiacs.

Peas and lentils were not held in high regard by the ancient Greeks. Peas supposedly increased the amount of semen but not lust.

Chickpeas enjoy a better reputation and Galen wrote that they stimulate lovemaking and increase semen production. An aphrodisiacal recipe in the Middle Ages included chickpeas and onions, with cinnamon, ginger and cardamom.

Artichokes, asparagus, leek are all stimulating vegetables, say the scholars. Asparagus is, according to the authors of an aphrodisiacal cookbook calling themselves "the cooking couple," "perhaps the most erotic member of the vegetable kingdom." Cheikh Nefzaoui recommended boiling asparagus and then frying them to make a very suitable dish to serve before lovemaking. In nineteenth-century France bridegrooms were supposed to eat several courses of asparagus "because of its reputed powers to arouse." The tomato was considered an aphrodisiac by the ancient peoples of Mexico and Peru.

Connoisseurs of what Lehman calls the love cuisine should use vinegar and lemons sparingly. Pickles and actually all things pickled are considered a love no-no. Although endives are considered stimulating, all other salad types are listed as weakening virility. Pomegranates, the holy fruit of Aphrodite, raisins, figs and most nuts are praised throughout aphrodisiacal literature.

On to the carbs. According to Lehman, rice has a better reputation than the potato. For the meat-lovers now a bit of bad news, at least the historical wisdom is that meat is not known to be an aphrodisiac. When the Romans partied they did serve peacock and other fowl, goat and various types of fish and shellfish including oysters. Casanova supposedly had 50 oysters a day. Their mythology speaks for itself. Aphrodite, the Greek goddess of love, came forth from an oyster shell and was the mother of Eros which adds to the myth as well. Pâté de foie gras, which dates back to Roman times, has kept its reputation of having stimulating qualities. Casanova apparently loved it.

So what validity do these traditions have? Perhaps it depends on what you choose to believe. Not many of these recipes have stood the test of time, but oysters have kept their reputation as aphrodisiacs. The French homeopathic doctor Guy Roulier believes in their effectiveness because of their high mineral content, such as phosphorus, especially zinc. The same applies to fish roe. According to some nutritional experts, ginseng is still considered an aphrodisiac. As for the rest, have some asparagus!

There is a remedy from nature's apothecary that medical experts do recommend to treat unspecific erectile dysfunction: yohimbine. Made from the bark of a tree native to Africa, this substance increases blood flow to the genitalia, thus promoting an erection. Some experts say it heightens libido, other doctors are more doubtful. It acts in the central and peripheral nervous system and has been used for over a century in treating erectile difficulties. And according to A. Morales, a urologist at Queen's University in Canada, that is precisely its problem. Since it is old, he points out, it does not "enjoy patent protection or commercial viability." And so, it remains in limbo. Studies in animals have shown good results but there have not yet been human clinical trials. Yohimbine hydrochloride is sold under various brand names such as Yocon. It is best to consult with a doctor about taking it. There has been a lot of research on yohimbine and in low dosages there are few side effects.

Then there are a large variety of penis creams and ointments. Some of them contain nitrogylcerin which increases blood flow to the penis. It is important that condoms be worn if these substances are used since they can cause headaches not only in the user but also in his partner. Overall, yohimbine seems to be the more reliable and efficient substance. Given the success of Viagra, it is clear that other substances aimed at sexual enhancement are coming round the corner.

Physicians may consider hormone therapy for a man who is reporting potency problems. But first, exact tests will have to reveal if a man really has a clinically relevant low testosterone level. Values of this hormone fluctuate over the course of a day, for example, which can falsify test results. Other more mechanical treatments for erectile dysfunction include vacuum pumps that get blood into the penis, or penis rings that prevent the blood in an erect penis from flowing back. Urologists point out that it is important not to pick a ring that is too tight as this can cause painful erections. And they recommend using a ring that can be opened in case of discomfort. Having erections for an extended period of time can damage penile tissue and needs immediate medical attention.

Looking After Your Testes, Your Semen, Yourself

The United States seems to have the most expensive urine in the world – due to its vitamin-rich content. In general, and unless a doctor has told you otherwise, if you eat a balanced diet you do not really need supplements or vitamins. Bodies prefer healthy lifestyles and environments and so do sperm. For a sperm, that is not an easy thing to come by. In a sperm's vicinity so-called free radicals abound – these are not members of some kind of political extremist group on their way to the next meeting of the World Trade Organization; they are molecules produced in the course of metabolism that are highly reactive and can damage DNA. They arise in many spots in the body. A healthy diet contains an appropriate amount of antioxidants, for example, vitamins C and E as well as beta carotene are all known to mop up free radicals. All of this is important for sperm because, as urologist T.B. Hargreave of Western General Hospital in Edinburgh puts it, within the testicle is the environment of spermatogenesis which is mutation-promoting. Within the testes, cells are constantly dividing, making sperm. It takes close to 380 cell divisions to create sperm and it is during these cell division stages that cells are prone to be injured through free radicals. Which makes the developing sperm, as British physician Sarah Brewer states, "sitting ducks for free radical attack."

To a certain extent, the body looks after its sperm itself. The vitamin C concentration in the seminal fluid is eight times higher than in other parts of the body. Bruce Ames of the University of California at Berkeley found that men with a low vitamin C intake had twice as much DNA damage in their sperm as men with an appropriate vitamin C intake. Smokers should be especially mindful as their vitamin C levels may be lowered.

The antioxidant vitamin E combined with vitamin C contributes considerably to protecting sperm. Sperm don't clump together so much and their motility is increased. Furthermore vitamin E helps to keep cell membranes flexible. Vitamin E is contained in seed oils, nuts and in various vegetables. It also helps to delay the ageing process to which free radicals contribute.

Beta carotene is also an antidote to free radicals and is thought to have a similar effect to the vitamins C and E. This vitamin A precursor contributes to sperm maturation in the epididymis. Because vitamin A can be toxic at larger quantities, taking beta carotene is the preferred option. Many vegetables such as carrots and broccoli, and yellow and orange fruit, margarine and dairy products all contain beta carotene.

Zinc: A Particularly Potent Mineral

More than 80 enzymes in the body require zinc to function properly. Zinc supports the immune response and is a vital structural element in all cell membranes. Zinc is also a member of the defensive line against free radicals and of major importance in the male reproductive tract. Zinc is needed to regenerate cells and it also seems to play a role in fertility.

Semen "knows" of all this and takes precautions: the concentration of zinc in semen is five times higher than in the rest of the body. With every ejaculation about 5 milligrams of zinc leave the body. Since the daily requirement for this mineral is about 15 milligrams, it is easy to see why it makes sense to replenish those zinc stores after prolonged lovemaking. Zinc can be found in meat, seafood, whole-grain products, pumpkin seeds, dairy products and beans.

Zinc levels are highest in the prostate, testicular levels are slightly lower. Zinc deficiency leads to testicular regression and creates glitches in sperm production. In semen, zinc is vital for sperm metabolism and it stabilizes the DNA, the precious genetic cargo, in the sperm's head. While in the prostate, the zinc is chemically bound but after ejaculation it is dispersed throughout the seminal plasma. The sperm take up zinc from the seminal fluid which helps them retain both their shape and their function. This zinc uptake is important because where the sperm are usually going, the female vagina, is a rather zinc-poor place. In the lab, if you add zinc to the seminal fluid, the sperm start swimming slower. They seem to be settling into a quiet phase. What happens is, they lower their oxygen intake and save energy. Once in the vagina, the zinc stores are tapped and there is an increase in sperm activity and mobility, so zinc is "acting like a mineral turbo charge," says Brewer. Zinc is an important element in fertilization because it helps to decondense the genetic material.

Lifestyle

Clothes

There are many good things to say about boxer shorts. And this is not just from a woman's aesthetic point of view. If the testicles are pressed too closely to the body, for example because underwear is too tight, their temperature rises. And that is not the best news for sperm production. Ron Weber and his colleagues of the Dutch University of Leyden did a study looking at temperature differences between men with boxer shorts and men who wear tighter underwear. And he says, "Boxer shorts are much better than tighter underwear."

"Look at us!," exclaims David Karabinus, andrologist at the University of Arizona. At a conference, he steps in front of his poster describing a new study and points to his genitals. I look, glad for the animated explanation. "All day long we sit on our behinds and wrap the testes in layers and layers of textiles." Then the slim man takes a few exaggeratedly bowlegged steps. "A bull's testes hang freely. That is much better." For his study he had wrapped bull's testes in cloth and found that the sperm quality dropped considerably. What is valid for the bull is seemingly also true for men. And mice. A study at University

Hospital Gasthuisberg in Belgium involved dipping mice up to their testes in water slightly above body temperature. And they found that these mice with "acute scrotal heating" had impaired sperm quality which were less able to fertilize eggs.

Scientists at the Harbor UCLA Medical Center in California took a studied look at jockstraps and had men wear specially devised ones. For one group the straps were lined with a layer of polyester, the other group wore a version with a layer of polyester and aluminium. In both cases the temperature in the testes rose by one degree and semen quality dropped. This is a significant change, but not enough, for example, to propose these jockstraps as a reliable male contraceptive.

Testes can also get too cold, but in a sense they can look after themselves because they can retract into the body. This occurs, for example, when a man jumps into an icy lake or pool. If they had a choice, the testes would probably not choose cold baths, but cool is definitely cool for sperm. Three to four degrees Centigrade lower than the rest of the body, that is what seems best for sperm.

A visit to the sauna is very good for the sweat glands, the skin and general circulation, but it reduces sperm production. The sauna does overheat the body and this is lethal for sperm. But this is not permanent – the testes replenish the stores. But you may not want to plan on fathering a child or delivering a sperm sample to a clinic right after visiting a sauna – the chances are that your sperm count will not be great.

Eating and Drinking

You are what you eat. Axel, 25, says, "When I masturbate, I sometimes swallow the semen that ends up in my hand. It tastes pretty salty, but is not unpleasant." Other men feel differently. Peter, 21, says, "Looking at it is fine, but tasting it … no, thank you." As previously described sexual therapist Barbara DeAngelis mentions in her book *Men – What Every Woman Should Know* that drugs, alcohol, stress and diet all affect the taste and consistency of a man's semen. According to DeAngelis, men who drink a lot of coffee and alcohol have more bitter semen and men who eat a lot of animal proteins, red meat in particular, have a more acidic taste to their semen. It seems only fair that before a man requests his partner to try his semen, he should try it himself.

DeAngelis has some advice based on her own experience as well as on reports of couples seeking her advice. She recommends having a male partner drink pineapple juice for several days which will make his semen sweet. Unprotected oral sex is a no-no unless you and your partner are HIV negative.

Bodybuilding

"In my practice I have seen several terrific male specimens – athletes and movie stars whose bodies looked like sculpted marble," writes American urologist Dudley Seth Danoff. These people had come to him because of a frightening development: "Their testicles had shrunk to the size of peas." They had been working out and had taken anabolic steroids to enhance their muscle development. "Enhance" is a mild way of putting it. Steroids can add amazing bulk to a man who works out with weights. There is certainly nothing wrong with exercise, it is healthy and muscles can go a long way when flirting. But steroids are not exactly harmless. And then, with all the bulk, at one point clothes do come off and that is when tiny testes will probably be unlikely to impress.

Anabolic steroids are chemically related to testosterone. As more of this hormone enters the body, the testes cuts back production – with the afore-mentioned results. Bodybuilding and taking drugs like these practically equals a chemical castration. Fertility can also be impaired.

Sports

Humorist Dave Barry believes it is a design flaw to have a man's privates out in the open, "like Harold Lloyd dangling from the face of the giant clock, waiting for disaster to strike."And he goes on to recount an episode where had climbed in his friend's shoulders to see a Republican campaign rally. He slipped off his perch and severely bumped his personals on his friends elbow on the way down. "I could probably hurt myself worse, but only if I had used power tools," writes Barry. In sports, games, lovemaking or plain old playful wrestling, the testes can get hurt. In that particular moment it seems hard to believe the pain will actually subside. Luckily, it usually does. But the experi-ence may remain with a man anyway.

A man in his early thirties came to a urologist because of his erection problems. After examination and tests it became clear that blood flow to the penis was impaired. The man thought for a moment when asked if he had sustained any blows to the groin and recalled a skiing accident several years prior, when he had crashed into a tree. The pain had subsided after several days and he had never consulted a doctor. The problems with erections only cropped up much later. In this case medication took care of the problem, but an operation was an option if that had failed.

In a study at the Children's Hospital Medical Center and at the Northeastern Ohio Universities College of Medicine, both in Ohio, physicians conducted a five-question survey among male athletes age 12–18 before a sports physical exam. As it turned out 54% of the young men did not know why the genitals were examined, 45% did not use testicular protection and the majority were unfamiliar with the symptoms of something amiss with the testicles.

"Mommy, ow." That is what her four-year-old, John, said. He had been climbing on the wrought iron gate that helped to keep their large dog out of certain areas of the house. The boy held his genitals in pain. Although the incident occurred seven years previously, his mother remembers vividly how frightfully worried she was. She whipped off his clothes and underwear and discovered a puncture at the base of his penis. At first sight she said: "Oh my God, he cut it off!" Panic-stricken, she rushed him off to the hospital emergency room. Her boy did not seem to be in too much pain and although the wound seemed deep, it was hardly bleeding. In the emergency room she had the doctors' immediate attention and they proposed surgery and a thorough exam to ascertain the nature of the injury. Even if not painful and not bleeding, genital injuries are serious. At any age. He might indeed have injured the penile tissue or the testes, or both.

Sports injuries do not automatically cause erection difficulties. But paying attention to the genitals pays off. A so-called true "urologic emergency" is frequent with male teenagers but it can happen at any age: acute scrotal pain often caused by testicular torsion when the testes twist around the spermatic cord. It is not always easy for physicians to diagnose this condition but time is the enemy in these situations. If it is testicular torsion, any delay in surgery can be deadly for the testicle. If it dies, there are no resuscitation methods and this situation can hamper both fertility and testosterone production.

In general, surgery in the pelvic region can impact on erections but not necessarily so. But there are many injuries which affect the arteries that supply the penis with enough blood for an erection. Injuries to the perineum are particularly tricky. Sometimes it just seems to be a bruise that heals but the internal damage may cause erectile dysfunction that may occur long after the original injury.

Sports trainers and coaches carry a big responsibility. They need to consider the men in their athletes and make sure all injuries, including those to the genital area are given full medical attention. For some sports, small changes can make a world of difference. According to some researchers, cyclists run a higher risk of impotence because the seat puts pressure on some important blood vessels. Special bike seats are manufactured that heed these delicate issues and are cushioned and hollowed out in all the right places.

Smoking

To non-smokers the thought of kissing a smoker is about as erotic as licking an ashtray. But the world is not populated solely by politically correct purists, so nicotine lovers can count on some concessions by other smokers and non-smokers. That said, it is well known that smoking is not a particularly healthy way to keep hands and mouth occupied. Some hints about the effects of smoking on the genitals may serve as an additional motivation to spend your money on healthier produce.

No blood vessel in the body is happy being constantly constricted. Since sexual excitement is coupled with an increased blood flow into the penis, free-flowing blood is very important. Men who have arteriosclerosis already have impaired blood flow in their bodies affecting also blood flow to the heart, the brain and the legs, as well as the penis. Impotence is generally more frequent in men suffering from arterial problems. Since smokers constrict their blood vessels and arteriosclerosis is more frequent in smokers, it certainly does not seem that cigarettes are doing a man or his penis much good.

Through no fault of their own, diabetics have an increased risk of arteriosclerosis. People with high blood pressure, high cholesterol and smokers with their risky lifestyle can change their habits, though. If they could, all blood vessels would express their gratefulness. Urologist Danoff says that smoking is just as bad for your penis as it is for your lungs. "If you want to be a man with penis power, say goodbye to nicotine."

The correlation as to whether smoking impairs fertility is not quite clear. Some scientists say there is ample evidence that smoking negatively affects sperm quality and others disagree. T.B. Hargreave of the University of Edinburgh thinks smoking only has minimal impact. In some studies smokers have lower semen volumes, in other studies the sperm concentration in the ejaculate is lowered. Other researchers found a decrease in sperm motility and a higher number of abnormally shaped sperm. However, there are also many studies that do not find any differences in semen quality between smokers and non-smokers.

The difficulty is exacerbated by the fact that statistically there are already many differences between smokers and non-smokers. Smokers are more likely to drink alcohol, for example. It is not easy to detect what effect is particularly due to cigarettes. Different diets also blur the results. Smokers generally have a lower uptake of linoleic acid from their diet. This could also have an impact on sperm production. If there was a distinctive impact it might be more noticeable in older smokers, as they have smoked longest. In a study at a German hospital in Ulm they found that the semen of younger men was more affected but did not have a clear explanation for that.

Sing-Eng Chia and his colleagues at the National University of Singapore found lower semen quality among smokers and wondered what chemical in cigarette smoke may be causing this effect. They pointed out that cigarette smoke contains almost a hundred different substances – apart from nicotine and carbon monoxide, for example, there are such heavy metals as cadmium and lead. Smokers have higher cadmium levels in their blood, and in animal studies cadmium has been shown to affect sperm development, but this has not been shown in humans. According to David Handelsman, andrologist at the Royal Prince Alfred Hospital in Sydney, on the whole, smoking seems to have a small effect on sperm production, function and fertility of otherwise healthy men.

There are always many aspects of a man's lifestyle that can impact on sperm production, be it seasonal rhythms or the fact that the participants of these studies did not adhere to the prescribed abstinence before they handed in their sample. When in doubt, however, and when a smoker is having difficulty fathering a child, he can count on a doctor suggesting that he kick the smoking habit.

Alcohol

Henny Goverde and his colleagues at the Dutch University of Nijmegen looked at the impact of smoking and alcohol on sperm quality in 5,000 men. More smokers than non-smokers had a lower than average amount of semen and excessive alcohol consumption increased the amount of sperm with abnormal head shapes. They conclude that smoking and alcohol consumption may not be contributing very much to poor semen quality but "high alcohol consumption may decrease further the degree of normal sperm morphology in semen of subjects with already poor semen characteristics."

Drugs

Marijuana can disrupt the body's hormones. Low sperm counts and a higher number of abnormal sperm shapes are more common in men who use cocaine. A study at Temple University indicates that cocaine can attach to sperm and thus piggyback its way to an embryo, perhaps harming its development. In the mid-1970s Theodore Cicero and his colleagues of the Washington University School of Medicine in St. Louis found that methadone users had a much lower testosterone level than either non-drug users or heroin addicts and sperm concentration was reduced as well. Prescription drugs can interact with both the body's testosterone production, sperm quality and the penis' ability to become erect. These issues will be dealt with in Chapter 6.

Stress

Positive stress turns into negative stress at different levels for different people. I have seen scientists at andrology conferences be ridiculed by their peers for their attempts to examine the connection between semen quality and stress. They were told that their statistics and data were not convincing. Stress is not easy to quantify.

Yet the effects are pretty clear when you ask around at sperm banks. "Sperm from a sample generated under stress usually has to be thrown out," says an andrologist at a US sperm bank. When giving their first sample, men are often nervous and stressed and the semen quality suffers. For that reason, the process often needs to be repeated. "The second time they know what to expect and are much calmer, and the quality of the sperm is much improved," says physician Ron Weber of the University of Leyden in Holland. Werner Gehring, the director of a private infertility clinic in Germany describes a couple desperate for children who had undergone long treatment in an infertility clinic before coming to see him. The husband explained that he was asked to masturbate in the restroom to provide a semen sample. The restroom was right next to the nurses' staff room, and their chatting during their breaks was easily discernible through the restroom wall. Days before his appointment in the clinic the man became terrified by the thought of having to masturbate there. "That man was definitely stressed," explains Gehring. "Needless to say, his sperm quality was lousy, hardly a living sperm." In the soundproofed and spacious rooms of

Gehring's clinic, the proud physician says, "the man's sperm was always top quality." The couple actually needed no further treatment. Just the fact that they had left the old clinic and had a conversation with a new doctor had dissolved the stress. The patient's wife became pregnant a short time later.

At a conference in the US, Weber reported that a lot was known about the influence of stress on women but very little on men. Here, as with many other aspects of male physiology, there is a considerable lack of information and research. According to Weber, a study of marathon runners found that their sperm were less mobile, but there was no clear explanation given for that.

In women, emotional stress, changes in diet, weight changes and sports can impact on ovulation. Girls who commence serious sport training before puberty appear to delay the onset of their menstruation. Prolactin levels rise when taking certain drugs and when under stress. It is known that increased levels of prolactin have a negative impact on libido both in men and women.

Weber tried to create an artificially stressful situation and observed that rats with higher prolactin levels had a lower level of LH. LH is the hormone that acts on the Leydig cells in the testis to produce testosterone. According to Weber, it is questionable whether these results can be applied to humans. Weber reversed the problem and said humorously: "I know, humans are a bad model for the rat." Richard Clark, an endocrinologist, pointed out the various forms of stress: environmental stressors such as hunger, disease and psychological stress. They can all have an impact on the male hormonal system and hence on sperm production. Lizards kept in cages and handled frequently have a lower testosterone level due to the stress this causes. Monkeys who were denied food for only a few hours also showed a stress related decrease in their testosterone level. Obesity, another form of physical stress, also has a negative impact on the body's testosterone levels. In a study at the Department of Health Services in Berkeley, California, it was found that men experiencing the stress of a family member's death had diminished semen quality.

Health Awareness

Every physician I spoke to dealing with men's health and sexual health in particular reported that their patients had little knowledge of their own bodies. "Sometimes they are really ignorant. They don't have a clue what they have between their legs," one andrologist said. As Lisa Tenover, an andrologist at Emory University, states: "Men do seem to speak less about their bodies, at least in our culture. Some of this may be due to the issue of men not wanting to complain or worry about themselves because of the cultural idea that men are strong and not supposed to get sick. That is seen as a sign of weakness." Peter, 21, says: "Of course I am interested in my own body ... even if men are not as wildly interested in it as women." He adds: "It is much more interesting to know more about the opposite sex."

So are men more knowledgeable on the vagaries of ovulation than their prostates? That does not seem to be the case. Overall, men I questioned said they preferred to postpone regular check-ups with the doctor as long as they could. "I don't want to go," "I don't have time for health stuff," were common responses. Actually I could not even convince a man to go to the andrologist just for the sake of seeing what it was like. Yes, testicular cancer or prostate cancer are just as frightening as breast or ovarian cancer are for women. With people like Michael Korda or Rudy Giuliani coming out and speaking about this disease and treatment options perhaps it will be easier for others to follow suit. Knowing your own body seems to make sense in order to deal with the stress of it when times are difficult. In times of general well-being, knowledge of this kind may well let a man use his natural tools in ways he never thought possible.

Potency Champions

Cinema can be educational. The same applies to so-called erotic adult videos which many men view for enjoyment and, so it seems, for educational purposes as well. "I watched 15 porno movies in order to find out what sex was all about," says Mark, 25. Of course many men say they watch porn movies to get turned on but they often say that they watch them to discover new techniques.

The particular shot that pornographic movies contain that soft porn does not, is the image of external ejaculation, or the "come shot." Visible male orgasm is essential to the plot of most stories in this genre, that are often a bit thin in the drama and dialogue departments. The "come shot" is sometimes called the "money shot," as this is the most expensive shot and male actors demand extra pay for it. But things are not always the way they seem. Reliable sources report that close-ups of ejaculations sometimes may be scenes edited in from other movies. They may not be from the actor and hence not authentic. Whether or not this happens often is hard to research. Obviously the industry does not want to admit to playing tricks.

4 Conversation of the Gametes: Getting Sperm and Egg to Meet

Men and Women

When a man meets a woman, there can be poetry, love and trust but also dislike, exploitation or even worse. And of course there can be anything in between. It is certainly helpful to have guidebooks as well as ideas on how to navigate the hills and valleys of relationship terrain. There are lots of books about the ins and outs of dating and relationships, but this is not one of them.

NASA does not seem to have a particular take on whether women are from Venus and men from Mars. The debates on the subject of gender differences may never conclude and instead may always lead to new questions, which actually keeps life interesting. Every debate has its context and these days it seems that biology sets the stage. The Human Genome Project, during which the basic genetic blueprint of humans has been unravelled, and similar projects underway on animals and plants as well as micro-organisms, are certainly all lending the science of biology a certain bullishness. It is tempting to look at pretty much every facet of life, including love and relationships, as a biochemical cascade programmed by genetics with a dash of spicing by the environment. As Roger Short of the University of Melbourne points out, "Human reproductive strategies are often a compromise," one that relates to the very different reproductive agendas of the two sexes. And this, in his view, is what fuels "the eternal tension between the sexes." Undoubtedly, biology is inherent to dating and mating. The question to what extent biology writes the script is part of a lively ongoing discourse on nature versus nurture. Would business school students really need to take negotiation strategy classes if we are all easy to analyze using biology alone? It does seem that the extremist view, "it's all biology" appears rather limited and limiting.

A major contributing factor to the fact that we are even here to debate these issues in the first place is thanks to the meeting of sperm and egg. Just how something as complex and sophisticated as a walking, talking and jamming biped arises from structures as minute and seemingly simple as egg and sperm has fascinated for centuries and remains fascinating to this day. The beauty and elegance of a developing embryo and the structures and events that give rise to it, confer a sense of awe. And so while nature and nurture make for intriguing and contentious debates, the events that occur in that biological date when sperm meets egg are just about as neat.

Female Influence

A sperm's career goal is to get out into the world and fertilize an egg. And being motile is key to sperm career advancement. At ovulation, vaginal conditions are pretty optimal for sperm travel. But sometimes something is amiss. Sperm and egg do not meet, perhaps over the course of one year of unprotected sex. And so medical attention of one sort or another may be necessary. Doctors will want to look at sperm–vaginal mucus interactions. To see how well sperm progress in the vagina, he or she may look at how sperm are faring right after intercourse. Or sperm and vaginal mucus will be placed together in a lab dish to see if there is "cervical hostility." In that case a woman must abstain from unprotected sexual intercourse before her appointment and a swab of mucus is taken from her vagina. Under the microscope sperm–mucus interaction can be observed. Or a so-called swim-up test is performed, in which the sperm must swim up and through mucus. This tells an examiner quite a bit about fertility problems. For this test, human mucus is not even necessary, vaginal secretions from cows will do as well. Another test method is to see if a human sperm is able to fertilize an egg, and a hamster egg is often used. Sperm are not that picky.

Egg and Sperm

Around the time of ovulation, vaginal secretions increase and many women express increased sexual desire. These secretions create a less acidic environment in the upper vagina and cervix, giving sperm an easier time to move on and up in life. The mucus also has a more streamlined structure creating a veritable sperm highway. This sperm-friendly path also protects sperm from the otherwise rather acidic and not exactly pro-sperm vaginal environment. Their survivability in this kind of setting rises from a few hours to a few days.

In addition to general hospitality there is even catering of sorts. Sugar levels in vaginal mucus are higher around ovulation than at other times in a woman's cycle. This sugar provides sperm a means to tank up on energy for their travels. And difficult ones those are. In the words of a pioneer of reproductive medicine, Ryuzo Yanagimachi of the University of Hawaii, they have to "negotiate the highly folded, mucus-filled cervix before entering the uterus."

Only a few minutes after ejaculation, some sperm may have already reached the cervix but most get trapped in the folds and niches around there and are slowly released over time. They essentially work their way up this sort of time-release staircase in the female reproductive tract. Sperm may camp out in the cervix for up to seven days. There are relatively few white blood cells there and the guests are thus less exposed to the equivalent of a biochemical clean-up crew as elsewhere in the vagina.

Sperm have their work cut out for them. As Martin Johnson and Barry Everitt note, "Human spermatozoa, a few microns in length, must travel some 30–40cm of male and female reproductive tract, or more than 100,000 times their own length, to reach the oviduct." It is, as they point out, a "long and hazardous journey, several major obstacles must be overcome, including transport between individuals at coitus." Just so you know the odds here: "Much less than one in a million of the spermatozoa produced ever complete the journey." Sperm cruise along at about 4 millimeters per minute which is certainly not bad, but not exactly fast enough to cover the obstacle course in the female reproductive tract to the uterus in the time they have. What nudges them on their way, besides their own tail swishes, are contractions of the uterus due to female orgasm. In addition, the egg will be travelling down the oviduct towards the sperm. Sperm are not immediately capable of fertilizing an egg upon arrival in the female reproductive tract. As Yanagimachi points out, "They gain this ability after residing in the female tract for some period of time."

To get ready for action sperm get shaved and showered through a physiological process called capacitation. Even after more than 40 years of discovering this reaction, it is still not fully understood. Part of it, as Yanigimachi notes, is "the removal or alteration of a stabilizer or protective coat from the sperm plasma membrane, which sensitizes the membrane to the specific milieu of fertilization and, more importantly, to the target of spermatozoa – the eggs." The changes involve sperm metabolism, in its nucleus, and the protective membrane around the sperm head.

As Ryuzo Yanagimachi explains, "We may assume that sperm plasma membrane is 'biologically frozen' when spermatozoa leave the male's body and capacitation represents its 'defrosting'." In order to achieve in-vitro fertilization it has been important to figure out which kind of combination of ingredients are needed in the medium of the lab dish to allow for fertilization. But not all sperm capacitate at the same time nor do all sperm undergo the process in the first place. But for the sperm who do go this route, capacitation begins within minutes of entering the female reproductive tract. From this point on the timeline, the job is all about getting enough capacitated sperm to the egg – and fast.

Researchers have shown that at mid-cycle the female uterus rhythmically contracts. Gerhard Leyendecker, a researcher and physician at the German city hospital of Darmstadt found that sperm are practically whirled upwards toward the ovaries with this help. Sperm can thus get from the cervix to the fallopian tubes within as little as a minute.

As the sperm move on they eventually reach a fork in the road, splitting off, as ob/gyn physician Luigi Mastroianni calls them, into the tunnels of love, the two fallopian tubes. So which way to the egg? As his friend Sheldon Segal, Distinguished Scientist at the Population Council in New York puts it in a conversation I had with both of them, "They really do not know where the egg is and some go up the wrong path." Some researchers believe that in addition to the muscle contractions that urge the sperm on, the egg gives off a perfume of sorts giving sperm a clue to her whereabouts. Sea urchin eggs do that. Michael Eisenbach and his colleagues at the Israeli Weizmann Institute postulate that the follicular fluid around the human egg exudes a scent that sperm pick up and follow. And he believes that this is actually a directed process in which there is a "recruitment of a selective population of capacitated ('ripe') spermatozoa to fertilize the egg." Other scientists are not so sure this is the way human sperm and egg come together. Sometimes cooperation does not work and Eisenbach wonders how cases of infertility may involve a lack of communication between sperm and egg. Communication problems? Sounds like one of those normal everyday-type relationship challenges.

Sperm–egg interaction makes for ideologically loaded questions. In the previously mentioned interview situation I inquired if the egg should be viewed as a slumbering beauty waiting for a gallant sperm/prince to saunter by? Sheldon Segal and Luigi Mastroianni both exclaim, almost in unison, "No, not at all." And Segal continues, "This is not about some macho sperm barging his way through the zona pellucida to get to the egg. As it turns out there are active hairs on the surface of the egg and these tiny microvilli are very actively involved in engulfing the sperm."

Of the approximately 100–200 million sperm of one ejaculate, the champions, the fastest and most motile ones reach the egg. The details are not quite understood, but the result is that of the whole ejaculate there is a select team of about 200 sperm that enter the finals. As Ryuzo Yanagimachi points out, it was originally thought that under natural conditions many spermatozoa surround each egg because that is what happens in the test tube. But actually, he states, "very few spermatozoa are present near the egg at fertilization." "During the course of fertilization, the sperm to egg ratio can be 1:1 or even less."

Upon arrival at the egg there are a few more tricky obstacles or, as one textbook puts it, "enigmatic variables" to overcome. One enigma is the cumulus oophorus, a loose cell matrix surrounding the egg for which the sperm need "considerable thrust to advance." Hamster sperm are reported to display a hatchet kind of movement to get through. According to Ryuzo Yanagimachi, the cumulus may very well be "one of nature's efforts to reduce individual variations in male fertility." Some factors in the cumulus stimulate sperm motility, others promote other reactions the sperm need to continue on in this microbiological version of the Iron Man contest.

The next challenge is the zona pellucida, a thick and elastic coat of glycoproteins around the egg. As it turns out sperm cannot keep up their habitual moves when they reach the zona.

As John Aitken of the University of Edinburgh states, "Zona penetration presents a different kind of physical challenge to the spermatozoon, necessitating the evolution of a second form of movement known as hyperactivation." One could be tempted to interpret this as excitement about nearing the end of their journey. It is assumed that wider movements of the sperm tails mobilize energy that the sperm need in order to penetrate the zona pellucida. This kind of sperm behavior is a bit difficult to study, they might be hyper one moment and then swim along cool as a cucumber the next.

Hyperactivated sperm will literally thrash and beat their tails in quite asym-
metrical ways. As Aitken explains, these hyperactivated cells are thought to be
generating the necessary propulsive forces needed to get through the zona.

Although it remains unclear if hyperactivation is essential to get through the
viscous vaginal environment or through the egg's zona, it is clear that timing
is crucial. According to Yanagimachi, "If spermatozoa undergo hyperactivation
prematurely in the wrong place in the female tract, it may result in exhaustion
of the spermatozoa and the failure of these spermatozoa to fertilize."

Propulsion is not all it takes, a sperm needs to recognize if it is knocking at
the right door. As Aitken states, "The specificity of this interaction is
extremely important because a spermatozoon may make contact with
hundreds, or even thousands, of different cells in the female reproductive tract,
none of which must be mistaken for the egg." Upon meeting, sperm and egg
exchange important recognition codes. The coding agents are proteins that
both the egg and the sperm have – if the match is right and essentially the key
fits the lock, the next step can ensue which is the fusion of sperm and the
protective membranes of the egg.

In fully capacitated sperm, molecules on the surface of the sperm then
firmly bind to the zona. A sperm beats its tail pretty vigorously, advancing a
little at a time, and appears, as Ryuzo Yanagimachi states, "as though its
narrowing front end cuts open the zona." There is a bit of controversy whether
this is happening through mechanical or essentially chemical means with
enyzmes plowing the way. Sperm are outfitted with what one could term a type
of warhead, or to be less militant about it, a loaded condom of sorts. Once
capacitated and near the zona, sperm go through a second reaction called the
acrosome reaction. The enzymes in the cap of the sperm, among them
hyaluronidase and acrosin along with others, escape as the membrane that
surrounds them at the sperm's tip dissolves. It seems that these enzymes are
helping the sperm gain access to the egg. This process can take quite a bit of
time, maybe even a half an hour. Once it passes the zona the sperm encounters
a space, called the perivitelline space. This is no chill-out zone since there are
still places to go. The sperm then fuses with the last barrier to entry, the egg
plasma membrane, and soon the entire sperm is engulfed by the egg cytoplasm.
And once that happens a cascade of biochemical and developmental changes
take place, the egg is activated and the formation of a new individual can begin.

The dynamics of sperm–egg interaction has been most extensively studied
in an organism slightly less flashy than humans: the sea urchin, a prickly
round marine animal. One of the intriguing facets studied in the urchin is that
right at fertilization the egg shuts her door to any other suitor. Not more than
one sperm can enter the egg, no matter how perky, strong or cunning. In
humans only one sperm can fuse with an egg. How others are kept out is not
precisely known but it is clear that there is this block to polyspermy since
multiple sperm entries do not lead to a viable embryo. In some animals more
than one sperm enters the egg but only one really gains access to the genetic

material and fuses with that to create a new individual. For the sperm who do not make it, the party is over: they perish.

Semen and Women

"I haven't thought much about my semen – only that some women find it very exciting when they see it," said Eric, 30. Sexual intercourse is one of the most popular and pleasant pastimes for men and women. Sometimes you get the impression that in the vaguely defined old days, people just did it, whereas today people talk about it incessantly or listen to others talking about it incessantly. In newspapers, on the radio, on TV and the Web, all thinkable aspects of sexuality are openly and frequently discussed. Maybe one reason for the frequent and blunt discussions is that in the age of AIDS, sex has not exactly become easier. But we still carry on doing it, enhanced by the knowledge about techniques and the mechanics of the act itself.

In the Hite Report, one man is quoted as saying, "I believe every man's dream is to have a woman who would, if you'll forgive the vulgarism, suck him off. If I could find the woman who would suck me off in the morning to wake me up, I would lay my life in the mud at her feet, for she would be one woman in a million." In sex surveys, men overwhelmingly describe how much they like oral sex. But because of AIDS, direct contact between any kind of mucous membranes and semen from men of unknown HIV status is risky. The virus is present in the bloodstream and in the semen of infected individuals and transmission of the virus via oral sex is possible. Dan Wohlfeiler, Education Director of the Stop AIDS Project in San Francisco, writes that one of the first questions he is asked when someone finds out what he does professionally is about the HIV–oral sex connection. Oral sex is a lot less risky than unprotected anal sex, is his reply, but he cannot say there is no risk.

The language of risk is actually the language of mathematics, but that might not seem to lead to a practical conclusion about what to do in bed. Websites and brochures set up specifically for gay men are very direct and no-nonsense about this issue. Even if you are not a gay man, the information can be helpful. The Centers for Disease Control in Atlanta does not beat around the bush on this subject either. "Yes, it is possible for you to become infected with HIV through performing oral sex," it says. The risk increases if your partner ejaculates into your mouth and if you have cuts or sores around or in your mouth or throat. A study called the Options Project at the University of California at San Francisco and funded by the CDC looked specifically at oral transmission of HIV. They found that 8% of recently infected men were probably infected through oral sex.

Fellatio – as oral sex with a man is also called – followed by an ejaculation into the partner's mouth is risky sex. So to be on the safe side, as the Stop AIDS Project puts it, "Avoid coming in someone's mouth. Or having them come in yours." Use condoms for oral sex. After all, there are thin condoms that come in all sorts of flavors. Licking and sucking the penis is of little or no risk as long as there are no small wounds present but pre-cum in HIV-positive individuals will also contain HIV. Some men told me that they had heard that gargling with whisky or mouthwash immediately after oral sex is supposed to do the trick. That is doubtful.

Pregnancy

On a sex education Website called Scarleteen.com, a young woman inquired whether her boyfriend was right in saying that a girl's cum has acids that can kill sperm. Her boyfriend had also told her that he didn't think he could get her pregnant because of how strong her cum is. The answer was: "Your boyfriend is completely mistaken." Around the time of ovulation, the vaginal environment is particularly suitable to sperm. Couples aiming for pregnancy should have unprotected sex as often as possible exactly at this time of the month. And avoiding pregnancy means not tempting biology around the time of ovulation. There was a scare about spermicides in the early 1980s linking their use to birth defects but other studies laid that fear to rest.

Semen and Cancer

Some women avoid intercourse before they go to a gynecologist because they fear semen could distort the Pap smear. This fear is unfounded. Under a microscope, sperm are easily distinguished from other cells that are of interest in this test. But it is true that a gynecologist can see if the woman had unprotected sex the night before.

All women fear the letter or the phone call after the test which mentions that abnormal cells were discovered. In most cases this does not necessarily mean cancer has developed. Unprotected sexual intercourse and cervical cancer are, it seems, linked, but in a not yet well-understood fashion. A study at the Weill Medical College of Cornell University showed that semen appears to influence the cellular production of so-called matrix metalloproteinases which are associated with cervical cancer.

Some Disadvantages to Semen

In rare cases, sexual intercourse leads to shortness of breath in women and this may not be due to their partner's breathtaking performance in bed. Particularly if breathing difficulties are accompanied by redness and swelling in the genital area, it can be a semen allergy. According to the medical literature this allergy may also be overlooked by doctors or misdiagnosed as a symptom of an infection. Australian gynecologists at the Flinders Medical Centre assume that taking histamines before coitus could alleviate the symptoms of this allergic reaction to semen.

Symptoms of this rare allergy can be quite severe and usually start a few minutes after unprotected intercourse. Most women thus affected immediately realize the connection to sex and seek medical attention. An 18-year-old female patient at the Vallabhbai Patel Institute of the University of New Delhi had struggled with post-coital breathing problems for two years. In spite of having unprotected sex, she had not become pregnant, but it was unclear whether her fertility was impaired by the allergy. The doctors stated that the allergy was hard to identify "because of social conditions." This careful phrasing hints at how difficult it is in some parts of the world to go to the doctor with these types of symptoms. As in the case of sexually transmitted diseases shame may keep people from going to the doctor. And a treatable condition may become a life-threatening one, which makes it all the more important to spread information about this condition. The biological trigger for this allergy is not clear, but one group of researchers postulated it might be linked to proteins in prostatic secretions.

A woman allergic to semen and who wishes to conceive will either have to endure the symptoms if possible or she might consider artificial insemination. In all other cases a condom offers good protection. Sometimes semen may contain another kind of troublesome ingredient. Through sex, a partner can react to medication a man is taking. A case study in the *American Journal of Psychiatry* mentions a woman who felt itching in the genital area after intercourse. This allergy had begun shortly after her partner had begun taking antidepressant medication. When he used a condom, she had no adverse reaction.

Diseases: Hitching a Ride with Semen

Sex was never risk-free. For those who did not wish to think about pregnancy risk or sexually transmitted infections, unprotected sex did perhaps appear risk-free. But AIDS has, in many minds, done away completely with the idea of risk-free, casual, unprotected sex. Given the long time the virus may be in the body before the illness breaks out, it is not paranoid but sensible to behave as if a sex partner is HIV positive, until a test confirms that he or she is HIV negative.

The male urinary tract is, according to experts, generally pretty sterile, except for the lower third part of the urethra and, in uncircumcised men, under the foreskin. As one medical textbook puts it, the microbial environment there is "complex and inconsistent."

The type of micro-organisms there depends on various factors, including age, personal hygiene practices, past illnesses such as urinary tract infections, sexually transmitted diseases and sexual practices, including gender preferences, degree of promiscuity, celibacy, monogamy as well as what one textbook terms sexual predilections that is whether you practise genital–genital intercourse, genital–anal, or genital–oral intercourse. When it leaves the urethra, ejaculate can be populated by countless micro-organisms and when infectious, semen can be the messenger of bad news.

The most worrisome viruses in the ejaculate are: the AIDS virus (HIV-1, HIV-2) cytomegalovirus (CMV), hepatitis B, hepatitis C, the human papillomavirus which causes genital warts and the herpes simplex virus.

Typical micro-organisms in the male urogenital tract and under the foreskin are staphylococcus, streptococcus, various types of *Enterobacteriaceae, Acinetobacter, Corynebacterium, Neisseria, Mycobacterium, Mycoplasma genitalium, Ureaplasma urealyticum,* and *Candida.* The specific disease-causing micro-organisms present can be: *Mycobacterium tuberculosis, Neisseria gonorrhoeae, Chlamydia trachomatis, Treponema pallidum, Haemophilus ducreyi, Calymmatobacterium granulomatis* and *Trichomonas vaginalis.* In one study at the Swedish University of Lund a total of 1,033 strains of micro-organisms were found in the semen of just under 100 men.

Since they populate semen, they can hitch a ride to a sex partner's body via the genital tract. The genital tract in both men and women is not void of micro-organisms, many of which are no problem. Yet, the range of potential infections is great and presents quite a diagnostic challenge for physicians. Tests will involve taking a swab from the urethra and in uncircumcised men one from under the foreskin as well. It some cases, the physician may choose to perform microbial analysis on a semen sample.

Sexually transmitted diseases are more common than is generally assumed. Reading down the list which includes syphilis, gonorrhoea, herpes, yeast infections, Chlamydia, genital warts, it begins to seem as if parachuting out of a plane poses fewer risks than sex does. At a conference, I was standing next to a researcher and we were reading a poster that described some new findings on the micro-organismal population of semen. "It is a wonder that women let us in at all," he said, not quite in jest. This is not a section of the book devised to advocate celibacy and abstinence. Sexual choices are private matters to be decided individually and without coercion from partners, neighbors, non-profit organizations or governments. But knowing about the risks can be useful and helpful, particularly when symptoms show up on your own body.

Chlamydia infections are one of the most frequent causes of female infertility. The challenge with this infection is that 75% of infected women and half of the infected men have no symptoms. A warning sign for men is discharge from the penis, urination accompanied by a burning sensation and swollen or painful testicles. In men, Chlamydia infections may also affect the prostate and the epididymides which can cause blockages that lead to infertility. It is not uncommon to detect these kinds of infections in couples attending infertility clinics. Patients are treated with antibiotics and of course both partners have to undergo the treatment if it is to be successful.

Say you get an angry call from an ex-girlfriend. It may very well be that she has symptoms and you do not. So before refuting all claims, it may be best to go to the doctor. After that, you may be able to send her flowers with a get-well card and a physician's note giving proof that you were not the source of her infection. If she says she has bacterial cystitis, for example, chances are it is not your doing although semen can make the infection worse. It is not really clear what causes this imbalance of bacterial cultures in the vagina.

Many of the infections of the fallopian tubes, the endometrium and the ovaries may be due to intercourse with an infected man. Urinary infections have many causes, one of them is nicknamed "honeymoon cystitis." The name refers to the fact that infection rates may rise due to frequent lovemaking. Some researchers assume that the bacteria in a woman's vagina are pushed into the bladder during intercourse, thus causing the infection.

Women are plagued more frequently by yeast infections than men. The fungus *Candida albicans* is generally present in the vagina. Overgrowth of this yeast leading to a whitish vaginal discharge, vaginal itching and burning and can have many causes including exposure to semen and even use of antibiotics. Sometimes a course of antibiotics is necessary to get rid of them; sometimes simple naturopathic recipes help, such as rinsing the vagina with yoghurt.

Trichomoniasis vaginalis can affect both men and women and has similar symptoms to Chlamydia. Human papilloma virus is actually a family of viruses that are transmitted when there is physical contact with a wart caused by the virus. Even if you do not have the warts you may still be able to transmit the virus to your partner. While there are several ways to remove the warts, there is no cure for this infection.

The best preventive method for people who are sexually active with people whose infection status they may not know, is the same as the method recommended for AIDS prevention: use condoms during sex since semen, blood and vaginal secretions can transmit the infection. If you have a hunch that there is something amiss, pull out those cocktail napkins with the numbers on them. See a doctor and call people you may have delighted with your sexual prowess but whom you may have infected. It is the courteous thing to do.

Etiquette

"We simply didn't think about it," said the young British couple who had taken over a hotel on the Mediterranean island of Menorca. At the end of their first season they inspected their mattresses and discovered much spoiling. And they bought what most hotels have: mattress covers. Guests will cause stains and most of them are caused by semen.

Sex can be a fluid-intensive business. At some point things get wet, as semen gets on the sheets or seeps out of the woman's body. Many women consider this OK or even sexy. But the experience, if it happens hours later, may be a bit unpleasant when she is maybe not in a position or in the mood to deal with it: on the tennis court, in the middle of a presentation in front of the board, in the supermarket checkout line. Condoms help avoid this situation.

So how do you decide who sleeps on the wet spot? In this day and age, it seems appropriate to be democratic about it. If you are practising safe sex, a man slips off the condom after his orgasm. And although a few drops may be spilled, generally the latex advantage is: no wet spot. If you are fastidious about it, the condom can then be knotted and immediately thrown in the trash bin. If drowsiness is too intense, the knotted latex can be discarded the next time you get up. Somehow it seems like a man's job, but that will be a private matter a couple can settle. A condom helps avoid stains and you can enjoy a few more minutes rest or a bit of post-coital glow. Stains may not be much of a problem outdoors, although there are probably people who call outdoor ejaculation just another form of littering. But wherever the location, clean-up will be called for. And yes, it is poor manners to leave spots on her sheets or to wipe your penis on her quilt, curtains or her favorite scarf.

Semen stains on sheets do often come out in the wash but some fabrics may be trickier than others. To remove fresh stains, soapy water should be sufficient. When the semen has dried up, one can try and brush it out, or wet it again and treat it with gall-soap or stronger agents. Baking soda seems to work pretty well, particularly on the more delicate garments.

Semen and Crime

In a book entitled *The Natural History of Rape: Biological Bases of Coercion*, the authors Randy Thornhill and Craig T. Palmer express the view that rape evolved as a form of male reproductive behavior. In an excerpt, they state: "We fervently believe that, just as the leopard's spots and the giraffe's elongated neck are the result of aeons of past Darwinian selection, so also is rape." Rape may have evolved, so they say, as a side effect of other adaptations, "such as the strong male sex drive and the male desire to mate with a variety of women." Craig Stanford of the University of Southern California calls the book "the worst that evolutionary psychology has to offer" in that it is more "an ideological rant than an empirical, well-reasoned analysis." Undoubtedly, rape, as many other human behaviors, is grounded in biology. But whether biology will provide all the necessary answers to this behavior along with the remedy for its prevention remains to be seen.

Right now, in most countries and cultures rape is an offense. In the United States, a so-called forcible sex offense is any sexual act directed at another person, forcibly and/or against that person's will; or not forcibly or against that person's will where the victim is incapable of giving consent. So this covers forced sexual intercourse without consent, both by stranger and acquaintance, forced sodomy, oral and anal sex, or forced penetration by a foreign object. According to a study by the National Victim Center and Crime Victim Research and Treatment Center there are about 683,000 rapes a year which boils down to a little over one rape a minute in the US. In 1999, according to the Bureau of Justice Statistics, there were 0.9 cases of rape per 1,000 members of the population age twelve or older. The US Department of Justice posts rape statistics on the Web along with many other crimes. The vast majority of violent sex offending involves males assaulting female victims, although the statistics include male as well as female victims and both heterosexual and homosexual acts of rape. Victim and offender are likely to have had a prior relationship. This is also true for rapes of children under the age of twelve who, in a high percentage of cases, are the victims of this crime. According to rape researcher Diane Russell, one in seven married women have been raped by their husbands. Depending on the study, around 10–20% of rape victims will report the incident.

Whatever the name or category, stranger rape, date rape, marital rape, multiple rape, acquaintance rape, rape involves the law. Unless a victim decides against pursuing the perpetrator, the case will be investigated by law officials. As part of an investigation of a rape leading to arrest and conviction of a rapist, a medical evaluation of the victim will be necessary. This will involve examining the victim for injuries, screening for STDs (sexually transmitted diseases) and pregnancy and gathering evidence for use in court as part of what is called a sexual assault evidence exam. Given the traumatic nature of the offense, the test is accompanied by counselling sessions tailored to the needs of the victim.

Up until the mid-1980s the biochemical methods used in rape cases were not very specific and narrowing down the circle of possible perpetrators was difficult. More recent developments in molecular biology allow a more specific identification of a sex crime offender. Using DNA analytical methods, semen, blood, hair samples can be examined and then matched with an assailant's DNA. A circle of suspects can be narrowed this way.

During the medical exam swabs from the vagina and cervix will be taken, clothes will be examined. The identification of sperm or constituents of semen is critical to tracking down the perpetrator, other evidence such as hairs will be examined as well. A victim will be asked if the perpetrator ejaculated or not. A question that may, understandably, be hard to answer. Even if the victims do not recall the exact details of the assault, officials will be intent on collecting evidence of the crime. Victims are urged not to wash or shower after a sexual assault, but even if they do, evidence can still be found on their bodies. In general, a so-called Wood's lamp, a UV lamp, is used to detect evidence of semen although some investigators have found it to be unreliable. Sperm, if found in the victim's body will be analyzed. If the man lacked sperm due to fertility problems, pathologists will be delivering evidence based on methods that use other cells found in semen. Any cell contains DNA. Methods that amplify DNA from very small sample amounts deliver sensitive testing methods that can reveal the identity of an assailant and can thus be used as evidence in court.

Contraception

If you are in a phase of your life during which you do not wish to have children yet, ever or already have a few and do not wish to add to the family, your plan may be to outwit your fertility. A man might choose to drink a lot, smoke a lot, take a few drugs or some heavy medication, go to the sauna often, use chemicals carelessly, take anabolic steroids, etc. That might kill off quite a few sperm. But the question arises whether the abuse is really worth it. And maybe erectile difficulties will result if the bodily abuse plan has gone a bit too far. There are better and safer ways to stop sperm in their tracks if need be.

According to the World Health Organization (WHO), over 500,000 women around the globe die from causes related to pregnancy and childbirth. Using contraceptives reduces maternal mortality and prevents unwanted pregnancies and lessens the need for unsafe abortions. Because it is women who get pregnant and because much is known about the menstrual cycle in women, most contraceptive methods are designed for women. Much of the data gathered by WHO is about women; for example, the percentage of women around the world who are of childbearing age and who use family planning. Even the WHO admits that many of their reports and activities have made little effort to consider men's health reproductive needs or to reach men. Slowly, as Paul F.A. Van Look, who directs the Department of Reproductive Health and Research at the WHO describes, that is changing. "According to WHO supported studies, men's opposition to family planning or use of a contraceptive method has been overstated in the previous studies and commentaries. Men in Kenya, Nepal, Brazil, and Turkey show interest in using a method and to share some responsibility for contraception."

According to *Family Health International*, male participation has recently become the focus of more attention in family planning campaigns; partly because of the realization that reproductive health is a woman's issue and a man's. Tradition is not easy to change. In any country. As one physician from Cameroon points out, men in Africa are brought up to think that family planning or reproductive health are women's issues.

Then there is the so-called KAP-gap, the gap between Knowledge and Practice. Studies have shown that there is a contradiction between the knowledge and awareness in men and their practices. As one study states "Men's contraceptive use is lower than might be expected, given their overall levels of approval and knowledge." But HIV has brought this whole issue to the forefront. Men and women need to be involved in these issues. Truth be told, despite HIV, condom use is still abysmally low in many countries of the developing world and not exactly brilliant in the developed world.

Contraception still seems to be pretty much a women's job. According to Paul F.A. Van Look and his colleagues, of the couples around the world who choose contraception, about 32% of couples use tubal ligation, 21% use an IUD (intrauterine device), oral contraceptives are chosen by about 14% of couples, coitus interruptus and periodic abstinence rank in at 14%, condoms make up 7% of the choices, vasectomy is chosen by 7%, vaginal barrier methods such as a diaphragm, jelly, foam tablets and other methods make up 5%. "After more than 30 years of female oral contraception the attitude of men towards new methods of male contraception has changed," says Eberhard Nieschlag of the German University of Münster. However, the numbers show that the change is indeed slow.

Sterilization

Vasectomy is the most reliable method for a man to keep his sperm to himself. It is, as the WHO puts it, one of the few methods that allows men to take personal responsibility for contraception. The operation, usually performed under local anaesthetic, only takes 10–20 minutes followed by a period of rest of about half an hour to an hour. In Britain, approximately 90,000 men each year choose this method of contraception. In the US about 500,000 men a year have a vasectomy. New Zealand has the highest rate of vasectomized men, at 23%. In the US and Europe it is about 11% and in China and India it is about 7–8%. Worldwide, in 202 million couples female sterilization is the contraceptive method of choice and an estimated 39 million couples have undergone vasectomy.

As the WHO states, "Acceptability and use of vasectomy varies from country to country. Often this depends on available surgical skills, the promotion of evidence-based counselling for vasectomy, including availability of information education and communication, and cultural norms." And as Nieschlag points out, "Generally sterilization in the male always competes directly with corresponding measures in the female, i.e., tubal ligation, which ironically has become increasingly popular because of improved techniques, although vasectomy was always technically simple." Vasectomy is not only simpler but also less costly than tubal ligation in women. Fees range from $250–1,000. Many insurance companies pay for sterilization but it will be best to check with your individual insurer. In Britain, the National Health Service pays for vasectomy. Some doctors may have moral objections to performing vasectomy, particularly on young men. In a sense they might, in some cases, be projecting their own fears of a "loss of virility" onto their patients. Having a vasectomy is something a man should think about carefully and couples will probably wish to make the decision together. If you feel a doctor is confronting you with preconceived notions about right and wrong and these views are not in alignment with yours, then you might want to get another medical opinion. The doctor–patient relationship should be built on trust not suspicion.

But doctors will and should ask explicit questions before the operation as they want to be sure that the man has made the decision voluntarily, that he is psychologically healthy and that he has not come at his partner's insistence. The patient can take the opportunity to reflect upon some questions that should be answered.

The consent form to be signed will contain passages referring to a man's voluntary decision and that he is aware that the operation will make him permanently incapable of producing children. Sometimes waiting periods are set up to allow for more thought before the operation. It is questionable whether one is obliged to discuss one's political and ethical views with a physician but a man must be prepared for such questions. What doctors fear most are legal consequences. This pre-op consultation is very important. It may seem like none of your doctor's business to ask if you and your partner have had all the children you wish to have, that other family planning methods are out of the question, or that you seek to enjoy sex without the fear of pregnancy. But these are valid issues.

Vasectomy will not solve marital problems or sexual problems you have with your partner. But it can make marital sex better. Steve, 37, says "I wanted it because my wife and I are through having children, we have three, and so I thought it would make sex more fun." Has it? "Yup!," he says. The consent form will also contain some frightening sections about all kinds of possible and actually pretty unlikely side effects. But as in every surgical procedure, possible side effects need to be mentioned.

There are two ways to do the operation. As one textbook puts it, "the patient must be well-informed and not be afraid of the procedure." OK, be brave. In both cases local anaesthetic is injected into the skin of the scrotum. Right. Men I spoke to usually wince right about now. If you can continue reading, please do. The doctor makes two tiny incisions in the scrotum and lifts out the tubes, the vas deferens. A small section of the tubes, 1–2 centimeters long, is cut out and the ends sealed. The incision is sutured. Voilà. Rest for about an hour. Go home.

There is another method developed in China called no-scalpel vasectomy and the procedure is true to its name. It is called "minimally invasive." No sharp instruments are involved. The skin of the scrotum is pierced and both tubes are manipulated through this one, small opening. No cuts, no stitches. The tubes are blocked the same way as in conventional vasectomy. It was developed by the Chinese practitioner Li Shungiang and his colleagues and is practised throughout China, Thailand and Indonesia. This procedure is even quicker than the other method. In a comparison "festival" in Bangkok, 1,200 men were vasectomized in one day – half of them by the standard method, the others by the Chinese method. Of the 19 cases of complications, 16 vasectomies had been performed using the standard technique.

Complications are extremely rare. The key is to separate the tube ends both to ward off infection and any kind of sperm transport. Rarely, the ends reconnect by themselves, restoring fertility. This only happens in about 0.5% of all cases, so it is not frequent at all.

Men report feeling sore for a few days after the operation, the scrotum will look bruised and there may be some swelling. But that will all be gone at the latest by a week afterwards. Basically people can have the procedure done on a Friday and be back at work on a Monday. Vasectomy does not affect sperm production; sperm are still produced but they are reabsorbed by the body. Libido is also unchanged as well as erectile functions and orgasmic abilities.

Some men reported that post-vasectomy their sex lives improved because the fear of unwanted pregnancy was gone. Ejaculation still occurs as before and the only things missing are the sperm. They make up only a minute fraction of the ejaculate so you will not be able to readily detect a reduction in semen volume. Actually it will take around 20 ejaculations, and possibly more, to clear your system entirely of sperm. There are even some reports that two to three years after the vasectomy the ejaculate of some men still contained sperm. One such case was reported at a medical conference and during the question and answer session the reason given somewhat laconically was, "Not enough intercourse." In some men, sterility may thus take a while to set in.

While vasectomy is theoretically reversible, that procedure is not always successful. Medical insurers often do not pay for vasectomy reversal, also called vasovasostomy. So it is best to be very sure about your decision when you make it. There are surgeons whose specialty lies in vasectomy reversal. The procedure constitutes sewing the two ends of the vas deferens back together. This is microsurgery since the channel of the vas is about the size of the dot at the end of this sentence.

When I interviewed men, the fear that vasectomy impairs virility came up repeatedly. The fear is unfounded. Vasectomy is not castration. In the past, studies have been published linking for example, heart disease with vasectomy as a long-term effect of the procedure. Studies about an increased risk of arteriosclerosis after vasectomy attracted much attention. At a conference Stuart Howards of the University of Virginia pointed out the fault lines in these studies. In one case it was based on only three monkeys who were fed a high fat diet and developed a higher rate of arteriosclerosis. Another study on rabbits concluded that the risk of arteriosclerosis after sterilization increased, but it decreased when the animals were held and stroked daily. For that reason Howards joked that men too have to be held and caressed on a daily basis. T.B. Hargreave, a urologist at the University of Edinburgh and the Western General Hospital, concluded after studying the current literature and research that "there is no indication of an increased risk of cardiovascular diseases after a man has had a vasectomy." There have been some studies seemingly linking vasectomy to a increased prostate cancer risk but the evidence is not quite clear. It is useful to speak to your doctor to get a thorough and up-to-date report on this subject.

After a vasectomy, a man may sometimes develop an immune reaction against his own sperm which means that they are perceived as foreign bodies. While this will not affect your health, sperm antibodies may affect your fertility if vasectomy is reversed.

One long-term effect of vasectomy lies in a different sphere as some men feel it enables sexual encounters outside their relationships. One woman reminisced about the long-gone pre-AIDS era: "There was this man who chatted me up in the disco. When we arrived at his place, I said that I didn't have any condoms but he just grinned and pulled out a medical document from his bedside cabinet confirming that he had had a vasectomy. After that we had a lot of fun." This kind of behaviour is extremely risky nowadays. Vasectomy does not hinder HIV infection or any other sexually transmissible diseases. Only the use of condoms will offer protection against STDs.

Coitus Interruptus

Coitus Interruptus is a fancy name for the withdrawal method in which a man deliberately interrupts sexual intercourse by withdrawing his penis prior to ejaculation. Withdrawal remains a popular method of family planning. And many men claim to have mastered this technique which, as one text puts it, requires "dexterity and self-discipline and reduces sexual pleasure." Its problem is its high failure rate, making it an extremely unreliable contraceptive method. After all, even the smallest drop of semen and even pre-ejaculatory fluid can contain sperm. And none of that should get either into the vagina or near the cervical mucus of a woman's external genitalia if pregnancy is to be avoided. Only if a woman is not ovulating can this method even be considered as a way to keep sperm and egg separate. The withdrawal method is an inappropriate method of AIDS prevention.

Periodic Abstinence

Periodic abstinence is sometimes called the natural method of family planning, limiting sexual intercourse to days of the female menstrual cycle during which the likelihood of pregnancy is low. The male contribution in this method is forgoing intercourse and, if he chooses, assistance with figuring out when the time for sex is right. The method has a high failure rate.

The Male Pill

"I would have to be sure that [a male pill] … had no side effects and [would] not harm my health in any way," says Eric, 30. Besides efficacy, the safety aspect is probably the one most dear to any man considering contraception. There is no male contraceptive pill yet. In the past 20 years, researchers have taken various approaches to male contraception. Clearly, it needs to be simple to use, reliable and safe.

Scientists have found pharmacological ways to suppress sperm production. "Right now men have to come in once a month and deliver a semen sample to see if the method is working. Couples are not going to accept that as a part of the normal mode of contraception," explains Frank Comhaire, researcher at the Belgian University of Gent. Considering the fact that every healthy man is a walking sperm factory with an output of 60,000 sperm per minute per testicle, male contraception has quite a job to tackle. Research into male contraception is run on a much smaller scale than studies on contraception for women, according to William Bremner of the University of Washington, one of the world's leading experts in this field.

Male appearance, genital and sexual development as well as male fertility are mainly regulated by the hormone testosterone that is produced in the testes – more precisely, in the Leydig cells. Compare, for a moment, a man to an aircraft carrier. The testes are the engine room. In the brain, in other words, on the bridge, the hypothalamus is in command. It issues orders to the pituitary, the First Mate, in the form of a substance called GnRH – gonadotropin releasing hormone. From here the orders are passed on by messengers, hormones regulating testicular function: LH and FSH. LH causes the Leydig cells in the testes to produce testosterone. FSH regulates sperm production in the coiled tubules of the testes. Chemically blocking GnRH production prevents sperm production. And presto: perfect male contraception. The side effect, though, is that this causes dramatically low levels of testosterone, putting an end not only to sperm but also to libido and potency as well as many other bodily functions. Not a happy end, obviously.

Suppressing sperm production entails suppressing both LH and FSH. If maleness itself is to be preserved, testosterone levels need to be kept up, by artificial means. Testosterone presents some challenges though. For one it must be injected intramuscularly and it does not have an immediate effect. Finding a pill with the same effect as the hormone is not an easy task.

Scientists are exploring various hormonal ways to obtain the desired results. Interestingly the hormones involved are not simply released into the bloodstream but are delivered in a pulsatile fashion and with feedback loops governing their further secretion. Intervention in this system means heeding this rhythm and these mechanisms.

The hormonal approach to male contraception uses substances that either are similar to GnRH, analogs, or ones that suppress GnRH antagonists, in addition to giving testosterone. Returning to the aircraft carrier metaphor for a moment, the methods work something like this. In the first case, there are stowaways on the ship and they present themselves to the First Mate with fake papers and seem to be model cadets. The pituitary releases LH and FSH. After a while their exaggerated diligence is noticed, and the computer in their department is programmed to ignore all incoming orders. The production of LH and FSH is suppressed. In the case of GnRH antagonists, undercover agents sneak onto the ship in the guise of sailors but they are basically not into working or passing on orders. There is no sperm production. As Nieschlag points out, these substances suppress sperm production from the very onset of treatment. And in general he believes this venue is promising for the development of a male contraceptive. "In the eighties more researchers pursued the idea of trying to find GmRH analogs, in the nineties many scientists returned to the GnRH antagonists," says Bremner. "In both cases one aims to impair the production of LH and FSH, and to keep the testosterone level normal."

As Eberhard Nieschlag puts it, "At first sight it would seem that testosterone offers the ideal substance for male hormonal contraception." It suppresses both LH and FSH. Since the 1970s efforts in this vein have been underway but the first WHO study only materialized in 1990. A recent study in Münster involving a combination of testosterone and the injectable female contraceptive norethisterone enanthate or NETE has been shown to successfully suppress sperm production.

One catch is the practicability of the intramuscular injections. Nieschlag, a realist, writes: "… a method requiring weekly intramuscular injections is not acceptable for broad use." In this recent study the injections were needed at six-week intervals. Still far from ideal. In an attempt to avoid this challenge, other studies have used an oral pill and testosterone depots, or implants. Roger Short of the University of Melbourne says he is not very impressed with many of the recent results. "The response rate is variable, it takes many weeks before the drug induces azoospermia, and men have to be incredibly motivated to keep taking it," he says. "But the principle objection," states Short, "is that it offers absolutely no protection to the man against the transmission of sexually trans-mitted diseases and we really can't afford any new contraceptives for either the man or the woman that do not offer some protection against STD transmission."

Intriguingly, the results for the same testosterone dosage are yielding different results along ethnic lines with sperm suppression being more effi-cient in Asian men than Western men. Both testes size and the number of Leydig cells differ with ethnicity, so dosages of potential male contraceptives will need to take that into account.

A drawback, in addition to the injections, and the delay in sperm suppres-sion is also the delay with which sperm counts reach normal levels after contraception is discontinued. Which would mean a man would need to say, "Sorry, honey, we have to wait, because my sperm count is still too low." Many researchers have their doubts about the male pill. Some say it is now leaving the "cloud cuckoo land" it has inhabited for a long time, others say it is scheduled to stay there.

Gossypol

Gossypol is a yellow pigment that is extracted from cottonseed oil and then heated. It has been widely researched in China and has been given a lot of attention worldwide. This substance suppresses sperm development in the testes. Unfortunately, it has been shown to be toxic, but newer studies in China using lower dosages are showing that this can be avoided while maintaining the contraceptive effect.

Trypterygium wilfordii

Trypterygium wilfordii is another plant-derived substance used in Chinese medicine. According to experts this substance has little chance of a wider application due to considerable toxic effects.

Pharmacological Methods

Sulfasalazine is a drug prescribed for stomach ulcers and it also interferes with sperm cell maturation. Unfortunately the drug has toxic side effects and is unsuitable as a method of contraception. This is also true for other substances like nitromidazole derivates.

Immunological and Biochemical Methods

Some research has focused on gearing the immune system toward contraception. For example, an immunized woman would have antibodies that would hone in, attack and destroy sperm. But efforts have not yet shown this to be a promising approach.

Joseph Hall, a biochemist at Norfolk State University in Virginia, created a synthetic compound which "blinds" sperm, at least in rats, so they cannot recognize eggs. When sperm meets egg, sperm latch onto a particular protein on the outside of the egg, after which an enzyme is released allowing a sperm begin to make its way into the egg's interior. The compound Hall found is a kind of decoy which binds to the enzyme inhibiting it. Fertilization is thus also inhibited. Human trials have yet to begin for this substance.

Ultrasound

Ultrasound interrupts sperm production, but the disadvantage is that the effect is irreversible so there is no incentive to use this method.

Heat

Subject the testes to normal body temperature and sperm production is reduced. It could be a very simple and chemical-free method of contraception to push the testes into the abdominal cavity called the inguinal canal. The body does this on its own on occasion and studies show that if the testes are kept there for extended periods, sperm numbers are reduced. Eberhard Nieschlag and his colleague Hermann Behr in Münster point out, "Whether wearing a special apparatus to reposition the testis in the inguinal canal will make this method acceptable is highly doubtful."

There is still no acceptable and safe method of contraception for men in sight. William Bremner states that research on male contraception started much later than for women. It is apparently not very well funded, and much less is known about how to influence the male reproductive system rather than the female one.

Condoms

Unless you have been in a deep-freeze for the last 20 years and were just recently thawed out, you will have heard of condoms as a way of preventing both pregnancy and AIDS. "There is not much to say about them – everybody knows about them," says George, 28. Yes, the AIDS virus does not discriminate and will infect anyone if given the chance. And while medication, with unpleasant side effects, is effective at keeping the virus at bay, AIDS still has no cure. So when the party is on, the party hat is indispensable. At times, it seems complicated enough to get someone to bed, without needing to think about accessories. And this one is not the greatest kind of accessory. As Stefan Bechtel and Laurence Roy Stains write in their book *A Man's Guide to Sex*, condoms, while necessary, are "the cod-liver oil of contraception." We have to live with them somehow.

If one partner insists on using them a bit too much, all of a sudden sexual excitement may wane since that implies there have been other sex partners. Unless both partners are virgins, that is only normal but in these types of discussions all of those partners seem to take a virtual seat on the bed in that moment. So is there a good moment to talk about latex? Somehow, when pants reach ankle level, that seems like a bit of an inopportune time. But the question of when will probably vary from one situation to the next. Better earlier than later. But despite the dangers, the warnings, the campaigns and the knowledge, a lot of times the party hat is kept off. The reality check yields some doubtful practices.

Eric, 30, says, "I have a lot of experience with condoms but these days I meet more and more women who can't stand them." He confesses that he does not always insist on wearing them. "Years ago, I got used to have condoms ready but sometimes I am stupid enough to have unprotected sex with women," he admits openly. "Last Friday I met this woman at a party. She is writing her thesis at the moment, and another acquaintance had referred her to me with a particular question. We had a long talk, and than we ended up making out on a sofa. Later we went to my place and to my bed. We had fantastic, wild, passionate and unprotected sex. The following day she explained that she did not use any contraception because she always knew when she was ovulating. The last woman who told me that has a little daughter now." Eric ended his e-mail tale with a little emoticon, a "smiley". He went on to admit, "I have no intention of fathering children unless I am in a stable relationship." So there it is, the female and male KAP-gap in action.

It has been known to happen. An intelligent, charming man utters the words, "I am impotent with a condom," or: "I can't feel you with a condom." This is about as acceptable as: "Trust me, I'll make sure you don't get pregnant." None of these sentences seem terribly manly. And so a date that could have ended in bed might very well end up with a man having to go home – without breakfast, too. In *Hot and Bothered*, journalist Wendy Dennis recounts a scene of safe-sex etiquette. One woman told her about a new lover. While he was passionately French-kissing her, her lover did a "deep back-handed retrieval from the night-table drawer and, stopping only momentarily to unwrap the package with his teeth, resumed kissing her while applying it, one handed, to his stalwart erection." The woman reported that she was both "utterly amazed … and totally impressed."

Allegedly, there are still men around who do not know or do not recall how to put on a condom. They think you unroll it like a sock and then pull it on. It seems easy enough to remember: what doesn't work for stockings, won't work for condoms. There are books, brochures and Websites that offer plenty of advice with illustrations and explanations. In a nutshell it goes like this: open the package and place the condom at the tip of the penis with the rim of the rolled-up condom on the outside so it looks like a sombrero. Then unroll the condom up the length of the erect penis leaving some space at the tip for semen. That's it, you're done.

For lubrication, avoid using baby oil, vaseline, or any kind of petroleum-based product because it will damage the latex. Use lubricants meant to pair up with condoms. Don't keep condoms in your fridge, on your dashboard or anywhere where it gets really hot or really cold. Throw condoms away if they are beyond the expiration date. Condoms can break and burst, so always make sure they are a good fit, not an asphyxiatingly tight one. A study at La Trobe University in Australia revealed that condom breakage is strongly associated with penis girth. The researchers recommend that condom manufacturers need to increase the range of condom sizes or their performance. As you roll the condom on, hold the tip and press the air out as it is rolled up. Condoms are intended for single-use only. When travelling to remote locations, or to places where you may not find your trusted brand, have a stash with you.

Fear of HIV and AIDS

"I won't get it," "The first time it won't happen," "It is a disease only gay men get," "I am much too old to get infected" – in spite of much clear information and many warnings, myths about AIDS abound. A while ago one could have possibly excused the myths because the disease was new. But today it seems hard to find good reasons for dangerous attitudes. Some sex therapists have found that many people feel that satisfying sex is supposed to be an act of spontaneity and a loss of control. Condoms seem to destroy all of that. That idea, though, may actually be mythologizing the sexual act. At least you need to wonder if that is the only possible definition of great sex.

HIV can be found in the blood and semen of HIV-positive men. Some studies have revealed that levels in semen and blood may differ. During unprotected penetrative sex, the virus can reach the bloodstream of a sex partner though the vagina or rectum. HIV can be transmitted by bodily fluids with a high concentration of the virus. It is found in the saliva, in tears and in the vaginal secretions of HIV-positive women, but for transmission the virus has to reach the bloodstream of the partner. If a tear of an HIV-positive person falls on unbroken skin, the virus will not be transmitted. AIDS is primarily a sexually transmitted disease and semen, of course, plays an important role in AIDS and in AIDS research.

If a man is HIV positive, his semen and sperm quality remain pretty much unaffected. When the disease manifests itself though, semen quality decreases. The virus can be found throughout the genital tract – in the testes, the seminal vesicles, the epididymes, the prostate and the urethra.

The amount of HIV virus present in semen of HIV-positive men varies individually. There are some studies indicating that HIV can hitch a ride on sperm; for example, by docking onto proteins on the sperm membrane. But HIV does not seem to infect sperm. HIV mainly infects white blood cells which are part of the body's defense system, thus making the disease difficult to treat. Researcher Deborah Anderson of Harvard Medical School pointed out at a conference that anal intercourse, sex during menstruation and sex with uncircumcised men all carry a somewhat higher risk of infection. To explain HIV infection she uses the metaphor of the Trojan horse story. The virus hides in white blood cells and travels with the ejaculate to another body. There it can leave its Trojan horse and wreak havoc in its new host.

Anderson has analyzed pre-cum, the pre-ejaculatory discharge from the penis and discovered that it too contains HIV if the man is HIV positive. Anderson says that she receives many calls from HIV-positive people, mainly men, who seek advice and new research results. She shakes her head: "This disease is bad enough. But it is worse when one's own assumptions get confirmed time and again." The discovery of the virus in pre-cum is a warning for all who, during sex, wait until right before orgasm to put on a condom. While vasectomy lessens the concentration of HIV in semen, it does not eliminate it in HIV-positive men. "It is sad, but it is better to know. And then you can adapt your behavior accordingly," she says. In these days of AIDS, uninformed sex can be life-threatening.

Roger Short of the University of Melbourne has proposed male circumcision as one important attempt to reduce the risk of HIV transmission. The WHO agrees with this view. "This evidence mainly comes from African countries and populations, and refers to men at high risk of acquiring HIV infection," says Paul F.A. Van Look. But male circumcision may not reduce the risk enough to replace other risk-reducing strategies. "Moreover, circumcision status is closely linked with deeply held cultural and religious beliefs so that such interventions may not be possible in many cultures," Van Look and his colleagues state.

There is a wealth of information available about HIV and AIDS in brochures and Websites, some of which are listed at the back of this book. Here is a short summary of HIV risks and safer-sex practices.

Vaginal Intercourse

If the male partner is HIV positive, the virus can be transmitted to the woman during unprotected vaginal sex. The risk of infection is high. The virus enters her bloodstream through tiny fissures in the vaginal mucus membranes. During menstruation, the risk of infection is even higher because as the uterine lining is being shed, HIV has easier access to a woman's bloodstream.

Anal Intercourse

Unprotected anal intercourse is the sexual practice with the highest risk of infection. The mucus membranes of the colon are particularly thin and very easily injured. Some researchers believe HIV can pass through these membranes even if there is no injury. The risk to the passive partner is particularly high. Even without ejaculation there is a risk in unprotected anal sex. Condoms, properly applied, offer very good protection.

Oral Sex

Stimulating male and female genitalia with the lips and tongue is considered low-risk. When licking or sucking the penis, it is not a good idea to get semen into the mouth. That is higher-risk sex.

To protect yourself and your partner, safer sex is essential because neither blood nor semen reaches the other person's body. Sometimes men may not feel comfortable suggesting a certain sexual practice to a partner and will go to a prostitute instead. Men are willing to pay more for unprotected sex, street-workers say. "I don't need clients like that," says a prostitute in Berlin. Most prostitutes will not have sex without a condom unless, for example, their drug habit leads them to make fewer choices in how they make a living. These prostitutes have a high rate of HIV infection.

Gerald, 38, a cab driver in Frankfurt, Germany, says, "Men have asked me to take them to the red-light district and one guy told me the address and said, 'Get me there quickly, it's a good place, the girls are all clean, and you don't need a condom.'" You can never tell if a person is HIV positive until the disease breaks out. And even then it may not be visibly apparent. Whether clean or dirty, rich or poor, aristocratic or homeless, the virus will go anywhere. And so these kinds of myths are unconvincing. In his doctoral dissertation, a German physician mentions an unusual-sounding case of HIV infection. A man became HIV positive after sex with a prostitute. But she was HIV negative. Her body had essentially acted as a conduit for the infection, since she had had unprotected sex previously with a man who was HIV positive. In having sex with her, the second man exposed himself to that man's semen and the virus.

HIV and Parenting

If you wish to conceive a child and live in a partnership you can conceive the so-called natural way. In case that does not work, at an infertility clinic you can use your own sperm or eggs or resort to either donor eggs or sperm and undergo in-vitro fertilization, depending on your individual situation.

Say you are an HIV-positive man, and in a partnership in which you both desire a child. German psychologist Ulrike Sonnenberg-Schwan reports that AIDS counsellors are often not clear on how to react when so-called HIV discordant or serodiscordant couples ask for advice on conceiving a child. The advice given to couples in which a man is HIV positive and the woman HIV negative is straightforward: practise safer sex. That of course will not do when you desire to conceive a child. And if these couples go ahead with their plan, both the mother and the future child are at high risk of being HIV positive.

HIV-negative partners in these relationships are often accused of being irresponsible if they want a baby by an HIV-positive man. After all, in the foreseeable future, so the argument goes, the baby will be losing a parent. But being HIV positive can also mean living a long life, even 20–30 years after infection. Combination retroviral therapy has greatly increased life expectancy for HIV-infected individuals.

There is a way to help these couples, says Sonnenberg-Schwan. "We think that the people who come to us for help deserve it. They really think hard about their desire to have a child and it will not be possible to prevent them from having one," she says. But if left to nature's course, the risks to mother and child are enormous.

The reasons for HIV-discordant couples wanting children are complex. Sonnenberg-Schwan explains that the couples do not make this decision on a whim but they carefully consider the possible problems. "The most frequent reason given by men is that they want to live on in a child after their death. With some women there is a clear wish to retain the loved partner in their life or they want a child as a symbol of their fulfilled partnership."

In several European countries, through a procedure pioneered in Italy and Germany, HIV-discordant couples can seek out special centers to help them conceive a child. What happens is that the sperm of the HIV-positive man are washed before being allowed to fertilize an egg in the test tube.

Augosto Semprini and his colleagues at the University Clinic of Milan offer this procedure to discordant couples, and people from all over the world come to him for treatment. In an editorial in the *British Medical Journal* he stated along with two British colleagues from Chelsea and Westminster Hospital, "There is no justification to denying treatment to parents who are HIV-positive." They point out that there are many similarities between HIV and once-fatal diseases such as diabetes and even breast cancer. "We believe that couples in whom one or both partners are infected should have access to the same fertility advice and treatment as non-infected individuals to allow them to conceive with the minimum of risk to their partners or children," say the physicians. In these approaches to assisted reproduction for serodiscordant couples in Italy, Germany, Spain, France and the UK, sperm are separated from semen and all other cells in the semen. Using a highly sensitive method called polymerase chain reaction, sperm are checked to assure they are free of HIV. And then in-vitro fertilization proceeds. This type of program is accompanied by extensive counselling, either in the clinic or over the phone. To date a total of 300 healthy children have been born after more than 3,000 cycles of sperm washing and assisted reproductive techniques. Not one seroconversion, or HIV transmission, has occurred in either mother or child.

Everyday, these clinics report numerous calls from couples in their respective countries and outside them. "Most of the people who call have been through a veritable odyssey in order to realize their wish to have a child. They have often been let down by gynaecologists, andrologists, general physicians and AIDS counsellors. One cannot simply dismiss it when people want children," say Sonnenberg-Schwan and her colleague physician Hans Jäger in Munich.

These efforts have been harshly criticized, mainly on ethical grounds, and some clinics have refused to cooperate with them. The ones who do agree prefer to remain anonymous. Undoubtedly, HIV-discordant couples with a strong desire for a child who are not helped, will go ahead and have unprotected sex to conceive a child, endangering both the mother and the child in the process. In the US, researchers and doctors report requests for assistance by serodiscordant couples. Despite the prospect of HIV infection of mother and child and despite the European experience, the Centers for Disease Control recommends against performing this procedure. Not everyone has the money to travel overseas, but if you do, that is currently your only option.

5 Nature and Culture

Semen and the Bigger Picture

While physicists groan about funding cuts, biologists experience sunnier days. Biology is on the upswing. This bullish trend is being propelled to a great extent by the efforts, a bit overhyped at times, to sort out the human genome. Some of this effort will contribute to knowing more about the underpinnings of diseases, leading, hopefully, to better treatments and cures. Finding out about how we work and develop tells us more about the mysteries of being alive. While this may seem a bit partial toward biology, many researchers find that watching organisms do their biological thing, whether human or microbial, is truly as exciting as going to the movies.

Not all sectors of biology are the darlings of the day; molecular biology in particular gets much limelight. Scientific publications that focus on genetic predispositions to alcoholism, homosexuality or aggression populate scientific journals as do studies on the genes determining body plan, eye color or the more arcane biochemical functions of cells and of functional units within cells. At times, molecular biology appears so predominant that it seems that is all we are, a bag of DNA. It certainly is not DNA in vacuum-sealed pack. Evolution has shaped and formed it, much as a ceramics master works with clay.

Certainly, most experts assert, not all modes of behavior are genetically determined. Fads and fashion, morals and education, schools and laws still retain their influence and are called upon most noticeably perhaps, when there is a need for a quick answer to issues such as school violence. "It's television's fault," say some; "It's the breakdown of the nuclear family," say others. But humans are indeed as biological as the next mammal. And so even though we may not be too furry, venomous or predator–prey focused as we sit in a traffic jam or an office cubicle, biological principles act upon us. And this influence is particularly marked when it comes to reproductive behavior.

Mating, so the humdrum explanation goes, perpetuates the species. However, as zoologist Tim Halliday points out, "the most cursory examination of the sexual behavior of animals reveals countless examples in which males and females treat each other with great hostility and are clearly not behaving cooperatively." Female spiders eat their mates, male sticklebacks are aggressive towards females. This does not look like working together toward a common goal. In recent years reproductive physiologists have been looking more closely at sexual strategies, yielding some startling findings. So with all due respect to men, here is a brief walk through the animal kingdom focusing on sperm and semen.

Stories from the Animal Kingdom

Pick up an andrology journal and you discover the newest biomedical research on the human male. And right along side them are studies on stallions, bulls, dogs, boars, bucks, rats, leopards, birds and many other animals. Some of them, like stallions, may get higher ratings on the macho scale than others. And if size really does matter, then whales get a nice wow-factor with a penis that can be over 3 meters in length and 30 centimeters in diameter – when it is not tucked away in its pocket, the urogenital slit.

At first, it may seem odd to look to the animal kingdom when thinking about male sexual biology and reproduction. But as Richard Blackwelder and Benjamin Sheperd phrase it in *The Diversity of Animal Reproduction*, "reproduction does occupy a unique place in biology, because it is central to heredity and thus to evolution." Zoologists are eager to learn about an animal's feeding habits and wake–sleep patterns, and are particularly keen on reproductive processes.

Human sexuality may appear – particularly in some magazines and Websites of a less academic nature – varied indeed. But it absolutely and positively pales in comparision with most goings-on in the animal kingdom. There is, for example, your very basic monogamy and promiscuity. Then there is hermaphroditism - when animals have both sexes in one body and self-fertilize. And that even has several shadings, there are simultaneous hermaphrodites which have both the male and female reproductive systems and fertilize themselves. And in some animals like limpets, one stage in their life may involve sperm production and they may change gender later. That is called protandry. Then there is protogyny where the animal starts out female and switches to male. Then there is the perhaps more familiar polygyny. Elephant seals, humpback whales, sea otters and polar bears, for example, are polygynous with males mating with dozens of females in a breeding season. Fur seals are often too busy for sex since they need to exclude other males from breeding with their harem. And they may only get around to about two or three copulations per year. Then again, some scientists think there may be some acts that occur at night and are not counted. Scientists cannot be everywhere. There is also sexual cannibalism when the female consumes the male as part of copulation, found in spiders and the praying mantis.

Studying mating behavior is not just some sort of government-funded way for researchers to get their kicks. An ecologist, for example, who studies animals in the wild will also be seeking ways to perhaps save a species from extinction. And that means knowing the conditions under which they successfully reproduce. "The lives of nearly all organisms turn around sex and breeding, and the strategy as well as the often bizarre morphology and behavior employed in each case have been designed to maximize reproduction," write James L. Gould and Carol Grant Gould in *Sexual Selection*. So reproductive biologists have particular license for a one-track mind. JoGayle Howard and her colleagues at the Smithsonian Institution are studying the reproductive habits, sperm production and semen quality in black-footed ferrets, for example. This ferret, the only ferret native to the United States, is endangered and an involved captive-breeding program was established. The animals were reintroduced into the wild and now there are about 200 of them. As it turns out, not all is well with the ferrets; for example, males in prime-breeding age are not reproducing as well as expected. So researchers are investigating the ferrets' reproductive physiologies and behavior to figure out why.

And doing that means accessing sperm. Gerald Schatten at the Oregon Health Sciences University, for example, says, "Sperm is like seafood, fresh is better. So for example, large apes and monkeys will masturbate and leave a clot in the corner." Three hours later the researchers can still find sperm in the clot for their use in research and breeding. "This is a noninvasive way of collecting sperm from the animals, a way to work with the system" explains Schatten.

For many of the men I spoke with, stallions seem to be a guy's kind of animal. In classified ads, both of straight and gay men, the stallion seemed to be the animal chosen to describe one's attributes in a nutshell. So perhaps it pleases the inner stallion to know about animals and to see if that knowledge delivers insight for humans. After all, neither the shape of the body attached to those nice pecs nor composition of male ejaculate have arisen from spontaneous combustion. So even if this feels like voyeurism, it isn't.

One of the earlier treatises on the chemical composition of semen was published in 1791 by Louis Nicolas Vauquelin. One of his followers was the German scientist Friedrich Miescher who published his collected writings on sperm and semen in 1897. Just like many of his contemporaries, he focused on fish spermatozoa. Fish were and still are popular in this line of research since fertilization takes place outside the body. They produce millions of eggs and sperm and deal with them in a most generous manner. Their reproductive habits offer quite the range. As David Price of the Plymouth Polytechnic writes, "Fish stand out amongst vertebrates in the range of sexuality which they exhibit. The various strategies employed include hermaphroditism, unisexuality and bisexuality."

As researcher Thaddaeus Mann pointed out, "The tardy progress of research on the spermatozoa and seminal plasma of birds and mammals was due in the main to the difficulty of securing enough material for experimental purposes; however, more rapid advances were made soon after Elie Ivanov (1907) and several other pioneers in the field of artificial insemination, perfected the technique of semen collection from domestic animals." During this period, the first trials in artificial insemination of cows were carried out. These experiments in turn, got more researchers interested in understanding how the ejaculate of a fertile animal differs from that of a less fertile animal.

And then in the late 1940s there was more and more interest in comparative research of humans and animals.

A grand man among the sperm researchers was Thaddaeus Mann, a prolific author. To this day his book *The Biochemistry of Semen*, published in 1954, is still considered a classic. "We still deeply admire the man," a doctoral candidate in veterinary medicine told me at a conference. Mann presented the first comprehensive collection of facts about human and animal semen. When he was given the opportunity to study spermatozoa and sperm, he did not hesitate because there were, as he wrote, many "peculiarities" that made semen such a "fascinating and attractive object of study." He analyzed human and animal semen as part of his quest to understand the basics of fertility and reproduction. The following tables of semen amounts of different animals are taken from his *Biochemistry of Semen*.

	Volume of single ejaculate (ml)	
	Normal variations	Most common value
Turkey	0.2–0.8	0.3
Bat	–	0.05
Cock	0.2–1.5	0.8
Fox	0.2–4.0	1.5
Man	2.0–6.0	3.5
Rabbit	0.4–6.0	1.0
Ram	0.7–2.0	1.0
Bull	2.0–10.0	4.0
Dog	2.0–15.0	6.0
Ass	10.0–80.0	50.0
Stallion	30.0–300.0	70.0
Boar	150.0–500.0	250.0

Looking at the concentration, the number of sperm per microliter, the list looks as follows:

	Sperm density in semen	
	Normal variations	Average value
Fox	30,000–250,000	70,000
Boar	25,000–300,000	100,000
Man	50,000–150,000	100,000
Stallion	300,000–800,000	120,000
Ass	200,000–600,000	400,000
Rabbit	100,000–600 000	400,000
Bull	300 000–2,000,000	1,000,000
Ram	2,000,000–5,000,000	3,000,000
Dog	1,000,000–9,000,000	3,000,000
Cock	50,000–6,000,000	3,500,000
Bat	5,000,000–8,000,000	6,000,000
Turkey	–	7,000,000

No matter how you shuffle the numbers, the human male ranks in humble mid-field on the scores of both semen volume and sperm density. Men I interviewed who looked at the list expressed surprise and there was even a bit of envy towards some animals with copious semen. Andrologists and urologists report that many male patients ask, a bit worriedly sometimes, if their penis is a "normal" size. Being big and having a lot of semen to deliver are both seemingly desirable features.

Different species have, as Martin Johnson and Barry Everitt note, "bewilderingly different" sex gland structures and also different semen volumes. Sperm can fertilize without semen but they apparently work best in a fluid vehicle which can, as Johnson and Everitt state, either be "exuberantly" supplied, as in the boar, or reproduction can work with the more "conservative" 3 milliliters or so in the human male. Zebras have particularly large volume ejaculates reaching on average about 300 milliliters.

The many animal mating rituals certainly do not correspond to the human idea of eroticism. Nobody really knows what stallions or other animals are thinking when they mate and it is probably futile to speculate about it. In explaining, for example, what he terms "animal sexual acrobatics," author Herbert Wendt wrote in the 1960s: "Everything takes place that historians of morals have brought to light in the way of strange, sordid, and diabolic behavior among humans: rape, cannibalism, vampirism, abuse of children, murder of spouses, and the wildest acrobatic tricks in copulation." He elaborates on episodes of marital fidelity, tenderness, touching child care, in order, in his words, "to make up for the erotic chamber of horrors." As a popularizer of the study of animal behavior, he took some liberty in his descriptions.

Even some researchers got caught up in the moral dimensions of animal behavior, such as natural historian Jean Henri Casimir Fabre who wrote of "orgies," "atrocities," "perverse lusts" and "bloodthirsty habits." But as Wendt explained in progressive 1962, "Nowadays we are aware that each organism obeys certain laws, and Nature does not in the least care whether or not we human beings like those laws."

When animals copulate there is definitely some sort of pleasure-seeking involved, and this can be even through intended or inadvertent masturbation. Yves recounted an experience when he was a young boy still living at home. The family dog had been in his room and was scratching himself vigorously when suddenly something white flew through the air and he knew immediately the dog had ejaculated. "I found that fairly disgusting and chucked him out of my room," says Yves.

Comparing sexual behaviors may seem a bit dubious but comparing sperm types is pretty neat. "You want to see sperm? Sure." Richard Harland, cell biologist and frog expert of the University of California in Berkeley and teacher in an embryology course I audited, was glad to oblige. Grabbing some previously prepared frog testes he squeezed a few drops of milky fluid onto a glass slide and added a drop of salt solution. Under the microscope I saw sperm with odd-looking heads. They were corkscrew shaped and the sperm were churning themselves through their liquid environment to get ahead. Human sperm are oval-headed and not unlike stallion sperm, but very much unlike sickle-headed rat, or the frog's cork-screw headed sperm. A round head and a longish tail are characteristic for the sperm of worms, insects and vertebrates. The dissimilar humans, the lancet fish, snails and fleas all have a similar sperm shape.

Sperm are often surprisingly large. In the fruitfly, *Drosophila*, a favorite in genetics labs, a scientist in the 1950s already remarked that their sperm "proves to be a most impressive gamete." The length varies from one species to the next but can be up to twenty times the 1.5 millimeter length of the fruitfly. No wonder their testes make up about 11% of their body weight. Interesting sperm are found in unassuming places. Another model organism in genetics is the nematode, *Caenorhabditis elegans*, an hermaphrodite which can self-fertilize its own eggs with its own sperm. To do so, the sperm do not swim but crawl into position.

Other sperm are unusual due to their overall shape. For example, the hermit crab has sperm that look like cone-shaped UFOs with long spindly landing legs. The moment sperm touches egg, the sperm explodes and drives its genetic contents into the egg for fertilization.

Another staple in reproductive biology labs is the sea urchin. In 1914, Frank Lillie postulated that the jelly coat of the sea urchin egg delivers a short-term kind of activation to the sperm. "Have you fertilized yet? You just have to," says Gerald Schatten, director of a reproductive biology course as I saunter snoopingly into his summer lab at the Marine Biological Laboratory in Woods Hole, Massachusetts. His statement, which might not make it past the political correctness police under normal circumstances, is typical banter in the most serious labs. Studying regulator genes or signalling cascades in cells may take biologists a bit far from where the process fits into the life of an organism. In reproductive biology, life seems more close at hand. Schatten takes me over to a styrofoam box next to the sink with two unremarkable beakers of milky fluid. From one he pours a small amount into a glass dish about a fingertip wide. "OK, now add the sperm." I take a small pipette and dab a drop from the other beaker onto it. Thinking this would never be enough, I go for another drop. "No, no," says Schatten, "that's fine." Schatten scans the slide's scenery under the microscope and says, "There you are, take a look." I look. A pancake. No, actually a sphere. Off to the side enter a swarm of tiny buzzing specks. Sperm on a mission. Out to buzz a girl, beckoned by an irresistably beckoning perfume, a pheromone. As I later learn in a lab down the hall, this attraction, chemotaxis, fascinates researchers. German scientists Ingo Weygand and Johannes Solzin are trying to figure out, in microsecond breakdown, how the signals are processed in the sperm to send them in the right direction after a particular receptor in their tails catches the scent. I stay to watch sperm entry and come back repeatedly to watch with fascination the first developmental stages of the embryo I had helped to create.

When sperm and egg meet, two sets of genetic material combine and the deck of genetic cards is reshuffled and the blueprint for a new individual takes shape. Not all animals reproduce in this way. Scientists estimate that there are about 15,000 species that have the choice of either reproducing sexually or non-sexually, that is without the fusion of sperm and egg. Instead, the creatures produce identical copies of themselves. At least 1,000 species – for example, some reptiles and fish – don't have this choice; they do completely without sexual reproduction. Micro-organisms just divide into two halves. Dandelions are completely asexual. If you walk over a field with lots of dandelions and touch the round seed heads, you initiate a reproductive process. The seeds are spread by touch and the wind. Bees can develop from unfertilized eggs. Water fleas and some crabs also practise this parthenogenesis.

For a long time it was not known that vertebrates too practise parthenogenesis, for example, the whiptail lizard in the southwestern US creates offspring which are exact copies of the mother. No sperm needed, no dads are around and the population is a bunch of female clones.

The unisexual lizards cannot simply do this on a whim, ovulation is necessary and it is triggered by pseudo-copulation, behavior akin to the sexually reproducing species.

As Tufts University biologist Jan Pechenik points out, "As terrestrial vertebrates, we think it is normal for individuals to be separate sexes. But in the ocean, many species, including Crepidula, are sequential hermaphrodites: they start off as males and eventually become females."

Crepidula fornicata, the American slipper snail; *Acera bullata*, the marine snail, and the European mud snail have versatile reproductive biologies. The fully-grown animals are mainly female. Males are only the young or immature. When a female snail meets a male, they start to copulate. During this process the male loses his virility and turns female. Another male snail nears and can mate with the now female of his species. Sometimes the animals form long copulatory chains of ten or more animals piggy-backing each other.

Some snails have both a penis and a vagina. During the mating ritual they shoot "love darts" at each other that often cause deep wounds. Then both extend their penis and penetrate deeply into the other's vagina to deposit the sperm. According to studies, the ejaculation is synchronized. Both "come" at the same time. In these animals there appears to be a discharge of muscular and nervous tension in a climactic moment. As Herbert Wendt writes, "Little factual information is available about orgasm in animals, since animals cannot talk and are therefore in no position to satisfy the curiosity of sexologists. But the curve of excitement in the sex of snails can scarcely be interpreted in any other way."

Squid use all their arms in love-play. Aristotle was already fascinated by their elaborate copulatory behavior that marine biologist Richard Hanlon calls a "nuptial dance." One or more of the tentacles serves as a mating tool. After quite elaborate caressing of his partner, the male pulls a packet of semen from his mantle cavity and deposits it inside her genital opening. On its way between the animals the semen pack, or spermatophore, swells as sea water rushes in and it explodes once inside the female, spreading sperm.

Many crustaceans also have special organs to deliver sperm, they are modified limbs. With these sperm-filled tubes, sperm are delivered to the genital opening in the female. Male spiders have different methods of depositing their sperm with the female. They use longish organs near the head, pedipalps, and load semen much like an injection needle, which is then deposited in the female's genital opening. While it is true that the male may occasionally not survive this act, particularly if he approaches her at the wrong time, he is not always the female's post-copulatory snack. According to spider biologists, the supposed aggressiveness of the female spider towards the male is pretty much of a myth.

The housefly has an acrobatic sex life. During ejaculation the male must twist his body completely around 360 degrees to place sperm correctly in the female. Mosquitoes are less agile, but vary positions during copulations, frequently starting facing each other and switching to a piggy-back position.

The variety of reproductive behavior in animals is staggeringly vast. While some people might agree with Mr. Casimir Fabre and find some aspects disgusting, others find them simply fascinating, both because of their elaborate nature and because of their significance for animals and the implications for humans.

Sperm Competition

Some seemingly far-fetched theories have arisen in the attempt to find the biological underpinnings to sexual behavior in humans. Robin Baker, a biologist retired from the University of Manchester, has postulated some extreme theories seemingly explaining infidelity, masturbation, frequent sex in a long-term relationship, casual sex, and homosexual sex. Using fictitious situations in the sex lives of men and women, Baker tries to show that sperm control many of our behaviors. A couple falls into a glum sex routine. Despite the lack of enjoyment, sex continues. In Baker's view this has to do with the fact that a woman is not naturally conscious of when she is most apt to be fertile. "In the face of such a powerful and effective female strategy, the man has no chance of being able to predict the best time to inseminate," states Baker. "As a result, the only subconscious strategy open to him is to try to maintain a continuous sperm presence in his partner."

In another scenario Baker devises a woman who sleeps with an ex-lover. Directly after that she has intercourse with her partner and deliberately increases the frequency of sex with him over the following days. This is because, as Baker states, "her body has already decided that, on balance, her ex-boyfriend would make a better genetic father than her partner." Her body is testing to ascertain if "his ejaculate is also more fertile and competitive." Hence, Baker says, "In other words, her body wants to promote *sperm warfare* between the two men, and this is probably her only chance ever to do so." Baker also names differing sperm types such as "egg-getters," "blockers," and "killer sperm". Killer sperm supposedly have head-to-head battles with competing sperm from another man. If you have your doubts as you read this, then you are not alone. Baker's ideas are not mainstream biology. Tim Birkhead, behavioral ecologist of the University of Sheffield, writes that Baker's ideas seem "ingenious" but he is in fact a "sociobiological zealot" with ideas that fail to hold up to rigorous scientific scrutiny. Evidence for Baker's theories, say other biologists, is "non-existent" and "figments of his imagination." Baker gives spermocentric explanations for every imaginable sexual situation – and includes himself in his theories as his book's biographical blurb states that "he lives with his partner in Manchester and (thinks he) has five children." Until widespread evidence of his ideas turns up, his sperm-based analysis of human sexual behavior is fraught with difficulty. Not so in the animal world.

Change is afoot in the study of animal physiology. According to Tim Birkhead, it has been known that both sexes can be promiscuous. He notes that "while males are renowned for their promiscuity, until very recently females were not. The discovery that females of almost all animal species routinely copulate with several males has … had a profound effect on the study of reproduction." A male animal mating with a female of his species will deposit his sperm. But his sperm along with that from other males will be competing against each other for the prized egg. Sperm competition as an evolutionary force is helping us to understand facets of our biology that were previously inexplicable, says Birkhead. At the same time, "the risk of cuckoldry, the drive to cuckold and the need to reproduce has opened not just a single Pandora's box, but a whole set of them," while at the same time it "has changed the way biologists view the world."

Geoff Parker of the University of Liverpool is considered the father of this field of sperm competition with ideas developed in the 1960s and 1970s that place the individual in the evolutionary spotlight. In his view, if females copulated with more than one male, sexual selection would favor the male whose sperm managed to somehow outchase others. Sex then is not about cooperation but each individual looking out for his or her own best interests. In Birkhead's words, "This is sexual conflict: the battle of the sexes, where males and females are out to screw each other for the best, selfish genetic deal they can get." When this theory was first advanced, it enraged many female researchers because sexual selection was presented as solely a male-dominated process. Over the years, the gender bias based on, in Birkhead's words, "a mixture of unconscious sexism" and "biological ignorance" has begun to shift.

There is dynamism between the genders. "Whenever one sex, let's say it is the male, constrains the reproductive success of the other, selection immediately favours an adaptation in females to overcome the constraint." Sexual conflict at least on the level of reproduction then becomes a race of adaptation and counter-adaptation between males and females. And this puts the particularities of reproductive behavior in perspective.

Who's Promiscuous?

In 1977, says scientist Roger Short at the Australian Royal Women's Hospital, as he was examining a tranquilized male gorilla, a chimpanzee and an orangutan in Bristol Zoo, he had an insight. "I was struck by the enormous contrast between the minute (18g) testis of the giant silverback gorilla (200kg) and the vast testis (60g) of the small (47kg) chimpanzee." Male gorillas may go for one year without copulating while male chimps copulate almost daily with any female in oestrous.

In subsequent studies Roger Short found that primates with promiscuous multi-mate mating systems had a larger testis to body ratio than the polygamous gorillas or the monogamous gibbons. According to Short, "the relatively small size of the human testis clearly indicates that we are not promiscuous by nature." In comparing sperm shapes he found that gorillas and humans have a high percentage of abnormally formed sperm in their semen whereas chimp sperm is pretty uniform. This shows, explains Short, that in species with multi-mate mating systems there has been intense sperm selection, "again highlighting the fact that humans are not, by nature, promiscuous." The testis is, according to Short, the witness of the mating system of a species. Which, of course does not say that humans do not practise promiscuity – it just implies that a chimp male would have an easier time saying "evolution made me do it." As it turned out, states Birkhead, in later studies what became apparent is that female chimps are also promiscuous so sperm competition is why males needed large sperm stores. Testis size and female copulatory behavior are linked.

As Tim Birkhead explains, paternity studies have slowly accumulated over the years from a number of species such that the idea of female and male monogamy has been practically eliminated for snails, bees, mites, spiders, frogs, lizards, snakes, birds and mammals. Cuckoldry is the rule, extra-pair paternity widespread. The rule is for females to copulate with more than one male, or in animals in which fertilization is an external event, the eggs are fertilized by different males. So part of the evolutionary dynamic is the evolution of behaviors to counteract the counteraction.

Protecting Sperm

There are many different ways to protect your competitive advantage. The red-sided garter snake in western Canada loves to love in a crowd. After having hibernated together – groups of males forgo feeding and stake out passing females. As the females exit their dens one at a time, they are greeted with a huge gang of males. As James and Carol Grant Gould write, "enormous, writhing 'mating balls' form around each departing female". The males vie for their positions and some have even been found to pretend to be female to confuse other males and to get closer to the desired partner.

Other ways to guarantee paternity are, as Birkhead notes, pre-copulatory mate guarding and frequent copulation. A male bird, for example, will guard a female for as long as her fertility lasts, which can be a period of several days from the time the first egg is laid till fertilization of the last one. "The frequent copulator award," writes Birkhead, goes to an insect, a water bug that lives in the streams of the southern US. The female sticks her eggs on the male's back and he carries them to term. So first he inseminates her, then she lays some eggs which she sticks on his back. Frequent copulation is assuring that the male's sperm are there to fertilize the eggs.

As part of a courtship dance, a male seahorse takes charge of a female's eggs. He adds them to his pouch and fertilizes them with his sperm. Another way of paternity assurance. But this is not a static arrangement, an adaptation arises and then other adaptations arise as attempts to circumvent this one.

In some cases being last gets you first in line; sperm from the last mating fertilize the eggs. As females copulate with several males, one male will try to be last in the line of mates. Some male flies offer a female a courtship gift – food. The female eats and the male takes this opportunity to mate. In some crickets, the male deposits two sperm parcels in her genital opening. The female tries to remove the unwanted gift from her spermatheca but only gets hold of the first capsule, which is nourishing, whereas the second one contains the sperm. When she has consumed the first capsule she leans forward and tries to remove the second one as well, but doesn't quite succeed. Now the sperm can move towards her eggs for conception.

In some salamanders some males wait to slip in their sperm packet. A male leads a female and releases a sperm packet which she walks over and pushes into her genital opening. A "cheater" slips in between the two, putting the female behind him. He releases his sperm packet on top of that of his competitor. She pushes them both into her cloaca but only one fits and the first suitor has lost out on a chance to produce offspring.

The highest prize offered is the male's own life – a connubial tragedy, as one natural historian writes. The females of some locust species tend to eat their partners during copulation. Before the meal is over in most cases the male has deposited his sperm and paid for it with his life. The same can happen to male spiders but some bring something to eat when courting to keep the female occupied while they are copulating.

Getting There

For some species, there is a very winding path that leads sperm to their destination. For example, a fish commonly known to amateur aquarists called Bronze Corydas catfish copulates with the female latching on to the male's genital opening. Then she lays her eggs. They are fertilized because she swallows the sperm and passes them through her gut. While this may be an adaptation to their life in fast-flowing streams, it also ensures that the female's eggs are indeed fertilized and a male is guaranteed his paternity.

When a cockerel grabs a hen and forcibly copulates with her, he transfers about 100 million sperm. As Birkhead explains, what she does is walk away and immediately squirts out most of the fluid and sperm from her cloaca. What appears like a waste is simply her way of reducing the amount of sperm in her body. And other factors further whittle down sperm numbers. There are many advantages to this strategy. Since sperm may also have fellow-travelers such as pathogens, females developed a variety of techniques – physical and chemical obstacles in the reproductive tract – to regulate the sperm numbers in their bodies and the number of pathogens they receive. The cervix, for example, is a formidable physical hurdle. Another reason for this mechanism is the need to avoid something called polyspermy, or multiple sperm entry to the egg. If two sperm enter at the same time, an embryo will not develop.

Another female strategy that Birkhead terms the "bank-vault strategy" is when the oviduct serves as a sperm storage site for a very long time. Spider crab females isolated from males for two years still produced viable clutches. In the Eastern box turtle sperm can be stored in the female body for years as well before use. Insects are also known to store sperm for extended periods; mammals are not known to do so. Sperm storage allows animals to unlink insemination and fertilization. In bats for example, copulation is in the autumn and females use the stored sperm in the spring to fertilize their eggs.

The Tool

In animals, the penis can take on many different shapes. Bulls have an elastic penis which is slightly hard even when resting. Stallions have a penis that swells like the human one and increases in length and circumference. Dogs, bears, wolves, and seals can't copulate very quickly. Their penis is reinforced by a bone, the os penis. After ejaculation, this structure increases in size until the female vagina is completely filled out which prevents the semen from flowing out again. Male and female remain joined for some time after copulation as the penis swelling decreases slowly.

Some creatures such as spiders have no penis but specially adapted feelers to transfer semen. Snakes, lizards and sharks have two penises, marine flatworms have dozens of them.

Post-Coital Games

Competition is not over after copulation. The females of one species of the African antelope copulate with up to ten males a day. As part of their mating ritual, the male conducts an elaborate courtship, often pushing his snout into her genitalia. It is assumed that this stimulates the release of certain hormones which cause her uterus to contract. These contractions help the sperm to swim upwards toward the egg.

As part of sperm competition, the dragonfly has evolved a most striking mechanism. At the end of his penis, the male has a kind of scoop that he uses to push out the sperm from a previous mating before copulation. Other males apply a kind of chemical chastity belt, a copulatory plug. In many insects and some rodents, the males essentially seal off the female's genital opening after copulation. This secretion not only protects the semen in the female's body but in some cases it renders her unattractive to other males and this inhibits further copulation.

In the adder, males seem to be transferring a renal sex secretion along with the sperm. This secretion causes a sphincter muscle in the back part of the female to contract and the muscles and tissue generally become stiff and hard essentially preventing further mating. Studies have also found this phenomenon in rodents. The exact components of semen with such anti-aphrodisiacal qualities are not known but they seem to carry a complex chemical punch.

Mariana Wolfner at Cornell University studies, for example, particular proteins in the seminal fluid that play a crucial role in fertilization. They are transferred to the female during mating and help to allow for the storage, displacement and even the replacement of sperm from a previous mating.

As Tim Birkhead puts it, the reproductive potential of males far outstrips that of females – this being the main difference between sperm and egg. At the same time males do not get everything their way, since the female reproductive tract is designed by evolution to make things hard for sperm. The male response is, in some animals, the development of longer sperm. And so it goes – adaptation and counter-adaptation. As Birkhead writes, "At any moment in time one sex may have slightly more control than the other, but the battle between sexes is an evolutionary see-saw – subtle, sophisticated, inevitable."

Semen Through the Ages

Before the microscope was developed in the seventeenth century, natural historians and biologists could only speculate about semen. Even without the instrumentation this postulation dates back to civilatory sunrise. Medicine and agriculture were widely studied in China, Egypt and India in 3,000 and 2,000 BCE. The questions "Whence the soul?," or "Whose contribution in the creation of new life is greater – the man's or the woman's?," were subjects of tumultuous theological and scientific debates and some aspects of these questions remain unresolved to this day. After all, if you figure out fertility, then you can also control it and can devise contraceptive methods. Politics enters the scientific picture.

In Roman, Greek, Indian and Arabic medicine, it was part of their elaborate inquiry into fertility to ponder the nature of male semen. Greek authors contributed much to establishing biology as a science. Their insights were a bit forgotten during the Dark Ages during which biology flourished in studies by Arabic authors. It took until the Renaissance (1300–1650 CE) for the questions and the quest for answers to resurface in Europe. Despite the long history, medicine has only fairly recently begun to focus in earnest on male fertility and infertility. Many researchers I interviewed stated that, compared to female fertility, little is known about the male reproductive physiology. It is not quite obvious why research on men has been lacking.

On this subject, mythology also has a long history. As Clara Pinto-Correia points out, "Knowing nothing yet about sperm and eggs, most people came to deify conception and the visible external structures involved in it" in the ancient cultures of India, Egypt, Rome, Greece, China, Babylonia and Assyria. Even the historically relatively recently published tome, the Bible, gives procreation and the male role in it, much attention. Given the special regard toward fertility in agricultural societies, statuettes of the female body or the phallus have traditionally been placed in fields to enhance crop yield.

For centuries, male infertility has been thought the result of sinister curses and punishments. The idealization of fertility is at least in part based on a fear of infertility. In order to avert curses, Roman boys wore an image of Priapus around their neck. Priapus, the god of virility, is normally represented as a man with a gigantic phallus. Apparently, in Rome women sat on the male member of his statue to ensure pregnancy. Today, priapus is the name given to a condition of prolonged and painful erection which can damage penile tissue if not treated promptly.

Castration

Before looking more closely at some of the historical ideas on sperm, some remarks on a particular aspect of history are in order. Throughout history, torture strategies did not exclude male genitalia. Apart from human sacrifice, the most common form of severe punishment was castration. In the 1950s, German historian Wilhelm Müller researched this topic and the following passage draws on his work.

Of all the rituals, castration during the Middle Ages to avert the onset of voice changes and maintain the high-pitched singing voices among choir boys is perhaps the most well-known. But other rituals existed too. In secret cults in Ancient Rome, the priests underwent voluntary castration. A man made this conscious decision to make a dire sacrifice to show how he honored God. Then there are the somewhat less noble political motivations for castration – in those earlier and rather short-tempered times, as Müller phrases it, castration was all about power.

In ancient China, the Empire gathered a good deal of experience with this procedure as a form of punishment. In the Sung and Ming dynasties, all civil servants were castrated apparently for security reasons. The Chinese sign for castration literally means "palace punishment." Harem guards in Turkey had their testicles and, frequently, their penis removed, perhaps because it was known that eunuchs could still be potent. In Europe, castration was sometimes used to deal with a political enemy or to remove the last members of a dynasty. In a monarchy, infertility massively jeopardizes a ruler's political career. In the eleventh century, the Bohemian Duke Boleslav had his brother Jaromir castrated to ensure his own succession to the throne. In case you find today's political debates tedious, perhaps it is reassuring that these methods belong to the past.

In the Middle Ages, medical castration was applied to treat violent behavior. One historian describes a case of alleged self-castration when a mad man tore open his scrotum with his fingernails, ripped out both testes and thus cured himself of his madness. He is said to have later been able to fulfil his marital duties with his pretty young wife. Church father Origines, seeking martyrdom and keen on demonstrating his devout religious dedication, castrated himself. According to some scholars this explains why he was never canonized. Another moving case, if one can call it that, was the famous and popular French scholar Pierre Abélard (1079–1142) who ran a school. He was living in the house of Canon Fulbert and got his niece pregnant. When Héloïse realized this, the couple eloped and married. However, Fulbert discovered where they were, entered their bedroom with a group of armed men and had Abélard castrated. The humiliated man found shelter in an abbey, and Héloïse became a nun.

Some views from antiquity may seem a bit odd when viewed today. Eunuchs, for example, were apparently numerous among the Scythes. The physician Hippocrates (460–375 BCE) explained that this was due to the injuries they had suffered while horseback riding which had been treated through castration. Claudius Galen (130–200 CE), another famous physician, contributed to the public debate about whether or not fighters should be castrated. Some contemporaries felt that an "uninhibited" man would fight harder than one who feared leaving behind a wife and children after his death in the arena. But Galen opposed this view since castration would cause a "loss of strength and male courage."

Throughout history there have been all kinds of quacks, wannabe magicians and dubious healers who offered various types of procedures to supposedly cure impotence or infertility. Many may indeed have been cured, by whatever luck or wisdom, but it is also clear that many men paid for their belief in these offers with their potency and in other cases their lives.

Whence Semen?

According to early ideas, blood, milk, semen, phlegm and other bodily fluids comprised human physiology. As historian Thomas Laqueur notes, according to ancient wisdom, too much phlegm which caused sluggish behavior could be alleviated with sexual intercourse since semen resembles phlegm. Around 520 BCE, Alcmaeon of Croton (500 BCE), who dissected animals and discovered, for example, the optic nerve, pondered the origin of semen and concluded that it came from "part of the brain."

At the time the brain was believed to hold a key role in most bodily functions, so it is perhaps not surprising that the brain was considered the semen production site. One of Alcmaeon's contemporaries, Hippon, favored the bone marrow for this function. Hippon's theory oddly seems to have lived on in myths about masturbation because he thought that after copulation, the bone marrow of male animals would be weakened. Other scholars at the time concluded that after sex males had not only spent their bone marrow but also some fat and muscle tissue.

Around 450 BCE Empedocles of Agrigentum believed that there were four humors: blood, phlegm, black bile and yellow bile, and these in turn were derived from the four elements – air, water, earth and fire – which composed life. In the fifth century BCE the so-called pangenesis theory was popular which stated that semen was produced in all parts of the body. As Thomas Laqueur explains, Hippocrates (c.460–370 BCE) specified the "anatomical pathways of interconversion; sperm a foam much like the froth of the sea, was first refined out of the blood; it passed to the brain; from the brain it made its way back through the spinal marrow, the kidneys, the testicles, and into the penis." Hippocrates also postulated that both males and females produced semen. Aristotle (384–322 BCE) thought that the male semen concocts "thoroughly the ultimate nourishment of the embryo" whereas the "secretion of the female contains material alone."

Neither Hippocrates nor Aristotle gave the testicles a large role in procreation. Plato (429–347 BCE) widened the discussion about semen as he was primarily interested in the human soul and its interaction with the body. Plato thought humans developed from bone marrow. Anatomically, his theory was that sperm was produced by the brain and the bone marrow and flowed from the head through the spine. Some part of the marrow, especially in the brain and the spine, was in his view, fertile. Aristotle, Plato's greatest pupil, differed in his opinion and thought that the blood contained the semen, writing, "Sperm is a product of the blood, which by being boiled thoroughly has the purest and most productive qualities." He poked fun at Herodotus' claim that Ethiopians have black semen "as though everything about a person with a black skin was bound to be black – and this too in spite of their teeth being white, as he could see for himself. The cause of the whiteness of semen is that it is foam, and foam is white … ." According to Aristotle, it was the combination of semen and menstrual blood that created a human embryo. The male provides the "form" and the "principle of movement", the female provides the body, in other words the material. The ejaculate, as Laqueur points out, was in Aristotle's view "but the vehicle for the efficient cause, for the sperma, which worked its magic like an invisible streak of lightning."

Creating New Life

In antiquity, it was generally believed that both sexes contribute to the creation of the new living organism. Alcmaeon stated that a baby's gender was determined by the amount of female or male semen. Semen that was too liquid was said to cause infertility. According to Hippon, the gender of the baby depended on whether the semen was either thick and strong or liquid and weak. In his view women did produce semen but it did not contribute to procreation, only the male semen did. Both semen consistency and the type of food eaten after conception were important in his view. If the woman's contribution in the domain of nutrition dominated, then that would determine the child's gender. Other writings in antiquity describe a kind of task-sharing model with the skeleton derived from the male semen and the female semen giving rise to organs and muscles. For other scholars, women were responsible for matter, for example bones and the male's task, as in the view of Pythagoras, would be a "hot breath" that stimulated the soul and emotions.

Empedocles (c.490–430 BCE) had other views entirely. Gender was determined by heat or lack therof, in the uterus in particular. As Aristotle summarizes, "if the uterus is hot or cold what enters it becomes male or female." It is also important that Empedocles was probably the first to consider a link between menstruation and procreation. Heat or cold in the uterus depended on menstrual flow, and the overall temperature differences could be explained by the fact that the human body was a sum of four humors: fire, air, water and earth. The male had more parts of the primary matter, fire, than the female. Later scholars altered his theories saying that only the temperature of the semen would determine the sex of the unborn.

Galen, too, was convinced that women produce semen with truly generative function. Man's seed was generally always hotter than a woman's in his view. In explanation of the complex question of whom children resemble, Empedocles assumed that when the father's semen was warmer and the mother's colder it would be a boy with his mother's features. If the mother's semen was warmer and the father's colder, a girl would result, resembling her father.

Right and Left

One ancient theory that survived for centuries was that male gender relates to the right part of the body and the female sex to the left. It is assumed that Parmenides around 500 BCE had developed this "right–left" theory. Aristotle observed that crabs often have larger pincers on the right side, and assumed the right side to be dominant. Right is better than left, he believed. As many other natural philosophers of his day, the question of sex determination fascinated him. After all this was a question of great importance to couples seeking an heir or animal breeders wishing more progeny of a particular gender. The Greeks who carried out anatomical studies on animals concluded that the uterus had two chambers and that the right one would be warmer.

Anaxagoras (500–428 BCE) thought that the male and female contribution to procreation were clearly separate. The sexual character would be already present in the semen. The germ for the male came from the right testis, for the female from the left. Empedocles said that semen entering a hot womb becomes male and if it entered a cold one, female; in other words gender is decided in the womb. Heat results from menstrual flow. Galen (130–200 CE) felt that the temperature difference between men and women had to do with the fact that the testicles were close to the liver.

The idea of heat was also tied to other phenomena such as baldness. Aristotle considered male baldness and inquired about the reason no man grows bald before the time of intercourse, and also why, when men are naturally prone to intercourse, they go bald. "The reason," he wrote, "is that the effect of sexual intercourse is to cool, as it is the excretion of some of the pure, natural heat, and the brain is by its nature the coldest part of the body; thus, as we should expect, it is the first part to feel the effect ... So, that if you reckon up (a) that the brain itself has very little heat, (b) that the skin surrounding it must of necessity have even less, and (c) that the hair, being furthest off of the three, must have even less still, you will expect persons who are plentiful in semen to go bald at around this time in life."

Other cultures also developed this theory of right and left. In ancient India it was assumed that boys would develop in the right side of the uterus and girls in the left. When the milk of the mother began to flow from the right breast, she could expect to have a boy.

Hippocrates and his followers viewed semen as a substance formed in the entire body of a man and that it contained an essence of all of the paternal characteristics to be passed on to the newborn. The followers of Hippocrates thought that the female contribution to the newborn was passive, giving matter waiting to be formed by the more active and shaping male contribution. But whether one was on Hippocrates' side or Aristotle's the basic picture of all of this did not change for a very long time indeed. Until science began to make inroads in this area, it became more popular to call upon astrologers and amulets rather than science in questions relating to fertility and procreation.

Albertus Magnus in the Middle Ages was not a reproductive biologist *per se* but developed fertility-promoting essences. Thomas Aquinas (*c*. 1225–1274) shared Albertus Magnus' views on new life arising from the mixture of male semen and menstrual blood. When Leonardo da Vinci made his dissections of cadavers and completed drawings that amaze to this day, he reasoned that sperm are not created from bodily heat processes but that they arise in the testes. As many scientists and philosphers before him, he reached his conclusions while thinking about the effects of castration.

The argument in antiquity about male and female contributions to reproduction was decided by Anaxagoras and Aristotle. The more active influence was to be found in the male sperm and the female part was restricted to caring and nurturing the new life. Similar ideas can be found in other cultures.

The Age of Enlightenment: Speculation and Strife

When Antoni van Leeuwenhoek (1632–1723) invented the microscope, investigation into reproductive biology began to progress. He was encouraged in his studies, but as historian E.G. Ruestow points out, he questioned the propriety of writing about both semen and intercourse. At first he examined semen, failing to detect sperm, and cut the experiment short because of his "disgust and nausea." Johan Ham, a physician and student of Leeuwenhoek's who is later purported to have become mayor of Arnhem, saw an estimated 1 million of these unknown creatures for the first time under the microscope. He was examining the semen of a man suffering from gonorrhoea, "the spontaneously discharged semen of a man who had lain with an unclean woman." He brought his specimen to his teacher, who then also saw the, as he called them "animalcules." He continued to study them, and included his own semen which he obtained, as he stressed, not by sinfully defiling himself but through the act of conjugal coitus. His wrote up his observations and findings and sent them to the Royal Society who published them as "Animalcula in Semine," as a series of letters. In his 1677 letter to the President of the Royal Society, he wrote, "If your Lordship should consider that these observations may disgust or scandalize the learned, I earnestly beg your Lordship to regard them as private and publish or destroy them, as your Lordship thinks fit." Fortunately the gentlemen in question were not the squeamish sort and published his studies on the semen of men, dogs, rabbits, cockerels, frogs and fish which attracted much acclaim.

Leeuwenhoek considered the testicles as the storage site for sperm and he also clearly recognized the link between fertility and sperm. When he could not discover sperm in the ejaculate of an older man, he concluded that this gentleman was "a retired soldier in the battle of love." With time, Leeuwenhoek became more and more convinced that the animalcules he saw were tiny male or female homunculi in which the next generation was fully present. The idea of preformation was very much en vogue in the mid-seventeenth century. This idea presumed that living beings came prepackaged in prior generations, like an incredibly large set of Russian dolls. As Clara Pinto-Correia notes in *The Ovary of Eve*, this idea dovetailed well with both Descartes and God's role in nature. It affirmed the brotherhood of all men, and that we had all been encased in the original sinner. At the same time, preformation allowed some first explanations about heredity or at least continuity between generations to appear. There were however two camps in this view – spermists and ovists. She notes, "In a colorful display of dialectics, preformation did not allow for compromises: either you believed that God had encased all life within the testes, or you held that God had encased all life within the ovaries." Leeuwenhoek, a spermist, thought sperm could develop into a child and his thoughts began to gather a following, "Spermism was definitely taking over," writes Pinto-Correia.

When Regnier de Graaf (1641–1673) published his work on reproduction, it had seemed that the egg was the true source of all life. For close to 100 years, ovists such as Albrecht von Haller (1708–1777) and Charles Bonnet (1720–1793) battled it out with spermists Leeuwenhoek and Nicolas Hartsoeker (1656–1725), and Jacques Gautier d'Agoty (1717–1785), all the while battling fiercely among themselves. French natural scientist George Louis Leclerc de Buffon (1707–1788) found both theories strange and held that sperm were organic particles. D'Agoty's image of the preformed fetus contained in the human semen, visible to the naked eye if the semen is delivered into a glass of water, or Hartsoeker's drawing of a teardrop-shaped sperm containing the embryo, are striking images of their views.

"Every sperm is sacred. Every sperm is great. If a sperm is wasted, God gets quite irate." The refrain in the song "Every Sperm is Sacred" by Michael Palin and Terry Jones from the Monty Python movie *The Meaning of Life* is a slapstick summary of the conundrum of spermism in the Christian environment in which it was developed. As Pinto-Correia notes, the spermists assumed "that God had placed all of our lives inside the testicles ... ." Given the clear message in both the Old and New Testaments that God disapproves of sperm waste, not only such sinful events as wet dreams and masturbation were a problem. Each normal act of copulation entailed the waste of millions of potential lives. Spermists went to great lengths to disprove that their theory postulated such ghastly ideas.

Even after their discovery, sperm were considered animals, parasites, artifacts, inactive fibers, signs of putrefaction or agents to incite males to the sexual act. As Pinto-Correia notes, the discovery of sperm "offers yet another reminder that being visible does not necessarily imply being credible." It would take much longer for sperm to finally obtain scientific acceptance.

For all researchers of the period, sperm held immense fascination. Charles Bonnet (1720–1793) wrote in a letter to Catholic cleric and biologist Lorenzo Spallanzani (1729–1799): "They are, of all animalculi of liquids, those which have most excited my curiosity: the element in which they live, the place of their abode, their figure, motion, their secret properties; all, in a word, should interest us in so singular a kind of minute animated beings. How are they found there, how are they propagated, how are they developed, how are they fed, and what is their motion? What becomes of them when the liquid they inhabit is reabsorbed by the vessels and returned to the blood? Why do they appear only at the age of puberty; where did they exist before this period? Do they serve no purpose but to people the fluid where they are so largely scattered? How far are we from being able to answer any of these questions! And how probable it is, that future ages will be as ignorant of the whole, as our own!"

Ironically perhaps, it was the ovist Spallanzani who settled much of the debate by proving that both semen and egg were needed for conception. In his work on frogs, he fitted males with tight-fitting taffeta pants and let them proceed with mating thus dressed. He was able to show that without semen, eggs that a female laid were not fertilized. Spallanzani is remembered as the first researcher to perform artificial insemination.

This work led others to think about semen and sperm in reproductive contexts – Albrecht von Haller (1708–1777) considered such facets as the influence of heat and toxins on semen. Other scientists, like Wilhelm Friedrich von Gleichen-Russworm, concluded that infertility was the result of a lack of sperm. He said pointedly that arguments between man and wife in childless marriages may well be helped by the microscope and light may be shed on some marital secrets with the help of this instrument as well.

As biologist Jacques Loeb pointed out in 1906, physicists have an easier time than biologists, since they need to find a formula that expresses a relation between a variable and a function with the independent variable mostly in evidence. "In biology the independent variable is generally unknown, and the main energy of the investigator must be devoted to discovering this variable." In his view the history of fertilization is "extremely instructive in this regard since it took close to 200 years from the discovery of the spermatozoon to the realization that embryo development begins when sperm enters the egg."

With the progress of studies, the wilder speculations concerning animalcules disappeared and knowledge about male fertility and infertility was gained in the course of the nineteenth century. But it took another century for the question to truly begin to be tackled, largely due to newly developed techniques.

Male infertility as a phenomenon was of course not unknown, although in the case of famous men, it often was kept secret. Historian Wilhelm Müller cites some examples.

VIPs and their Problems

Caesar Octavianus, later known as Emperor Augustus (63 BCE–14 CE) is thought to have contracted an illness before the onset of puberty and, according to Wilhelm Müller, was unable to fulfil his marital duties. Supposedly he fathered many children but upon calculation it turns out that the moment of conception was always when he was travelling or on the battlefield. His uncle Gaius Julius Caesar, who had many affairs apart from Cleopatra, apparently contracted gonorrhoea at some point of his life, causing infertility. Henry VIII apparently was also rendered infertile due to a sexually transmitted disease. Müller and the historian Francis Hackett analyzed his family history and found that his marriages either remained childless or the children were fathered during an extramarital affair. Henry rightfully feared a rebellion in his kingdom should he die without leaving a male heir and reacted with anger to every hint that his fertility might be impaired. Ann Boleyn's brother, with whom she had betrayed the king and who had fathered her child, was sent to prison because he is supposed to have said that the king "was a boring bedfellow, and that he was impotent."

Prussian Frederic the Great was sickly all his life but nevertheless had the reputation of being a womanizer. Müller mentions that as a young man Frederic succumbed to the seductions of the Saxon court. He probably contracted a sexually transmitted disease which was responsible for his many illnesses and his premature ageing. The reason could also have been various childhood illnesses or a severe fall from a horse.

Louis XVIII of Bourbon, the brother of beheaded Louis XVI, had several childless marriages even though he once bragged that he had been "four times happy" with one of his wives in one night. One of his mistresses said that the king kept women "like luxury objects, comparable to his many horses which he never mounted either." After his death, the court physician discovered in the autopsy that he had phimosis, an affliction his brother also had. The physician is reported as having said, that Louis had not been in the position to "give his women practical proof of the feelings which they seemed to have elicited in him."

Karl III, a great grandson of Charlemagne, was apparently infertile, which had dire political consequences. Without an heir, Charlemagne's empire crumbled following his death.

Infertility and its Treatments

From writings, it is clear that the Egyptians had knowledge of contraception and how to encourage conception. The Old Testament and the Talmud contain much information on the subject. In the Talmud for example, one view is that the penis has two ducts, one for urine and the other for semen. If a man held back urine often, it would cause a rupture in the thin membrane between the two ducts leading to infertility. One remedy for infertility was a potion mixed from saffron and wine.

Medicine in ancient India dedicated much attention to male infertility. According to Ayurvedic medicine semen is like the sweet juice of the sugar cane. Blood is developed from the primal bodily fluid, Chylus, then comes flesh, then cell tissue, bones and from that the semen. All diseases can have an impact on the semen, the testes and fertility. Herbal treatments were discussed for such disorders as "semen stones," worms, enlarged testes, and impotence. To cure "semen faults" one should ingest a mixture of boiled milk, syrup and butter.

The Arabs, Persians and Syrians also had many different treatments for male infertility. In the tenth century, the Persian Haly Abbas developed an elaborate method of diagnosis. In his view and in accordance with the Greek physician Hippocrates, riding horses was detrimental to male fertility. The Arabic physician Avenzoar working in Andalucia refers to climacterium virile, the male menopause, and also considered the link between testicular function and infertility.

In the Middle Ages, Constantinus Africanus, a monk originally from North Africa who spoke many languages, managed to obtain old Arabic medical texts and reintroduced them in Europe. In his view three things were necessary for intercourse: the "appetitus" that had its seat in the liver, the "spiritus" from the heart and the "humor" from the brain. All three were susceptible to various malfunctions. Humor and spiritus, stated Constantinus, were the basic elements of the semen which treatment had to address.

At the same time various books of herbal remedies were published in praise of aphrodisiacs and the healing power of plants. Hildegard of Bingen's work *Causae et Curae* remains a highly respected work of mediaeval medicine. In her view, semen was a foam boiled in the heat of passion. For male infertility she recommended a recipe consisting of hazelnuts, pepper, campanula, the liver of a young but virile male deer and raw pork."This meat is to be taken with bread that is dunked into the broth until one gains fertility from its strength – if God in his grace allows it to happen."

Albertus Magnus dealt with sperm production and infertility in his work *Secreta Mulierum et Virorum* that he compiled with the assistance of his scholars. He maintained that the constellation of the planets, especially that of Saturn, impacted upon male fertility. To rejuvenate male fertility, a dish of pig's liver and pig's testes was recommended.

As the Dark Ages receded, printing was established, universities were founded, medicine progressed and physicians were more able to diagnose the various disorders of the male reproductive system. It was known, for example, that obesity could decrease male libido and that excessive consumption of drugs such as opium could lead to infertility.

Much superstition also flourished but researchers from the seventeenth century on were more intent on looking for scientific evidence on which to base their assumptions. Usleber, Bellovacus and other physicians tried to understand the external factors that might influence proper functioning of the testes and sperm production. To cure infertility they prescribed vitriolic spirit, mercury, soda in amber water, pharmaceuticals with souring properties and spicy food. Bellovacus applied his extensive anatomical knowledge and mentioned prostate and epididymal problems. He also had a take on genital hygiene for men. "Aesthetic considerations are also important for successful intercourse." He recommended that men shave their pubic hair, "because otherwise there might be flat and many-legged animals in this area."

6 Fertility

Semen and Male Fertility

Being involuntarily childless can cause great strain, distress and heartbreak. Once a couple has decided to have a child they might begin preparing themselves and their surroundings for a baby. They buy toys, clothes, perhaps a crib, start looking around for birthing classes, hospitals, pediatricians, daycare programs, schools. In some cases couples try to conceive and yet pregnancy does not occur. For a while that may not be an issue. But if the situation continues and the desire for a child is strong, both partners will begin to suffer, as expectations remain unfulfilled and life turns into a hurry-up-and-wait kind of loop. If after about one year of unprotected intercourse pregnancy does not occur, that is usually when a physician will agree that an appointment is a good idea. But if, for example, a woman knows that her cycles are irregular or a man knows his sperm count is consistently low, a couple may wish to seek assistance earlier. Many people have slightly lower fertility than what is called "normal."

Fertility experts say that they have been seeing an enormous increase in the number of couples who are involuntarily childless. Some scientists even call it an epidemic.

The World Health Organization estimates that 8–10% of all couples experience infertility in one form or another. According to the scientific group the Endocrine Society, only half of couples trying to become pregnant achieve pregnancy easily, and about one in six American couples of reproductive age are involuntarily infertile. While knowing this will not solve your particular personal quandary, it is perhaps reassuring to know that many people face the same difficulty and have also explored possible remedies.

Given these numbers, it seems a bit surprising that "reproductive medicine" has only slowly advanced to becoming a recognized field. More and more hospitals have sections and departments that carry this name but smaller clinics and doctors in private practice may not use this term. This field offers a variety of medical subspecialties, so there is no clear and right term for the physician you might be seeing. He or she might be a board-certified reproductive endocrinologist, which is someone who, in addition to their ob/gyn training, pursued additional study for a number of years in this field. Or it may be an ob/gyn who has basically learned by doing. Or a urologist. A urologist whose subspecialty is andrology. For a first consultation, specialists may be hard to find and this is particularly true for andrologists who are not readily listed in the yellow pages.

Resolve is an advocacy organization geared towards helping both men and women deal with their fertility issues. And as Resolve Medical Information Director Diane Clapp points out, being listed in the yellow pages or even being a member in certain professional organizations "[does] not qualify one to become an infertility specialist." "It is often up to you, the patient/consumer, to determine by means of self-education that you are not getting the kind of medical care you need," she says.

As in other medical circumstances, it might seem best to ask around in your circle of friends, family and acquaintances for doctors others can recommend. Then again, a search for help to conceive is not exactly the same as looking for a dentist. For many couples, it just feels too intimate to talk about this subject with people even if they know them well. Often they feel they should just "keep trying," swinging themselves and their mental state from menstrual cycle to menstrual cycle.

As one couple said, "We did not even feel we could talk to our friends about it. There was something too raw about it." So if it seems a bit daunting to figure out who to talk to, the Web is a great place to turn for information and support networks. In addition, there are some organizations that also offer anonymous and free phone counselling on a variety of topics. They can tell you, for example, where there may be physicians, clinics or organizations in your area to meet others in a similar situation to consult, either via e-mail or in person. Some of these resources are listed in the back of this book. It is true, however, that much of the information available is geared toward women.

The good news is that more than half of all couples affected can be helped just by talking to the right people and through counselling. Seeing a doctor about your situation does not necessarily mean extensive examinations and investigations. And you are not immediately obliged to sign onto the most modern methods of reproductive medicine. But after seeking out information you may wish to do so. But before entering into what some call "miracle medicine" and others more sourly term the "fertility mill," it may help to map out a strategy for the terrain ahead and be aware of options along the way. After all, your choice will take time, effort and money.

"It's my fault," says Sue, 38, who has been trying to conceive. "At least that is how I felt." Actually, battling with infertility is nobody's fault. And it is not more common for a woman to have fertility problems than a man. Equal distribution of work does extend to this field. As fertility specialist Sherman Silber of St. Luke's Hospital in St. Louis, Missouri, says, it is "a problem of the couple, and cannot be easily attributed specifically just to the husband or just to the wife." In approximately 40–50% of cases it is the man who is infertile. Some experts believe that figure may increase in the future. Some say this is due to a rise in male infertility overall and other believe it is due to medicine giving males more attention now than in the past. As the Endocrine Society states, "Despite the relative importance of infertility due to the male, infertility evaluations have traditionally focused on women, because women tend to seek gynecological care and because men are often reluctant to seek advice."

Because most women have regular gynecological check-ups, they have an established relationship with a doctor they can consult. Only a minority of men see their doctor regularly, so for their questions and examinations these men are on virgin territory. And even if they go for regular check-ups it is a whole new ball-game to talk to a doc about fertility, men told me. In addition, it may be hard to find the right doctor quickly and specialists may have long waiting periods for appointments.

It helps to know what to expect at a consultation. A doctor may speak to a couple together and may also speak separately with partners. If a man is referred to an andrologist, he may well be alone or the doctor will at one point, ask his partner to leave briefly. A man will face plenty of questions – ranging from his past medical history, including childhood illnesses, operations, injuries, as well as sexually transmitted diseases; his desire for a child; previous fatherhood; his sexual practices, since all of these factors are necessary to give a complete picture. The questions are not standardized, but you will find some in the section "Questions" p. 173. Physical exams are discussed in Chapter 2.

When can talking do the trick? Sherman Silber describes one couple who came to see him. They had been infertile for many years. The wife had a picture-perfect, regular ovulatory cycle. Which was part of the problem. Because as it turned out, she always ovulated on a Tuesday or Wednesday. Her husband, a "travelling, workaholic businessman" was only in town on the weekends. Their infertility was based on the fact that they were having sex on the weekends. So the doc's prescription was to recommend rescheduling their sex life a bit. The woman got pregnant rather promptly.

Some men suffering from premature ejaculation have difficulty fathering a child because sperm are not getting to where they need to be to fertilize an egg. In these cases too, a doctor can recommend techniques that can help remedy the situation. So part of conceiving is essentially strategizing and plotting out how best to get sperm and egg to meet. The solution may very well be low-tech.

The Ejaculate

If a fertility test is called for, a man will need to produce a sample for a doctor to examine. One of the main methods used is masturbation. As one medical textbook states: "As most adult men have some experience with masturbation it is considered a physiological method which allows," according to another text, "a method of getting semen directly into a vial." The container in question should be wide-mouthed in order not to lose any of the specimen. If a man doesn't like this "physiological method" or cannot do it, he can produce semen at home. There are special kinds of collection condoms used for this purpose. If a couple lives too far away from the infertility clinic, and they do not wish to produce a sample in the practice, the sexual act might have to take place in a nearby hotel using one of these special condoms. The preparation for the procedure, described in a handbook by the WHO, includes instructing the man to first "empty his bladder," then "wash his hands and penis with soap." The soap "is to be rinsed off carefully" and the penis "dried with a clean dry towel."

There are many reasons why some men find it difficult to produce semen in a clinic; psychological effects may create hindrances or religious or cultural beliefs may be decisive. "I understand that. It is alright when they do it at home, as long as they bring the sample in immediately afterwards," one doctor in an infertility clinic said. After an hour or two, though, many sperm may have died or lost much of their motility, which is why most physicians prefer if a man can produce a sample on the premises. Sperm need to be kept warm. If you are delivering your sample from home, you will be asked to keep the semen sample close to your body, or to carry the container under your armpit. Often women bring in their husband's sample. One women undergoing treatment for infertility reported seeing a number of women like herself rushing down clinic hallways first thing in the morning a bit hunched over, carrying something that was covered from sight. "We all knew what we were doing, but averted our eyes for some reason," explains Joan, 39, who carried a baby to term that was conceived through artificial insemination. "In hindsight it seems a bit funny, actually. But at the time I was worried about getting the sperm to the right place in time."

German gynecologist Dirk Propping, who has allocated a small intimate room in his practice for the purpose of producing a semen sample, said, "I always ask my female patients how they would like it if they had to produce an orgasm on command." A sexual experience at the drop of a hat in a strange and not exactly erotic environment is not an easy ordeal. It also is a strange kind of sexual encounter. While his wife is lying next door, perhaps slightly sedated, and ready for fertilization, her husband is working at something else in his cubicle, which, more often than not, will show a distinct lack of charm.

Usually men are requested to abstain for about two to three days before delivering a sample. Some physicians recommend a few days more. Saving it up for a longer period than that in order to deliver an even higher sperm count does not work. Unlike most animals, the epididymis in men does not store a great deal of sperm. The capacity of this coiled organ explains many animals' capacity to have repetitive ejaculations in quick succession. Men are not equipped with that kind of an epididymis.

Frequently, women undergoing fertility treatment complain that men do not empathize enough with their hopes and fears that the whole process causes. The drugs they are taking also have less than pleasant side effects. Christine, 35, said that during the infertility treatment she felt absolutely horrible, nauseous and very easily irritated. "As a man I am not really as directly affected as my wife in all of this. Although I do not really know what she is going through physically and emotionally, I can tell when her mood is on the downswing," said Herbie, 40. "It is like using opera glasses. It gets me close to the action, but I don't understand a lot."

The techniques of modern reproductive medicine involve both men and women but women are more taken to task in a physical sense than their male partners. Men often say that while they don't like to see their partners and wives suffer, they would like to be able to speak about their ordeal, too; for example, about their anxieties about being under pressure to produce high-quality semen.

After producing a sample, semen undergoes many tests and evaluations, which is not exactly a relaxing thought. The whole affair resembles a sports event, because timing is everything. If, for example, the physician decides it is time to retrieve eggs from the woman and he would prefer to use fresh semen as opposed to a frozen sample, then he needs semen immediately. A father-to-be must then postpone everything else – business meetings, trips or errands – because an on-the-spot performance is required. It is not surprising that the whole procedure can be mighty stressful.

"I kept my eyes on the tiled wall and got the job done," says 37-year-old Andy who had risen to the task. The location where you might be producing a sample will have varying levels of appeal. According to one textbook, "A private room should be available, adjoining sanitary facilities, appropriate illustrated literature, background music, and/or video tapes should provide a suitable atmosphere." Another text recommends a quiet environment: "A quiet and clean room is of course necessary, to enable the patient to concentrate." In reality these rooms are often sorry sights. They may be in or adjacent to rest-rooms, or even right next to the reception area of a practice, often not soundproof. They might be tiled or painted cubicles in more or less pleasing shades of grey or white. Others might be much cozier. There may be a table or a chair, and the range of stimulating accessories will vary. There might be a dog-eared stack of pornographic magazines, a VCR with an X-rated film. In many clinics the physicians report that the porn videos frequently go missing. One fertility clinic sent out e-mails to patients and former patients requesting the films be returned, anonymously if need be.

"Unspeakable," said Susan Rothman, who after years of research at a clinic in Ohio, started her own infertility practice. "I wanted to create a different environment for my patients. I did not like the atmosphere in the hospital at all. People who want to start a family are not ill in the usual sense. The archi-tecture, the interior decoration and the room colors are very important. There needs to be a certain atmosphere, that calms the clients and gives them hope. We want the client to feel welcome and relaxed." The room in her practice intended for producing a semen sample has two comfortable armchairs and a small table on a soft green carpet. Another physician in Germany said, "I want to help these people, and my office and facilities should reflect that."

Many men complain that fertility treatment entirely disregards the role of men. They report feeling reduced to their semen and its quality while their emotions and thoughts on what is going on, are, for the most part, ignored. As Susan Rothman says, "A couple needs to feel that they are not helpless but in control of the procedures." While interviewing Dr. Rothman at a medical conference some of her colleagues listened in attentively and nodded their heads. They admitted that their own facilities for obtaining semen samples were not adequate and that allocated funds were more easily spent on equipment and supplies than on interior decorating.

Mary Claire Mason's sensitively written and informative book *Infertility – Men Talking* decribes the experiences of many men coping with various degrees of fertility problems. One man, Parry, told her that while tests for women involve charts and blood samples, for men "it is masturbation at 9am in a white tiled room with only girlie mags for company. Who can blame them for finding it hugely distasteful?" Due to time constraints some men have to produce samples at work. As one man she interviewed explained, "This was the first of my love affairs with small plastic containers and, like a lot of first love affairs, it was a painful business. This was because there was a tiny plastic shard attached to the rim of the container where the two halves joined. I did not notice this booby trap until I was trying to direct my ejaculation into the neck of the bottle. In my excitement the little shard nicked the end of my penis, causing a momentary halt in the proceedings. Have you ever gone to work with the end of your penis wrapped in cotton and elastoplast?"

An important reference book in fertility labs is the "WHO laboratory manual for the examination of human semen and sperm-cervical mucus interaction." Somehow, the idea that there are norms for semen may seem a bit odd and men I interviewed did not find the existence of such a manual very reassuring. The WHO's semen parameters are not attempts to define a man. The goal is to standardize laboratory methods so that labs in different parts of the world or within a country can compare results. This kind of standardization can contribute to many facets of research in reproductive medicine for which semen analysis is needed. Knowing that may not be much consolation when you see your semen analysis report from the lab and which your doctor may show you. It will include the date of specimen collection, the number of days since the last ejaculation and if a man is taking any kind of prescribed medication. It then breaks down semen analysis into many categories such as the color, viscosity, pH, the volume in milliliters, the percentage of motile sperm, the percentage of forwardly motile sperm, sperm concentration, the total sperm count given in millions of sperm per milliliter of semen, the number of white blood cells, the degree of agglutination or clumping, the percentage of sperm with normal morphology and the so-called Penetrak score, in millimeters. Here is a bit of information about these parameters.

Examining Sperm and Semen

In his writings, the Greek scholar Aristotle mentioned that a water test could be used to test for male infertility: "the thin cold semen quickly diffuses itself on the surface, whereas the fertile semen sinks to the bottom." Although this is not a current state-of-the-art technique, this passage shows how old the idea of semen analysis is. Here are some of the current methods labs use.

Liquefaction: Semen liquefies within 20–30 minutes. Extremely quick liquefaction may indicate an infection.

Color and odor: Normally, semen is greyish-pearlish and opaque. The opacity is an indicator of sperm concentration. The color may vary in accordance with the length of sexual abstinence and may also vary with particular foods or drugs a man has ingested. Shorter phases of abstinence result in a clearer ejaculate. As men age, their semen might have more of a yellowish tint but this can also be a sign of infection. The tint may also occur if some urine is mixed in with the semen, for example in men with disturbances of their bladder neck function, when it does not completely close during ejaculation. The odor is described in the literature as resembling chestnut blossoms. A lack of scent can indicate a prostate problem.

PH level: The pH level which indicates the acidity of semen is usually somewhere between 7.2 and 8.2, and pH results outside this range may indicate an infection of the prostate or seminal vesicles.

Volume: can vary but is usually around 2–6 milliliters, or from a half a teaspoon to a teaspoon.

Sperm motility: The next step is to observe sperm under the microscope. The most important question is: Are there any sperm? If not, further investigation is necessary to discover what is occurring. If the ejaculate does contain sperm then their motility is evaluated. And how the sperm move is classified as (a) rapid progressive motility, (b) slow, sluggish progressive motility, (c) nonprogressive motility, (d) immotility. Fertility physicians are looking for at least 50% motile sperm and it is good news if 25% or more are rapidly, progressively motile.

Sperm movements are thoroughly analyzed for the clues they might be giving as to a man's fertility, some sperm may be sluggish or just flickering on the spot. Stewart Irvine at the Reproductive Biology Unit of the Medical Research Council in Edinburgh told Lawrence Wright of *The New Yorker* that he watches for particularly motile sperm. "From previous work that we've done, we know that these sperm tend to do quite well in achieving pregnancy, because they've got good propulsive force," he said. And this is what most clinics will be looking for. As Wright describes sperm, "The tail is one long snapping filament. Altogether, the sperm is an elegant testament to form following function. It is pure purposefulness – the male animal refined into a single-celled, highly perishable posterity-seeking rocket." The speed of that rocket differs greatly. Some sperm race across the viewing field of the microscope. Others dawdle. If the sperm are not moving or flickering they also have limited capacity to make headway in the vagina. The reason for this is often the existence of antibodies on the sperm's surface. Perhaps surprisingly, according to WHO standards only up to 50% of a man's sperm are expected to be forwardly mobile, which also means that half of them can be lazy or unable to swim properly.

Are the sperm progressing and mobile or are their movements patholog-ical? Do they swim in circles? Are they shaking? Because of the many variations in the way sperm can move, performing the correct analysis takes a lot of experience. D.H. Douglas-Hamilton, vice-president for research and development of Hamilton Thorne Research, a company that produces instru-ments for computer-based sperm analysis, concedes: "The eye is 10,000 times more intelligent than our computers." But the high-speed computer analysis of sperm mobility and shape can avoid a backlog of tests in larger laboratories. And researchers can track facets like the sperm's "head size" or "track velocity." Most scientists rely on their eyesight, though. But they admit that the computer sometimes detects more than they do. "Eyes can be tricked," Douglas-Hamilton explained while presenting a new model of his instrument at a trade exhibition. On the screen, a projection of what is happening under the microscope, some sperm wriggle by. "Under the microscope some sperm appear to be quite motile but maybe they are only swimming in a large circle," he said. "That is quite alright, but a man with too many sperm of that type will find it difficult to achieve a pregnancy," said Douglas-Hamilton. The computer system tracks a sperm's path and speed.

"Nonsense," a scientist behind me hissed at the trade fair, summing up his impression of the instrument, while a colleague of his contemplated buying one. Computer-assisted sperm analysis may be similar to other areas of automation. They accelerate the work, but the human mind and eyes are needed as well.

Shapes and Standards

Sperm, like humans, come in all shapes and sizes. Their heads can be longish or round, cigar-shaped, very small or oversized like a balloon on a string. Some sperm have two heads, no tail or a bent one, no mid-piece. Fertile sperm usually have oval heads. A laboratory will try to determine the proportion of "normal" sperm in the man's ejaculate. A certain kind of defective sperm may indicate the cause of infertility. Round-headed sperm, for example, lack the acrosome that would enable them to fertilize an egg. While the WHO stan-dards in 1988 stipulated that 50% of the sperm had to be of normal shape, in 1993 the threshold was lowered to 30% as the higher percentage was deemed unrealistic. So 70% of sperm can be odd-shaped.

Sperm and More

Apart from sperm, a lab will also record and count all other cells present in the semen. There is a lot of cell detritus. One andrologist said at a conference: "It is a miracle that the women let us in at all. Semen contains so much garbage." This is true for both the men with fertility problems as well as men with textbook-perfect ejaculate. The testes hold many surprises. Even in semen that the WHO would call "normal," there are bacteria, spores, immature blood cells, cells from the urinary tract. If there are too many white blood cells, the police force of the body's immune system, there may be an infection requiring treatment. The number on the semen analysis report will be 1 or less than 1 if semen is in a normal range. That means there can be up to 1 million white blood cells per milliliter of semen.

Motile sperm can sometimes be herd animals of sorts, sticking together. When this happens they can form large clumps of sperm attached head to head, middle to middle and tail to tail, none of which are conducive to fertility.

Fuel

Examining seminal plasma is also part of semen analysis. Since it stems from different glands, such as the prostate, and the epididymides, the composition and concentration of particular substances indicates how a particular gland is functioning. Zinc, citric acid and prostatic acid phosphatase are evidence of prostate function. Prostaglandins and fructose are secreted by the seminal vesicles and if fructose is low there may be obstruction in these glands. To ascertain the function of the epididymides, the marker substances L-carnitine, glycero-phosphocholine and alpha-glucosidase are considered important. Fructose, known to decrease slightly as men age, is also the substance that gives the sperm their energy. If it is completely lacking, this may indicate a problem of some sort in the epididymis.

At conferences, a good way to get some researchers hot and bothered is to ask what they think of the WHO norms. "They are too strict," said the German andrologist Walter Krause. Ron Weber of the Dutch University of Leyden laughed and made a gesture as if to rip up fictitious paper and to express his critique of the WHO manual. Geoffrey Waites, one of the authors of the WHO document, is not too happy about these kinds of reactions, although they are not exactly infrequent. In his view, there is a bit of confusion about the manual. The standards were set up as lab standards and not as diagnostic tools to determine whether artificial insemination is called for. Having standard sperm and semen is no guarantee for fertility, nor are abnormal sperm an immediate indication of infertility. "Normal is," according to the andrologist Carl Schirren, "when a baby is the result of intercourse between man and woman. And that is possible even when there is a much lower concentration of sperm in the ejaculate, when there is less motility and when there is a lower percentage of sperm than are considered normal."

Sperm in the Mix

A number of tests may be employed to see how well sperm fare in the mucus of the female reproductive tract. One of these tests may be the post-coital test which is performed on the woman 9–24 hours after unprotected intercourse. The goal is to look at "the disposition" of sperm in the vagina. If sperm are motile, that is considered a normal result. Another test looking at the compatibility of mucus and sperm is done in the lab. A drop of semen and a drop of vaginal mucus are placed on a slide. After a while one should be able to see motile sperm making inroads into the mucus. The Penetrak score is about how far and how well sperm can swim in cervical mucus. This test may also be performed with cervical mucus from cows.

The micro-penetration assay test or hamster-ovum penetration test, uses human sperm and tests their fertilization capabilities. Rather than use human eggs, specially prepared hamster eggs are used. A more frequently used test is the swim-up test which is performed by filling thin capillary tubes with mucus or an otherwise hospitable medium for sperm. Then the researchers look to see how far sperm will swim up. Are the scientists getting more accurate in their sperm classification systems or was sperm better in the old days? Some scientists are very clear about it. "Men produce a lot of bad sperm." At a conference one scientist said that a bull or stallion producing such bad quality would have been taken to the slaughterhouse a long time ago. Sperm with substandard shapes might have more sperm with genetic flaws, but this correlation is not quite clear. An abnormally shaped sperm may have DNA in fine shape.

Before sinking into a depression about how poor men's sperm quality is, it may help to consider the fact that humans are the product of evolution and not of ambitious breeding. That may not explain all. There is no denying the fact that nature affords a high degree of faulty sperm in humans for which nobody has a plausible explanation. Although things look a bit bleak under the microscope, perhaps not every sperm needs perfection since only a few are destined to reach the egg. Maybe it is like sports – not everyone has to be fit enough for the Olympic Games.

Infertility Treatment

Sometimes a couple wishing to conceive try and try to achieve pregnancy, timing intercourse just to coincide with ovulation … and still nothing happens. Then, months later, when they may have given up entirely and yet continued the practice of unprotected sex, pregnancy may occur. Then again it may not. There are a number of causes.

Psychological Factors

In the 1940s and 1950s, it was common to view infertility in connection with certain personality traits. Judith Bernstein from the Faulkner Center for Reproductive Medicine in Boston calls this the "era of scapegoating." Psychology does play an important and intricate role in involuntary childlessness. But it is not, as was once believed, hostility or anger toward the marital partner that is causing the infertility. A couple desperately wishing for a child will experience much pain during their waiting and hoping. The stress can manifest itself physically and it can lead to anxiety, doubt, depression and isolation. As Bernstein explains, in the 1960s and 1970s the insight emerged that infertile couples are "normal" but that indeed it was important to understand the relationship between emotional distress and infertility.

Doctors are under much pressure, as are their patients. Although not readily admitted, the drop-out rate at most clinics is significant and people switch doctors frequently. Many of these incidents are caused by false hopes and others by insensitive physicians. Some aspects of the stressors involve facing the fundamental question of having a child. Questions such as: "Is it the right time? Am I really up to this?" are very common in couples trying to conceive. Some couples may fear that having a child might damage the relationship between the spouses. According to experts, these thoughts are quite normal and part of what goes on when a couple decides to start a family. But if a phase of involuntary childlessness is extensive, the focus on having a child "at all costs" can put an enormous strain on the relationship and the individual partners. As Bernstein elaborates, there are various stages that have been identified that go along with infertility treatment, such as "diagnosis, assimilation, hope, intensifying treatment, spiralling down, letting go, quitting, and shifting focus." But no matter how you define the stages or label them, there are differences between genders when it comes to coping with infertility. "Men are generally less directly involved," Bernstein notes, "less obsessive and depressed, but more hostile and angry in their reaction to infertility." They are more likely to view the experience as a threat to their marriage. "This may reflect the effect of stress on the couple's sexual relationship as attention shifts from making love to making babies."

Couples with fertility problems are under a lot of psychological pressure even before they start treatment. Sex is supposed to be leading to pregnancy and is not. It becomes a chore. And if particular sexual issues on the part of the male partner, such as erectile problems or premature ejaculation, are contributing to the problem, then these issues will certainly come up in conversation with a physician if a couple decides to go for treatment. The overall pressure can be expected to increase during treatment. Studies show that involuntarily childless couples have sex less frequently. Sex becomes an event run by timing issues rather than the right mood or moment. So if there are sexual problems in your relationship in addition to a seeming fertility problem, then you will need to be prepared for having all of these issues surface. That is the bad news. The good news is, they may be resolved.

Reproductive medicine seems to offer a cornucopia of possibilities to have a baby. The drawback is that a couple may feel almost obliged to try to explore every option which entails more emotional stress. Andrologists who treat men for fertility problems say that the men are not willing to start any kind of long treatment plan. "It has to be quick," said the German andrologist Walter Krause. "Women are more willing to look for information, to admit to weaknesses and to talk about that. Men don't really want to talk. They simply expect us to do something for them and to solve their problem." "Women have a much lower threshold for going to see a doctor than men," explained andrologist Abraham Morgentaler at Harvard Medical School. "Infertility treatments are both hard on men and women, there may not be much of a gender difference. They both have more trouble performing on demand, on command. But infertility affects men profoundly, it is not masculine to be infertile."

Many men I interviewed said that they were very proud when their wife told them she was pregnant. "It might sound silly, but I felt that my manhood was confirmed," explained Jake, 33. Some men who are diagnosed as having fertility problems experience a drop in self-esteem. As Mary-Claire Mason reports in her book, men may feel "defective" or "like a failure" upon receiving a diagnosis that they have a low sperm count. Others report being ashamed or angry. Everywhere they go they see people with children, and are thus exposed to situations in which they cannot partake.

At family gatherings, they might be openly reminded of their situation, often in not very subtle ways. It is alright for a mother or a father to want grandchildren but it can be difficult for their offspring to explain their difficulties. A mother who knew about her son's problem said that she somehow felt responsible when her son told her that his sperm count was very low. George, 35, reported that his cousin offered to stop by and "see to his wife." "He was drunk when he said that, but jokes like that have the same effect as a kick into the balls," the man explained. "I never could stand that guy, and now he was capable of doing something I could not do."

"So far everything has been fine," Peter, 21, told me in an interview. "Why should there be any problems with my fertility?" Most men assume that everything is normal. And when a man has never had any doubts he will have a family someday, the diagnosis that he does not have enough sperm or that they are not motile enough can be an unexpected shock. Life, all of a sudden, is not going as planned and there seems little to do about it. As Mason points out, experts have found that many men seem to believe that being competent is being potent. "Impotence is seen as feminine, undesirable behaviour, something to be avoided at all costs."

In talking to Mary-Claire Mason, Jeffrey said that he clearly remembered the diagnosis given to him in his early twenties, even though that was ten years ago. "It was a dreadful experience. My two brothers had children so I just assumed I would be all right. It was pretty difficult dealing with the news at that age. I felt as though I had gone into a brick wall. There was just nothing to prepare me for it. I'm tall, hairy, masculine-looking and yet I had no sperm. It was a bombshell and there was no reason for it."

Therapy and counselling can help to deal with emotions that can be difficult for the man and his partner. But then again, that is not a path many men choose. And male support groups for these issues are available but not nearly as many as are available to women. Studies on the psychological impact of infertility diagnoses on men are about as rare. "I am the sperm donor – that is all," said one man sarcastically and a bit sadly. Trying to conceive can turn into a job. It can destroy a relationship, a spontaneous and joyous sex life. As one man admits, "For a long time we didn't want sex for sex sake. The only purpose was trying to make a baby. When sex turns into work, I lose interest." Maybe it can help a bit to know the different causes for infertility. Yes, the whole thing may all be in your head and that will entail therapy. But there are other causes as well. And it is not always easy to figure them out – one man described the whole process of figuring out what was going on in his body and his testes as "walking through a maze."

No Effect Without a Cause

There can be many reasons for male infertility. It can be a psychological issue. It can be a genetic disorder, gastrointestinal disease, infection of the genital tract, the prostate, cirrhosis of the liver, drugs, tumours, sport injuries, hormonal problems, external factors like heat or chemicals or even a short illness like flu. In some cases the problems are only temporary. And even when the urologists or andrologists know their job well, it is possible that they will not find the cause of the problem. This does not mean they are poor doctors.

Hormones

In contrast to female infertility, male infertility is only rarely caused by a hormonal imbalance. Nerves transmit their messages from the brain to, say, a muscle via a direct link. Hormones work indirectly as messengers to elicit a particular function. No serious andrologist will be sitting in his or her office with a loaded needle full of testosterone as a quick-fix. To figure out if a man has hormonal deficiency, complex tests are needed. Hormone treatment in men who do not have a deficiency has not proven successful.

Medical or Surgical Intervention

Approximately 15–20% of all men develop a condition called varicocele which is something of a varicose vein in the scrotum. Sometimes this condition disappears untreated, in some cases an operation may be necessary. Some experts say they are sure varicocele can impact fertility. Other say "bah, humbug." As Eberhard Nieschlag and his colleagues at the German University of Münster state, "While this makes varicocele the second most frequent pathological finding …, it gives no indication of the importance of the finding as a cause of infertility." They call the connection between varicocele and fertility "less clear" and note that "varicocele does not exclude paternity." If varicocele is diagnosed, and surgery is immediately scheduled, it is best to get a second opinion before consenting to surgery.

Unknown

"Idiopathic infertility" is the scientific expression for infertility without an obvious cause. Up to 20% of all couples face this diagnosis. Knowing a cause obviously raises the hope that a solution can be found. So this diagnosis can be very disheartening for couples trying to conceive.

Very often it is difficult or even impossible to pinpoint the exact reason for a fertility problem. As D. Stewart Irvine and Allan Templeton, of the MRC Reproductive Unit in Edinburgh and the University of Aberdeen respectively, point out, "Our ability to provide accurate diagnosis, and therefore rational management, for the male partner of an infertile couple remains poor, largely as a consequence of our lack of understanding of the causes of defective sperm function at the level of the cell biology of the spermatozoon." Some doctors have their own methods they swear by that offer solutions to fertility issues of this kind, but other physicians find less positive things to say about such approaches. Among the substances prescribed to men with idiopathic infertility are androgens, HCG/HMG-therapy, gonadotropins, gonadotropin releasing hormones, anti-oestrogen and aromatase inhibitors, and all of these substances have yielded varying results. Some caused severe side effects.

In 1962, a scientist named J.H. Blair reported an unexpectedly positive effect on the sperm quality of a man who was receiving medication for depression. Other studies followed, some with "astonishing results," but no recognized therapy has resulted from that. Many trials would be necessary before a therapy to increase the sperm quality in this fashion could even be considered. As Eberhard Nieschlag points out in summary, "Pharmacological approaches to the therapy of male idiopathic infertility have been highly disappointing."

Kallikrein

Most research on kallikrein has been carried out by the German scientist Wolf-Bernhard Schill at the University of Giessen. He is convinced that kallikrein has a positive effect on sperm motility and that it can be used as a treatment regimen when idiopathic male infertility is diagnosed. Other scientists regard his claims skeptically. One drawback of the substance is that pre-existing infections in the epididymis or prostate may be exacerbated through this treatment.

Pentoxyphyllin

Pentoxyphyllin can increase sperm motility in the test tube and increase fertilization rates. But when delivered as a medication it has not been shown to improve sperm function or production.

Vitamins, Trace Elements and Antioxidants

The vitamins A, B and C are vital for sperm production. Trace elements also play an important role but their connection to fertility has not been fully explored. According to some studies, vitamin C counteracts the agglutination of sperm, when they clump together. After a dose of vitamin C sperm showed a better ability to lock onto the egg's membrane. Heavy smokers sometimes have vitamin C deficiencies and taking vitamin C may help enhance their sperm function. Glutathione, an antidote to free radicals, has been shown to increase sperm motility. Vitamin E has also been shown to enhance the binding of sperm to the egg's membrane.

Zinc is a trace element that is of major interest to reproductive scientists. Some studies have suggested that taking zinc can improve fertility but the results have not been confirmed. So as yet, there is no such thing as a recommended zinc therapy. Zinc can be detrimental to sperm function in high doses so it is not a good idea to simply take zinc megadoses.

While most physicians are not willing to put these substances on their prescription pads or to claim that they will cure a particular condition, there is increased research interest in the therapeutic effect of antioxidative vitamins on fertility disturbances. And that means that products are in the works which may indeed have a positive effect. Pentoxyphyllin is also an antioxidant but it apparently has an adverse effect on the activity of the egg. So it may actually not help to treat fertility problems. Of the substances mentioned, most physicians will probably not approve of more than a low-dose vitamin regimen.

Supplements

There are a number of dietary supplements on the market that claim to enhance sperm quality. For example, they may contain a substance called L-carnitine, a semen component. Before taking any kind of supplement, it is a good idea to consult with a physician, even if it is an over-the-counter substance.

The Influence of Medication

Dependent on the dose, the length of administration and individual aspects, many prescription drugs can impair potency. Sperm can be damaged in many ways by prescription medications and at many developmental stages. In some cases, sperm metabolism can be disturbed or their motility impaired.

Of course, many patients rely on their prescriptions and cannot simply discontinue them. This section is not intended to encourage men to not take their prescriptions. But it is a reminder that if you are trying to conceive and cannot find out why, you might need to consider your medication as a possible cause. Your physician will be taking down a list of any prescription medicine your are on for just this reason. In some cases, a replacement can be sought that will have the same therapeutic effect with less impact on male fertility. When in doubt, consult your physician.

Antibiotics may in some cases impair sperm quality by decreasing their motility, for example nitrofurans (nitrofurazone or nitrofurantoin) and macrolides (erythromycin). The drug sulfasalazine used to treat colitis, the anti-fungal drug ketoconazole, and azulfidine, a drug used to treat ulcers, have all been implicated as potentially harmful to male fertility as they may impair sperm development. Opioids have been shown to be associated with fertility problems. Cytotoxic drugs used, for example used in the treatment of cancer, damage sperm. Which is why a man undergoing treatment for testicular cancer will be asked to give a sperm sample before he starts his treatment. These drugs are also used for the treatment of other diseases such as psoriasis.

As T.B. Hargreave notes in a publication on the subject, Amiodarone, an antiarrhythmic drug may be toxic to the epididymis. A number of drugs may interfere with the "hypothalamic/pituitary/testicular axis" including high-dose corticosteroids, androgens, antiandrogens, estrogens. The beta blocker group of drugs used to treat high blood pressure can impair sperm motility and potency. Sedatives and antidepressants can cause erectile dysfunction. And the list goes on. So, to be on the safe side, if you are trying to conceive and on prescription for a medication or about to go on medication for a condition that might be totally unrelated to reproduction or sexuality, it might be a good idea to ask if your physician knows if the medication impacts on libido, erectile function, sperm development and function.

Fertility and the Workplace

Work can be risky business. And not just for bodyguards or stuntmen. And the risk may mean more than the perhaps more obvious and possibly job-related illnesses such as stomach ulcers or heart attacks. At a multinational pharmaceutical company, a spokeswoman was apparently baffled by my question as to whether the company took the reproductive health of their male workers into consideration. "We have never had a question like that," she said. Cold calls to other companies and in other industries yielded similar reactions, although the firms did make a point of stating generalities on how important employee health was. Male reproductive health, however, did not seem to be targeted in any specific way.

Some researchers have attempted to see if erectile dysfunction could be related to stress at work, night shifts or physically taxing labor, but no conclusive correlation could be found. An occupational health administrator in one company pointed out a dilemma for the employer. Erection problems can have such a multitude of triggers that it was going to be impossible to blame an employer for them. The company representatives I spoke to were only willing to speak off the record on this, apparently hot, subject. General medical exams at companies do not normally include semen analysis. As one company representative told me, "I could never get my workers to do this." And of course there are other ways to ascertain a man's health, so semen analysis may not be necessary. But if something about the workplace is impacting fertility, and there are no exams or questions on this subject, then male employees may be faced with some difficult situations on their own.

A Hint

Dibromochloropropane (DBCP) is a nematocide, a chemical that was widely used to control pests in banana and other fruit plantations. At a conference, C. Alvin Paulsen, an andrologist at the University of Washington, said that a coincidental conversation got people thinking about this substance. Some men who worked at a Californian pesticide factory where DBCP had been produced since the early 1960s, were at lunch one day and discussed the fact that none of them had fathered any children, even though they and their wives wanted to be parents. Five of the men went in for medical check-ups and the physicians found that the men had no or few sperm. And the sperm they had were not very motile and there was a high percentage of abnormally shaped sperm. A year later, a similar report emerged from a pesticide factory in Israel. Systematic studies came to the conclusion that workers who had been in contact with the pesticide indeed had become infertile. As Jaana Lähdetie of the University of Turku points out, "During the late 1970s and 1980s, a massive sterilization of male workers at Costa Rica banana plantations was reported, at least 1,500 workers had become sterile because of the use of DBCP." Production and use of DBCP was subsequently restricted in the US but use in developing countries continued. Follow-up studies showed that it took many years for sperm production to return to normal after exposure ceased. For some men, sperm production and hormone levels have not reached levels found in unexposed men. DBCP had been shown to have a detrimental effect on the liver, kidney, lung and testes in laboratory animals. As Gad Potashnik and Avi Porath of the Ben-Gurion University of the Negev in Israel point out, "Workers reported in the present study were not aware of the need for daily change of clothing and proper use of masks. Because skin contact and inhalation are the main routes of DBCP absorption, their actual exposure is estimated to be highly intensive."

According to Lähdetie, "DBCP is by far the most impressive occupational testicular toxin in men." So far no other chemicals have been found to have this targeted an effect on the testis but, he adds, "it is obvious now that all new chemicals should be scrutinized for effects on spermatogenesis." As David Handelsman of the Royal Prince Alfred Hospital in Sydney, Australia, notes, "Although this was not the first agent identified to cause human male infertility, the effects of dibromochloropropane were so dramatic and clearly related to the industrial exposure that the incident became the classic example of occupational male reproductive toxicity."

Occupations and Risks

Some places of work are far from ideal for the testes and their precious contents. "At work, high performance is expected, regardless of mood and motivation," writes Jens Kämmerer in his dissertation on the impact of various occupations on semen quality, based on data gathered in the 1980s. Kämmerer compared the semen quality of self-employed men and men in upper management with academics, farmers and manual workers, civil servants and white-collar workers. In his evaluation he compared parameters such as fructose levels and sperm concentration. He was trying to ascertain if various stressors such as nightshifts or a subjective sense of workplace hazards were impacting the men's semen quality.

In his study, younger men between the ages of 31 and 40 generally had sweeter semen than men over 40, a fact which has been confirmed in other studies. These values change as men age, but he did find variations within occupations with the self-employed and top managers leading on the sweetness scale followed by civil servants. White-collar workers ranked in next and a bit further on were the farmers and manual labourers. Academics came in last. All of the men considered in this study had either normal or higher than normal levels so these differences were not of clinical significance. Only if fructose is far too low will physicians see a cause for concern and look for a cause. Fructose levels can vary if the body is warding off an inflammation or infection of some sort. Why managers had higher fructose levels is open to speculation.

When other parameters were compared, the ranking was different. In terms of semen volume, the academics made first place, followed by the civil servants, the farmers and manual laborers; the self-employed and male managers ranked at the bottom of this scale. In terms of percentage of normal sperm, the sequence was similar: 1. academics, 2. civil servants 3. white-collar workers 4. farmers and manual laborers, 5. self-employed and managers. When realigned for sperm density academics once again took the lead, followed by the self-employed and managers; farmers and laborers were next with civil servants and white-collar workers showing the lowest sperm density in their semen.

Men who worked irregular schedules showed a higher percentage of normal shaped sperm with greater motility than men who worked more regular hours. Although men who worked nights complained of various health-related conditions, such as digestion issues, sleeping problems, they did not have reduced semen quality in comparison to men who worked daytime hours. Men who felt exposed to hazards in the workplace did not show a lowered semen quality. Yet, men who were feeling stressed in their jobs did show a higher percentage of abnormally shaped sperm than their unstressed colleagues. In this study, however it was not completely clear if the men were experiencing stress at home as well. Stress in general does negatively impact sperm quality, as andrologists in infertility clinics report.

In a study at the National University of Singapore comparing sperm quality between various occupations, it turns out that "plant and machine operators" have a higher risk than "senior officials and managers" and "people working in transport and communication" of having lower sperm counts which may cause fertility problems. The authors of the study point out that exposure to excessive heat may be responsible for the effect.

Every once in a while alarming reports pop up. Some studies have pointed to painters, car mechanics and farmers as being at particular risk of fathering children with congenital defects. But the results are not conclusive. In 1990, a study was published according to which the wives of painters and workers in wood-processing plants who worked with solvents had a 2.5 times greater risk of miscarriage in the first three months of pregnancy than the general population. Some researchers postulate that the men's sperm harbored damaged genetic material.

Whether farmers observe all the safety precautions when handling pesticides is not generally known. Some occupational health experts report having heard many farmers say that they choose not to dilute substances in the correct proportions in order to improve the efficacy of, say, a particular pesticide. By so doing, these people can suffer higher exposure to the chemicals. According to a publication by the Danish Ministry for the Environment, workers in greenhouses can be particularly affected as they are in confined spaces while working with pesticides. The workforce there is mainly female but not exclusively so. The approximately 5 million migrant and seasonal farm workers in the US are, according to researchers at the University of California at Davis, "the most underserved and understudied populations." Understanding how the farm work exposures, including pesticide-related illnesses and reproductive health problems affects them "are vital to characterize and reduce the occupational health risks in farm workers." For example, they are looking at the effects of solvents which are suspected of impairing spermatogenesis. In the early 1980s, a Finnish study was published showing a nearly 30% miscarriage rate among seamstresses. The reason was not their workplace but that of their partners and husbands who worked in a nearby metal factory where they were exposed to toxins such as solvents. A study by the Aarhus University Hospital in Denmark found that in farmers, exposure to styrene, a toxic solvent, seemed to cause a decline in sperm density, but the study was, in the authors' own words, still inconsistent in its results. This study is part of a program in Europe called ASCLEPIOS which focuses on occupational hazards and male reproductive capability and involves a collaborative effort between occupational physicians, epidemiologists and andrologists from ten European countries.

The Occupational Safety and Health Administration lists many diseases that have been linked to the workplace, some of them pertaining to the reproductive capacities. Scrotal cancer, for example, has been found in automatic lathe workers, metalworkers, coke oven workers, petroleum refiners, tar distillers and chimney sweeps.

An occupational group that is fairly closely monitored for occupational hazards are physicians, and radiologists in particular, and professionals exposed to anesthetics. And then there is the military. Some studies revealed exposure to radar as a hazard to reproductive health while other studies could not confirm the results. A study of men working at an Air Force installation paint shop showed slightly less motile sperm in their semen than men who were not exposed to the paints and solvents.

Historical Remarks

Work-related health problems as they relate to reproductive health are old news in some ways. In 1775 a disease called "chimney sweepers' cancer" referred to the rates of scrotal cancer among chimney sweeps, attributed to their exposure to soot. In the 1950s, studies showed radiologists and employees in the nuclear power industry to be particularly at risk for various diseases. In some British and US nuclear agencies employees were advised not to marry colleagues because the combined radiation damage might be harmful to their offspring.

In the 1950s some studies mentioned that soccer players who regularly wore "protective gear in the loin area" should have their fertility checked, "especially as sports people also tend to take a lot of hot baths." Occupation-related fertility problems were discovered in workers at gas and coke plants around 50 years ago. Roland Hoferer of the University of Würzburg in Germany wrote back then, "Heat related fertility problems can arise among professional soccer players, Europeans who spend extended periods in the tropics, stokers, drivers, steam engine drivers, bakers, steel industry workers, chimney sweeps and welders."

"If the world is facing a decline in human fecundity," writes Jörn Olsen of the Danish University of Aarhus, "which has roots in environmental exposures, research should be directed towards populations with the highest exposure, which are often specific occupational groups." Is that a principle pursued? To a certain degree and for some illnesses. "If today's rules and regulations at the workplace are observed, there should be far less work-related cases of cancer in the future," said Andreas Zober, Director for Occupational Medicine and Health at the German chemical manufacturer BASF. Time will tell if he is right and if the efforts undertaken are sufficient. Reproductive health poses a par-ticular challenge since, as Olsen notes, "Fertility problems are sensitive matters which are difficult to accept and talk about for many, probably because they relate closely to fundamental biological issues of human life."

People just Love Chemicals

Be it car tires, paints or all things plastic, there is hardly an object in modern households that has not been touched by some chemical manufac-turing process. While some people deem these products and the substances used in their production toxic and evil, others are less alarmed by them. Initially, the chemical industry mocked Rachel Carson's book, *Silent Spring*, published in 1962, which dealt with the environmental effects of pesticides. These days, such stark reactions are less likely. But that may depend on your perspective. The literature on the cancer-causing, cancer-promoting or other-wise harmful properties of various substances is vast. Substances seem to go through a scientific and then a cultural risk assessment cycle of sorts. Asbestos, widely used in the past, for example, is now generally recognized as a hazardous material. CFCs, or man-made chlorofluorocarbons, have been shown to eat away at the earth's protective ozone layer. And there are other chemicals associated with products we are loath to be without and which have been shown to come back to haunt us. Even the Chemical Manufacturers Association does not deny these issues.

Some environmental organizations would prefer it if man-made chemicals were first generally considered guilty until proved innocent. While that may lead to great safety standards, the principle does not seem easy to practise. And then again many everyday, all-natural substances may prove harmful as well. Who knows if even pepper and salt would actually obtain FDA approval if they needed to. That does not get man-made substances off the hook. There are a number of cases in which, despite better knowledge and test results, man-made substances became ubiquitous and they later turned out to be causing harm. A number of chemical manufacturing companies have maneuvered themselves into the positions of the villain and because of these incidents are regarded, by many, with general suspicion.

On environmental issues it seems easiest to turn fundamentalist. You can either pick:"Get rid of it all!," or the antidote, "That's nonsense, everything is fine!" Figuring out if a substance is harmful or not can take years. The evidence may then not be as conclusive as was hoped. Despite differing opinions a consensus may be found on what to do. And possibly, production will cease, probably not uniformly in all countries.

Actually, investigating the effects of substances often does not only require looking far and wide for consequences. More often than not, the effects can be felt close to home, as the people who work with these substances may also have the greatest exposure. These people, however, are not necessarily the first to be heard. In Scandinavian countries and several Western Europe nations occupational health seems a bit more in the forefront than, say, in the US.

In general, if a product that is already on the market is shown to be harmful, as the tobacco, asbestos and CFCs cases illustrate, it is not easy to have them removed from the marketplace. After all, that can be quite involved and costly as any company involved in asbestos removal can attest. Everyday products have to be safe for consumer use. A car dashboard should not exude toxic fumes when hit by sunlight. The same protective principles should apply to the workplace. Production workers should not be in danger because of the chemicals they handle.

During the manufacture of certain chemicals such as pesticides and paints, employees in a production facility encounter a number of potentially toxic substances. There are regulations and laws that stipulate the use of protective eyewear, clothing, gloves, and there are permissible limits of exposure. Some companies, though, ignore these safety precautions, and the workers are exposed to substances that can harm their health. In other cases the negative effects of a particular substance are overlooked. An occupational health expert said, "For years agencies have been focused on carcinogenic substances, but it is not unlikely that other effects have been overlooked." Sometimes health problems and diseases only manifest themselves years after exposure to a particular substance. If a certain problem occurs more frequently in one company, it might be possible to link the symptom to a cause but this is not always easy. Often, of course, a company will keep the statistics under wraps. In some cases, there is very little known about the effects of a substance and yet it makes its way into a manufacturing process.

If a pregnant woman smokes, drinks alcohol or is malnourished, her baby will suffer. As the National Institute of Occupational Safety and Health (NIOSH) points out, "It is not well known, however, that a man's exposure to substances in the workplace can affect his ability to have healthy children ... ." There is no master list that contains all the substances known to be hazards. There are some the research community agrees on, others being debated with some countries reaching different conclusions than others. Since new chemicals are being developed all the time which all require testing and the synergistic effect of these substances also requires testing, the whole field of toxicology is sure to never be out of work. As far as studying the male in this context is concerned, things have really just started. As NIOSH states, "scientists are just beginning to understand how these hazards affect the male reproductive system." And in particular the study of the effect of substances or external effects on male reproductive health is still in its early stages as well. As Gladys Friedler of Boston University Medical School points out, "Male-mediated effects were not systematically examined until the early seventies when independent studies reported adverse effects in both experimental animals and human offspring after paternal exposure to several drugs or to paternal interventions."

If your occupation exposes you to hazards you do not like, then, given the opportunity you may wish to re-launch your job search. That, of course is not always an obvious and easy way out. What else can you do to lessen the risk if a job involves exposure to potentially hazardous substances? Besides making sure they are properly stored and handled, follow the writing on the wall in the washrooms: wash hands. Avoid direct contact with hazardous materials, wear all the prescribed protective gear, avoid bringing contaminated clothing home. Some workplace hazards may have immediate effects, you may feel ill upon coming home from work. And contacting a doctor in that case is essential. Other effects may be more subtle and difficult to detect. If you suspect something at work is making you ill, contact a doctor. The following are some of the substances and environmentally induced hazards affecting the testes and sperm production:

Heat is not good for the testes. In 1958, a study at the German University of Würzburg stated, "Of all the dangers to the gonads heat damage is at the top of the list. The effect of high temperatures on sperm production has been known for a long time ... ." The impact of heat on sperm production is so definitive that time and again scientists have discussed the possibility of developing a contraceptive based on light scrotal-heating.

Men exposed to heat in their work environments, such as the high temperatures of the ceramics industry, have shown a higher percentage of sperm with pathological characteristics in their semen. Welders, for example, in the steel industry, are exposed to both heat and fumes. In some studies, but not all, welders have been shown to have lower semen quality. Some researchers have found lower sperm counts among professional drivers. A fever may actually have the same kind of effect. As work by Richard Levine at the National Institutes of Health has demonstrated, human sperm counts are generally lower in the summer. He suggests that there may be a kind of built-in clock to the male reproductive system, perhaps coupled to the length of daylight. In the US and in warm climates throughout the world, there are fewer births in the spring. Yet, in Canada and Europe, the birth rate is highest in the late winter and spring. The explanation for this variation is not quite clear. Studying men who worked in New Orleans, Levine found that in men whose workplaces were not air-conditioned, semen quality deteriorated in the summer. For a later comparative study he picked men who worked outdoors and who lived with their wives near San Antonio and who were trying to achieve a pregnancy. In all men, semen quality deteriorated in the summer leading to a low number of children born in the spring. The lower the sperm concentration at the outset, the greater the reduction in sperm concentration and the motility of the sperm in the men's semen during the summertime. It is not obvious to what degree the seasonal variation in semen quality may be playing a role but it may be more relevant than the effect of outdoor workplace heat on the men's testes.

The testes are special sites with sperm output ongoing 24 hours a day, seven days a week, producing about 150 million sperm a day. Particular toxins can damage sperm at practically every stage in their development. That is not exactly easy, since the developing germ cells are protected by the so-called blood–testis barrier. Not everything in the blood reaches the testes. But there is an exception to this protection. While the germ cells are protected by this border, the cells from which they arise are not. The so-called spermatogonia are outside the blood–testis barrier. Sperm can be and are affected by external factors although how that occurs is not always clear.

Sperm themselves may be destroyed, somehow impaired or their genetic material, their DNA, can be damaged. And this damage is not always readily detectable. While a deleterious change in his genetic material need not express itself in a man, it might very well do so and it might also be possible for him to pass it on to his children. The endocrine system may also be affected by external factors. In order for the testes to function properly, hormones such as LH and FSH are important. Impacting the hormones can have far-reaching consequences.

Radiation damages sperm and this has been known for a long time. High levels of radiation exposure can permanently damage the testes. Researcher Liane Russell at Oak Ridge National Laboratory has found that sperm are particularly vulnerable to ionizing radiation in their early and late developmental stages. This is where the high vitamin C content of semen comes into play. This vitamin, an antidote to so-called free radicals, may be a helpful adjunct in the body's own system to repair radiation-induced damage. The tricky part about radiation is that the germ cells may survive but they may have sustained chromosomal damage. Radiation damage is also a problem for men undergoing treatment for cancer, although scientists debate the degree of risk.

In the US during the 1970s, the testes of more than 100 prison inmates, supposedly volunteers, were irradiated with various dosages showing suppression of sperm counts up to complete infertility. Men involved in clean-up activities after the nuclear accident in Chernobyl have been shown to have decreased sperm counts and various degrees of disturbed sperm development. Georgian soldiers (from the Russian Republic, not the American state) who were accidentally exposed to high levels of radiation had ulcers on different parts of their body, testicular damage and semen quality problems. In the UK there is an ongoing study called the Nuclear Industry Family Study in which a database of the employees' reproductive health and the health of their children is being collected.

In 1990, British epidemiologist Martin Gardner set off a controversy when he reported that children of men working near the nuclear processing plant Sellafield were more than ten times more likely to have congenital leukemia. Previous studies in Nagasaki and Hiroshima seemed to indicate that radiation exposure in men did not cause a higher leukemia rate in their children. To this day experts argue about methodological errors in the Sellafield study particularly because there is no data from the region from the time before Sellafield went into operation. Long-term exposure to low levels of radiation is probably a different phenomenon than high levels of exposure from nuclear incidents, making it difficult to compare data from these two classes of events. Scientists assume, though, that long-term low-level radioactivity might very well be a problem if it causes genetic damage that can be passed onto the next generation. Laws and regulations are in place to protect pregnant women from excessive radiation exposure and traditionally much research has focused on reproductive effects on women. It is considered normal to view women, particularly women of childbearing age and pregnant women as deserving of special protection. Only slowly are fathers and fathers-to-be taken into serious consideration when it comes to male-mediated effects on reproduction.

Technicians with occupational exposure to *microwaves* with high-frequency electromagnetic fields have been shown to have a lower semen quality. The potential health effects of exposure to extremely low-frequency magnetic fields such as those emitted by mobile phones have come up consistently in the discussion. The current consensus is that the risk is minimal but the long-term risks are being studied. It would seem that mobile phones might be of particular interest since men often wear them around their belt, not far from their genitals.

Diethylstilbestrol (DES) is a *synthetic estrogen* that was used in the US and other countries as a prescription drug for pregnant women to avoid miscarriage. Men occupationally exposed to DES experienced hormonal imbalances. Fertility problems have cropped up in male workers involved in the manufacture of contraceptive pills which involves exposure to synthetic estrogen. Singular instances, such as an embalming professional who began to feminize due to the embalming cream he used, show how active these substances can be. Textbooks and studies point out a number of substances that have damaging effects on sperm – for example, *glycol ethers* and solvents such as *carbon disulfide*.

Reports of carbon disulfide intoxication date back quite a while since this substance was used to manufacture viscose, cellophane, and rubber, as well as reports of specific chemicals such as carbon tetrachloride. A report from 1856 describes carbon disulfide poisoning. "He who works in the 'sulphur' (CS2) is no longer a man." The effects extend well beyond loss of potency to include such general effects as memory loss, reduced will power, and lowered self-esteem.

Spermatocytes are sperm that undergo a cell division called meiosis. During this developmental stage there is a lot of genetic activity which makes the pre-sperm particularly vulnerable to attack with serious consequences. One spermatocyte toxin, as the Australian researcher David Handelsman points out, is *2-Methoxyethanol* (2-MEA), used in varnishes and paints. The chemicals 2-MEA, 2-Ethoxyethanol and 2-Ethoxyethanol acetate belong to a group of chemicals called glycol ethers that are used as solvents in many applications such as cleaners, commercial printing inks, paints and coatings, and they are also used in the production of plasticizers, as de-icing additives in jet fuels and in electronics manufacturing. Particularly because of their reproductive and devel-opmental health effects, the Occupational Safety and Health Administration has readjusted the permissible exposure limits to these chemicals.

Some chemicals target particular cells in the male reproductive tract in their biologic effect but this knowledge is based pretty much only on animal experiments. For example, phtalates, used as plasticizers; nitroaromatic compounds which are formed in the production of dyes and explosives and particular kinds of solvents have been shown to be toxic to Sertoli cells. These cells play, as Handelsman puts it, a "a cardinal role in regulating and supporting spermatogenesis, forming the scaffolding of the seminiferous tubule, and creating its unique milieu."

Heavy metals are found in many workplaces and they, too, can affect the male reproductive system. High exposure to *lead* is associated with testicular damage. The data for studies of these health risks were gathered mainly from research on welders. As the Canadian Centre for Occupational Health and Safety points out, low to moderate exposures to lead have been shown to have "significant harmful effects" in the male reproductive system; for example, low sperm count and abnormal sperm structure and motility. In the former Yugoslavia, 101 male workers had been exposed to both low and high levels of inorganic lead and experienced reduced semen volume, lower overall sperm concentrations as well as fewer viable and motile sperm and a higher number of abnormally shaped sperm.

Cadmium is suspected of having a negative effect on the testes but so far there has not been conclusive evidence. *Arsenic* and *zinc* also damage sperm. Some reports mention mercury poisoning of female workers in battery facto-ries. The wives of workers in Spanish mercury mines had a 40% higher rate of miscarriages, stillbirths and birth defects. German researcher Roland Hoferer mentioned in 1958 that there was evidence of chronic *mercury* poisoning of men working in factories manufacturing explosives, mirrors and thermometers.

Rules and Regulations

Work is generally not supposed to harm your health. As the Occupational Safety and Health Administration of the US Department of Labor states, their goal is "to send every worker home whole and healthy every day." The Health and Safety Executive in the UK has a mission "to ensure that risks to people's health and safety from work activities are properly controlled."

There are laws and statutes – in the US, for example, the Occupational Health and Safety Act – standards and rules, regulations, inspections, and compliance directives. There are TWA PELs, or time-weighted averages of permissible exposure limits, that regulate exposure that cannot be avoided in a workplace. However, work is not an injury-free zone, although it is true that since 1993, injury and illness rates have fallen in the US by about 30%. But there are still 5.7 million work-related injuries and illnesses. In the UK around 2 million workers and former workers have some kind of work-related health problem every year. Of course not all of the injuries and illnesses pertain to the male reproductive tract, and effects are usually not limited in that way.

Every country has its own risk assessment policies which are often based on the laws and conclusions in the international scientific community or on research in that particular country. One part of this procedure is to determine safe exposure levels – the threshold at which toxic effects are shown. This will vary from compound to compound. Nordic countries in Europe are particularly active in this field of study, but research is also conducted by groups at the WHO as well as the Scientific Committee for Occupational Exposure Limits at the European Commission. The tests involve studying how a substance is taken up by the body, how it is absorbed, distributed, metabolized and excreted and what kind of effect it has while in the body. Both short-term and long-term effects are studied. Historically, in many countries the maximum exposure to a particular substance is often determined in relation to pregnant women and women of childbearing age.

The National Institute for Occupational Safety and Health (NIOSH) in the US conducts investigations into possible health hazards in the workplace and calls them HHEs, or Health Hazard Evaluations, which means that upon request by employees or employers the place of employment can be specifically evaluated. NIOSH also maintains lists of chemical hazards which will tell you what the exposure limits of a particular substance are and what the symptoms of overexposure may be.

Safe Limits

Hazardous substances are classified in various ways, according to their biological effects, such as carcinogenic properties, or so-called teratogenic properties, their ability to cause birth defects. Some toxins may cause damage upon skin contact.

If continuous monitoring of safety limits is not possible, there are sporadic check-ups, either several times a day or a week in order to compile a profile of the effects of a potentially hazardous substance. And since some regulations do not reflect the latest scientific findings, a company may decide to set its own safety levels. The problem is that, often, these studies may be retrospective studies, establishing that company X has a higher frequency of bladder cancer in Department Y. For the workers who have become ill, this news comes much too late. These findings can thus only be used to prevent such occurrences from happening again.

In order to obtain governmental approval to market and use a particular substance in the first place, a battery of tests must have been performed. These will include animal studies as well as cell-culture studies. If there are research results from other exposures that have been recorded, these too will be taken into consideration. One challenge lies in the study of long-term effects. Cancer may develop many years after the first exposure with a particular toxic substance. By then someone may have already switched jobs or retired.

Safe Workplace Environments and Fertility

As NIOSH points out, "Although more than 1,000 workplace chemicals have been shown to have reproductive effects on animals, most have not been studied in humans. In addition, most of the 4 million other chemical mixtures in commercial use remain untested."

Many workplace safety pratices have focused on women and their unborn children, and while their risk might be greater, there is no reason to leave men out of the picture. Their health and the effects they may pass onto their children do not deserve to be disregarded. Asking a man about his libido, sexual potency and whether he is experiencing involuntary childlessness as part of a routine medical exam at the workplace may not be possible because of the invasion of privacy these types of questions entail.

"There are good reasons to believe that human sperm can serve as valuable indicators of toxic and eventually genotoxic effects of occupational and environmental exposures because spermatozoa are produced in large numbers, are easily available, and carry on the important genetic material to the next generation," according to Jaana Lähdetie of the University of Turku in Finland. So does this mean that semen analysis will be a routine job on the job? Even at the DBCP plant some workers refused to provide semen samples and were given jobs elsewhere in the plant. It may be more attractive to find different ways of monitoring a worker's reproductive health. A man may also choose to discuss such issues with his own doctor rather than a company doctor. And physicians will need to take workplace hazards into account when giving their male patients their yearly check-up.

Some researchers have advanced the idea, and not even in jest, that men exposed to noxious chemicals or radiation at their workplace be given a 90-day preconception leave, just enough time to produce an unexposed batch of sperm. Cleaning up a workplace may be a better alternative but may be harder to do if the studies are not giving a clear-cut view on whether the chemicals are indeed hazardous or if the person's lifestyle habits are the main cause of the fertility problem.

Environmental Influences

"Sex has become the least important of man's sensory pleasures." The fact that contraception was no longer an issue did not free sex for new and imaginative delights. In the mid-1990s infertility had become universal and semen testing compulsory. In 1995, the last human was born. The human race – an endangered species – was unable to reproduce and was drifting toward a looming end. This is the scenario of a thriller by P.D. James called *The Children of Men*, published in 1992. A sombre and unlikely story of a world hit by the cruel impact of pollution? Maybe. This is a most pessimistic view of the state of affairs. Perhaps, things aren't quite that bad. So you may decide to just forget about the pollution debate altogether. Let's say, though, that a man is diagnosed as having no sperm. It might make sense to consider the many reasons why this may be the case.

"Sometimes I feel like a plumber," one doctor told me. "Most men who seek my opinion seem to expect a quick diagnosis and an even quicker recovery. They expect us to take out the spanners, stop the leaks, tighten all connections and – end of problem!" "My male patients consent to just about everything, as long it is over quickly," said another doctor. Sometimes there are simple remedies. Men with a stressful life have – perhaps unsurprisingly – stressed sperm. And in some cases it appears sufficient to reduce stress for adequate sperm production to return. Sometimes, however, more complex treatments are necessary. But these, too, sometimes fail. In order to develop better treatments, it is essential to look at other kinds of sperm and testes stressors.

Male fertility and sperm quality are not given equal importance in every country. Denmark is a country with heightened radar for these issues, it seems. A debate about sperm quality was touched off by a publication by Niels Skakkebaek, chief of the Department of Growth and Reproduction at Copenhagen's largest hospital, Rigshospitalet, and his colleagues. He treats men with potency and fertility problems as well as children with hormonal problems or developmental genital abnormalities. Denmark has an unusually high rate of testicular cancer; a disease which seems to be on the rise in several countries. The cancer registries in European countries reveal an upward trend for this disease. As the Danish Environmental Protection Agency notes in a report, "… testicular cancer is now the most common malignancy of young men in many countries, and although it is still rare compared to the malignant diseases most prevalent in old age, the lifetime risk of developing testicular cancer now approaches 1% in a country such as Denmark." In many countries testicular cancer is the most frequent form of cancer in young men. There are very efficient treatments for this rare cancer.

Skakkebaek had noted the rise of abnormalities in the male reproductve tract including testicular cancer as well as non-descended testicles. In this condition, the testes do not descend to their position in the scrotum but remain lodged in the body. British scientists have found the incidence of this condition to have doubled between 1962 and 1981. Research in Sweden and Hungary obtained similar results but the epidemiology of this condition does not offer clear-cut numbers and trends. While non-descended testicles are treatable through surgery, they are associated with lower fertility and a higher testicular cancer risk. Skakkebaek had studied the germ cells of aborted fetuses and discovered precursor cells to testicular cancer which suggested that this condition may begin to develop when the fetus is in the womb even though it may not appear until later on in the boy's life.

Decreasing Sperm Quality

Skakkebaek had been wondering why Danish sperm banks were having such a hard time recruiting good donors. And so the team set out to study sperm quality, leading to the publication in 1992 of a study that made headlines, caused alarm around the world, and created a furor in scientific journals and conferences that has yet to subside fully.

The overview was a so-called meta-analysis of 61 studies about semen quality published between 1938 and 1990 involving a total of about 15,000 men, all of whom had no fertility problems. They conclude: "reports published worldwide indicate clearly that sperm concentration has declined appreciably" in that time period, "although we cannot conclude whether or not this decline is continuing." The mean sperm concentration in an ejaculate had decreased from from 113 million per milliliter of semen to 66 million. The decrease was dramatic – nearly 50% in 50 years. If this was true, things were looking dismal for the human male and the human race.

What seemed especially alarming was that the percentage of men with a sperm concentration of less than 20 million sperm per milliliter seemed to have increased steadily over the period. The WHO considers this figure as the lowest threshold for fertility. Men with less sperm have little chance of fathering a child. Skakkebaek and his colleagues surmised that there was a link between the increase in testicular cancer, congenital abnormalities and decreased semen quality. And they point out that they "are probably due to environmental factors rather than genetic factors."A possible cause may also be "some common prenatal events."

Skakkebaek is not the first to do this kind of study; over the years several studies have found a marked reduction in sperm numbers and there has been speculation about an incriminating environmental factor of some sort.

Not everyone agrees with the Danish interpretation. Other researchers criticized the statistical models used, the possibility of bias and the perhaps questionable reliability of the data analyzed. As I.S. Tummon of the Canadian University of Western Ontario and David Mortimer from the Sydney IVF Pty Ltd. asked, "How good was quality control in andrology laboratories in the 1940s and 1950s?" The Skakkebaeck group was relying on unreliable numbers, they said. Perhaps the comparison of recent findings with historical data was unacceptable. "The greenhouse effect, global warming, declining sperm counts – all may be true; we just don't know," they wrote. Skakkebaek replied that lab techniques may well have changed but questioned whether the changes have been so dramatic as to show such serious sperm-count differences.

As the Danish study brought up more questions than answers, scientists around the world began investigating sperm quality in particular regions. A falling sperm count has been reported in studies from Scotland, Belgium and England. Compared to previous studies' figures from different countries, a generally lower sperm count was found in Nigeria where the average was 64 million sperm per milliliter of ejaculate; in Pakistan, 79 million; in Germany, 78 million and in Hong Kong, 62 million.

Pierre Jouannet, a reproduction biologist at the Parisian Hôpital Cochin, was skeptical of the Danish study and analyzed sperm samples in his own clinic closely, collected over the course of 20 years for artificial insemination. Although he had set out to disprove the Danish results, he discovered that in the French samples, a sperm concentration of 89 million per milliliter in 1973 had dropped to 60 million in 1992, which is 2% per year. Could this decrease be explained by changes in lifestyle? At least in regard to ejaculation not much had really seemed to have changed for French men – then as now, a 25-year-old man had on average 9.3 ejaculations per month. When Jouannet examined the figures for men in the same age group, he found an even bigger drop – 3.7% per year. He and his colleagues suggested that chemicals in the drinking water or pollution might be the cause.

Another study, in the French city of Toulouse, revealed no change in sperm quality between 1977 and 1992. Scientists at the university hospital wondered whether the debate was due to environmental factors, mentioning air and water quality as well as lifestyle differences between the two cities, such as commuting time. Potentially this could trigger a politically heated debate in France about life in the stressful and cloudy north versus the relaxed and sunny, and apparently more fertile, south of France. Then another study came out in France showing no change to sperm quality.

"No decline in sperm counts" was reported by Harry Fisch and his colleagues at the New York Columbia Presbyterian Medical Center and the Albert Einstein College of Medicine after a large study in 1996 on samples from sperm banks in New York, California and Minnesota. No drop was also reported by C. Alvin Paulsen of the University of Washington who referred to similar results by Finnish colleagues. New York generally seems to have high sperm counts. As Larry Lipshultz of the Baylor College of Medicine points out, "To date no one can explain why the New York data, even when examined historically, appear to demonstrate consistently higher sperm densities." And then there are the Finns, and the cause for what is informally known as the Finnish Testicle Mystery.

Finnish men have an average sperm concentration of 114 million per milliliter of ejaculate, nearly two and a half times higher than Danish men.

Testicular cancer rates are also considerably lower in Finland. What is so special about Finnish testes? In the little town of Kuopio in Finland, a man with a sperm concentration of 133 million sperm per milliliter of ejaculate was reported – which is the highest number recorded in the last 50 years anywhere in the world. Finnish andrologists Jyrki Suominen and Matti Vierula have surmised that one reason might be the Finnish climate. In general, sperm production varies with the seasons and is generally lower in the summer. Maybe the relatively cool summers in Finland don't impact on sperm production as elsewhere. The Danes smoke more and the country is more densely populated.

Risto Santti, a reproductive biologist at the University of Turku, does not believe in the superiority of Finnish men. They eat as much fish from the polluted Baltic Sea as the Danes, and their paper industry has polluted many rivers. "Fish in rivers close to the factories have shown to have a damaged reproductive system," he said in an interview. According to some Finnish scientists it is only a matter of time before modern developments would be reflected in the sperm quality. Men living in cities have a considerably lower sperm count than in rural areas. A study at the University of Helsinki seems to confirm this. Whereas in 1981 56% of all men had normal sperm quality, this figure sank to 26.9% in 1991.

So what good is all this comparision? Are magazines going to start publishing world fertility maps indicating cities and regions with men of known high fertility? Single women on the prowl for a mate and potential father of their child would then preferentially travel and hunt there. But there is a snag. As a report by the National Research Council puts it, "Although multinational trend studies are consistent with a downward trend in mean sperm concentration, this pattern may be confounded by local geographic variation." The data on sperm quality are not as good and clear as one might wish. There goes the map proposal.

So given the geographic variation, the doubts, and skeptics, are we to worry? Even the very low sperm concentrations found in these studies are still above the 20 million sperm per milliliter of ejaculate that the WHO set as a minimum standard. So there are still enough sperm to go around. Some men have low sperm counts. But an average value is not an individual value. A trend is not saying all there is to say about an individual. And a man is, after all, more than the sum of his sperm.

The variability is a crucial point in this debate. Harry Fisch of the Columbia Center and Erik Goluboff of Einstein College take this discussion to the point: "We found that substantial geographic difference in sperm counts are evident worldwide and therefore need to be considered when analyzing data from different locations over a finite period of time." Semen is not the same everywhere and at all times. Every country, every region, whether urban or rural, has its idiosyncrasies that are reflected in the sperm count. "All results seem to differ geographically and that is to be expected for a problem that has an ecological dimension", said Alvin Paulsen of the University of Washington, a worldwide renowned expert on male health. "There is no uniform worldwide development that effects all men in exactly the same way." Paulsen regards a London study, which tried to relate reduced sperm quality to drinking water quality in particular areas, of great interest. "So far nobody has had a look at the water in that particular district," he said. He also thinks that with research at its present stage, more research is urgently needed. "Something is happening and we all have to try and find out the reason for it."

For example, a group of scientists and physicians at the Medical Research Council's Reproductive Biology Unit in Edinburgh have embarked on a study of men aged between 20 and 30, to do just that. The Project aims to discover the current state of reproductive health in Scotland, as a baseline against which to judge future changes. The group also hopes to establish the extent to which environmental and/or other factors may contribute to the changes which have been reported. In Scotland there is evidence of declining sperm counts in some studies.

Congenital malformation in the male seems to be becoming more common – for example, testicular non-descent. "Although one could argue that the increase may simply reflect increased awareness, it should be noted that there has not been a corresponding increase in equivalent malformations in the female," the group states. Other studies in the UK are looking at the environmental risk involved in hypospadias, as well as the epidemiology of prostate and testicular cancers.

Some researchers believe there are environmental reasons which are causing or contributing to these problems. If for example, a particular substance is causing a result, then it might have the strongest effect where it has the highest concentration. In environmental issues, this type of causality is extremely difficult to build. But the risk for the villain, if there is one, is quite large. After all, identifying a harmful substance can lead to lawsuits with claims that can threaten entire industries. Then again it might all be a bad scare. Maybe there are researchers who are too busy counting sperm and unable to see the wood for the trees. The jury is still out on this case and will not be in by next Tuesday. No upcoming indictment. What is worth looking at is the jigsaw puzzle of evidence. Reproductive integrity, in both men and women, which includes sperm and the tonic they swim in, is crucial to our survival. So when a topic comes up that some tabloids term "eco-castration," it hopefully piques interest.

Various Findings

Why is the number of damaged and deformed sperm rising? Why do men suffer more and more from testicular cancer? "These are urgent reasons to increase research into the threat to the male reproductive system," state Niels Skakkebaek and his colleagues in Copenhagen. Are these physical signs reflecting high stress modern lifestyle in some way? Indeed it is known that sperm production can be affected rather quickly by external factors. As author Lewis Wright states, "From the sperm's perspective, modern life abounds with perils." Medication, tobacco, venereal disease, stress, X-rays, temperature are but a few factors.

Rachel Carson had noticed something seriously amiss when birds began plummeting to the ground, dead, after aerial spraying. As it turned out, the reason for spring to turn silent was a man-made product, a pesticide called DDT. Her book, published in 1962, led to a public outcry and intensive studies. The chemical was subsequently banned, although to this day it is still not banned in some countries where it is used to combat malaria. Carson's work certainly raised awareness about the fact that chemicals could have haunting and unexpected modes of action.

Another substance group that has found widespread use in the chemical industry since the 1930s are PCBs – polychlorinated biphenyls. These compounds have been used in flame retardants, adhesives, hydraulic fluids, in electrical transformers and capacitors, as well as in lubricants and seals. PCB production was banned in the United States in 1977. As it turns out, PCBs are highly persistent in the environment and can be found practically everywhere – in soil, in rivers and lakes, in fish, in polar bears, in women's breast milk, in men's semen. According to some studies, the PCB levels in infertile men's semen are higher than in fertile men. Studies of occupational exposure to PCBs reveal a slight increase in cancer rates.

In wildlife, exposure to DDTs and PCBs has shown to skew the sex ratios in gulls and cause egg thinning in many bird species. A PCB spill in the 1980s in the Saginaw River led to deformities and population declines in terns. Mink fed with fish from the Great Lakes in the 1960s and 1970s where the PCB levels were high, showed reproductive problems, stunted growth and behavioral abnormalities. Seals exposed to fish from the highly PCB-contaminated Baltic Sea showed a depressed immune system making them more vulnerable to a variety of diseases. When PCBs accidentally leaked into rice oil that was consumed by the residents of a town called Yu-Cheng in Taiwan, a depressed immune response was also reported as one of many effects. A follow-up study on the children of mothers who had ingested the contaminated oil showed various health problems including decreased sperm quality with prenatally exposed boys showing a higher percentage of abnormally shaped sperm. Babies of mothers in Wisconsin who had consumed PCB-contaminated fish showed higher incidences of infectious illnesses, but some researchers question the validity of this study.

More than Cancer?

John Harshbanger of the Smithsonian Institute in Washington, an expert on cancer in animals, believes that large outbreaks of cancer in fish are connected to the impact of man-made chemicals. Fish that live in the sediments below discharge pipes from industrial manufacturing plants have repeatedly shown to develop cancer. Cancer is frightening. Although treatment has advanced greatly, with surgery, radiation and chemotherapy showing great success in many cases, most people are acutely aware of the many times the treatment fails and results in the death of a loved one. As preventive health measures and early detection take hold, treatment will become easier. Nevertheless, cancer remains troublesome. Undoubtedly, many cancer-causing agents are man-made. Which brings environmental issues close to home.

Unfortunately, much of the data for deleterious effects of chemicals arises from accidents. For people in a contaminated neighborhood, information may help them avoid health impacts but it may also be too late, the damage might already be done. Researchers hope that insights won from these incidents will allow similar events and their consequences to be averted. Usually, much attention is given to a population exposed to a chemical because health effects may not be known. Accidental spills do not necessarily deliver a straightforward view of how a chemical may affect health since the substance amounts released in an accident are much higher than general exposure. At the same time, accidents may point out a type of health impact that may have otherwise gone unnoticed.

In 1976, there was an an explosion at a pesticide factory in a small town north of Milan, Italy. About 3,000 kilograms of chemicals were released and the cloud of toxic material contaminated a heavily populated area about 6 kilometers long and 1 kilometer wide. The event became known as the 'Seveso disaster,' named after one of the most heavily contaminated towns. Among the chemicals in the cloud were a few kilograms of a compound called TCDD or 2,3,7,8-tetrachlorodibenzo-p-dioxin. TCDD is a byproduct in chemical manufacturing of chlorinated products, for example pesticides, and is also produced when plastics or paper is burned in incineration facilites. Due to other chemical accidents in the US, Germany, the Netherlands and the UK, the toxicity of this compound was rather well-known. The first sign of problems in Seveso was people with skin lesions and persons exposed to the cloud developed a skin condition called chloracne, that is associated with dioxin.

Since the accident, the population in Seveso has been under close surveillance by the health authorities. There seems to be no clear association between cancer deaths and the area of residence, as one ten-year mortality analysis revealed but there has been an increase in soft-tissue tumors. Another insight on TCDD comes from the military. TCDD is the major contaminant in Agent Orange, a defoliant used by US forces in the Vietnam War under the name "Operation Ranch Hand." The substance has had a health impact on both the Vietnamese population and the soldiers who were exposed to it. Some studies on soldiers revealed decreased testosterone levels correlated to the exposure. According to the National Research Council report, there is a link between herbicides contaminated with dioxins as TCDD and soft-tissue cancers.

Men: An Endangered Species?

History teaches lessons. And some incidents of environmental contamination have led to efforts to find the cause, stop it and clean-up the contaminated sites. When the so-called water in a river leading into Lake Erie caught fire in 1969, the symptoms were obvious and a clean-up effort began. The incidence of fish tumors decreased and so things got better for both the wildlife and the people who lived in the Great Lakes area. Or so it seemed.

In 1996 Theo Colborn, Dianne Dumanoski and John Peterson Myers published a book called *Our Stolen Future*. In it, Theo Colborn describes being puzzled about the Great Lakes region. The wildlife was having problems, but it was not cancer. As the authors write, "For the past three decades, the words 'toxic chemical' have become almost synonymous with cancer not only in the public mind but in the minds of scientists and regulators as well." They continue by stating that "this preoccupation with cancer and mutations had been blinding her to the diversity of data she had collected." Reproductive difficulties, developmental abnormalities, immunosuppression, population decline. What Colborn and others realized is that the studies were pointing in a different direction; not to tumor development but to disruption of the endocrine system. The hormones in the body of an animal or in humans were being affected.

The endocrine system is the body's own Internet, with a networked system of hormonal glands such as the testes and the ovaries as well as the adrenals and pancreas, the thyroid gland, and glands in the brain such as the pineal gland, the hypothalamus, and the pituitary. The most famous hormones are estrogen and testosterone; another is insulin which is produced in the pancreas.

While this idea of endocrine impact might seem like not much more than scientific hairsplitting, the hunch has many members of the scientific community intrigued and worried. In essence, this hypothesis means that there are more subtle expressions of damage than "just" the development of a tumor. And here is where the road splits again with some scientists calling it all hogwash, saying the evidence is insufficient to speak about these effects with certainty. But before joining in on either side of the choir, perhaps it is interesting to get a glimpse of what some of the findings are.

Studies reveal that sometimes man-made or natural substances can be similar to the body's hormones, for example estrogen, and act as hormonal imposters. Expose a body at the right time and in the right dose to this chemical mimick and the hormone balance in the body can be disrupted. The Environmental Protection Agency says endocrine disruptors "interfere with the synthesis, secretion, transport, binding, action, or elimination of natural hormones in the body that are responsible for the maintenance of homeostasis (normal cell metabolism), reproduction, development and/or behavior." Thinking about the disruption of the hormonal systems in the body is not exactly old science, with much interest and research due to the reaction to *Our Stolen Future*. Researchers are still putting together evidence how this might work.

"Concern has been raised in recent years regarding potential adverse effects of various environmental contaminants often called 'endocrine disruptors'," reads an in-depth report by the National Research Council published in 1999. Various governmental agencies commissioned a study on these so-called hormonally active agents in the environment. In the US, the UK, Germany, Denmark, Sweden and Japan as well as other countries, research continues on this issue.

One of the most frequently quoted examples of a species in the wild that has been affected by hormonally active chemicals in this way is the alligator. Lake Apopka, a large lake in Florida, had great bass fishing and clean water. That was at the beginning of the twentieth century. Since then the lake has had a rather turbid history, and it is now better known as Florida's most polluted lake. Drainage north of the lake exposed fertile soil which has been intensively farmed since World War II, which is when restoration of the lake began. Then there was an accidental spill of a pesticide called dicofol – contaminated with DDT – as well as sulphuric acid.

Louis Guillette, zoologist at the University of Florida, knows the lake well. He and a number of his colleagues discovered that the alligator population declined dramatically in the 1980s following the spill. The alligators showed many developmental abnormalities – both males and females – with various types of reproductive problems; for example, abnormal testes and ovaries. The males had smaller penises than males in other lakes and their testosterone levels were reduced. In alligator eggs, high levels of a DDT metabolite as well as other pesticides were found. DDT has a nasty habit of remaining in the environment and the body. And DDT's egg-thinning effect has been shown in other creatures such as birds. As the report states, "Many wildlife studies show associations between reproductive and developmental defects and exposure to environmental contaminants, some of which are HAAs [hormonally active agents]." HAAs are what the researchers call hormonally active agents. What Guillette proposes in his studies is that hormonal disruption in the alligators is caused by the pesticides, their hormones becoming affected during their embryonic development and early life.

A hormone is a sort of a latch-key child. Travelling through the blood, this is a substance with a home in mind, a lock to which the key fits. The lock is a protein called a receptor. When the hormone finds its home, the key binds to the lock and a slew of physiological reactions occur, causing a particular event or a cascade of events in the development or metabolism of an organism. Hormones are not released by the pound, the amounts are small with timing being everything.

High levels of DDE, the DDT metabolite were also found in the tissue of another Floridian, the endangered male panther. One frequent developmental abnormality in these animals is testicular non-descent and some scientists suggest that there is a connection between DDE levels and the testicular problems in panther cubs.

Fish have also been shown to have altered physiologies in polluted waters. In the early 1990s British researchers at Brunel University in Uxbridge found male fish with ovotestes, testes filled with eggs. As it turned out, they were living upstream from a sewage treatment plant. In subsequent studies by John Sumpter and Susan Jobling, it was found that male fish when placed in cages downstream from such plants had elevated levels of vitellogenin in their blood. Normally the levels of this hormone are minimal in males because this is a protein involved in egg yolk production in female fish. The levels in these male fish were 500–100,000 times higher than in male fish in non-polluted waters. Throughout England the testing began and the same levels were found in many rivers – sewage treatment effluent was causing the male fish to feminize. Among the chemicals that seem to be having this effect were octylphenol and nonylphenol, which are used in a variety of products such as detergents; bisphenol-A, used in plastics manufacturing; DDT and PCBs, all hormonally active agents. The chemicals build up over time in the tissue. Fish brought to the effluent in cages developed these high levels of vitellogenin after about two or three weeks there. Other studies at other locations such as along the Mississippi River have shown similar results.

In addition to fish and alligators, effects on the reproduction and development in the wild have been found in birds, turtles and amphibians. As a report published by the MRC Institute for Environment and Health at the University of Leicester states, there are many possible ways in which these compounds may act on an organism's physiology. J.A. McLachlan proposed that there are some chemicals that may act at a hormone receptor site as a mimic, causing a particular response, and others which act as hormonal blocks and stop the normal reactions. The effects may be varied; thyroid dysfunction in birds and fish, decreased fertility in birds, fish, shellfish and mammals, behavioral abnormalities in birds, demasculinization and feminization in fish and birds and compromised immune systems in birds and mammals.

Sewage treatment plants are not the only facilities to have been studied. In the Great Lakes, both synthetic and natural hormonally active agents contained in the effluent from paper mills have been shown to alter the reproductive physiology of fishes.

The National Research Council report notes that in the course of assessing the effects of chemicals with estrogenic properties or anti-estrogenic properties, it is important to consider the species exposed since steroids differ and endocrinology may differ from one species to the next. "The developmental stage at which exposure occurs in particularly important. The effects of exposures occuring at a critically sensitive period in the lifetime of an individual, such as during embryonic development, have been termed 'organisational effects' as they may lead to permanent structural modifications of the reproductive, immune or nervous systems." These effects usually manifest themselves in early life but can extend to adulthood. In adulthood the effects on the endocrine system have been given another name, "activational effects," as they are more commonly transitory in nature.

Old and New Chemical Risks

Richard Peterson of the University of Wisconsin has found that with dioxin exposure in rats, only a relatively high dose caused damage to the genital tract. When pregnant rats were given a dose 100 times smaller, the male offspring suffered from impaired fertility. Their reproductive organs were smaller, the sperm concentration lower and they displayed behavior more common to females. These studies and others show that the time of exposure is crucial. Only embryos in a particular developmental phase seemed vulnerable.

As *Our Stolen Future* explains, Ana Soto, an endocrinologist at Tufts University in Boston, and her colleagues were studying the mechanism that regulates cell growth in normal cells and cancer cells. They detected a substance that stimulated the growth of breast cancer cells but could not readily identify what it was. Human breast cancer cells are responsive to estrogen and she was looking at the reaction of the cells to various levels of estrogen. But the cells grew the same as in the control groups to which no estrogen had been added. The researchers were disappointed. However, after months of tests they discovered that their results had been tainted by contamination. A chemical in the plastic tubes that were part of their experimental set-up had been leaching into the cell cultures. And it was hormonally active. They eventually identified the compound, wreaking havoc in their experiment but delivering an important insight, to be an estrogen-like chemical that was enhancing the growth of the cancer cells. Another chemical with similar properties was discovered in 1993 at Stanford University.

Because of these and other observations in recent years, some scientific interest focuses on the effects of substances on the human endocrine system. The spotlight is on substances contained in paints, detergents and pesticides, alkyl phenols, and phthalates that are used to manufacture plastics. Phthalates are probably one of the most common synthetic chemicals known to mankind.

In this case, too, an accident delivers an important lesson. DES, a synthetic estrogen, was prescribed to women thought to be at risk of miscarriage. In the words of the report by the National Research Council, the "physiologic rationale for this therapy ... is difficult to reconstruct." Then again, the field of reproductive endocrinology was in its infancy. The panel calls the prescription practice "hormonal assault." In the US an estimated 4 million women and their fetuses were exposed to this drug between 1947 and 1971. In so-called DES mothers, this drug has been linked to higher breast cancer risks and the DES daughters run a higher risk of developing gynecologic cancers; for example, a tumor called clear-cell cervicovaginal cancer. Other problems include various abnormalities of the reproductive tract and reduced fertility. For the sons of DES patients, some studies revealed higher incidences of genitourinary and reproductive abnormalities. Much of what is known about hormonally active agents is based on studies of the effects of DES. As the report by the National Academy states, "no known environmental toxicant has been shown to be more potent than DES." Some scientists believe it is a model for the way other hormonally active agents may act on the body.

What has become clear in the studies is that prenatal exposure to DES affects fetal development. "Studies show that exposure to DES during the critical period of organogenesis can profoundly disturb differentiation of the reproductive organs. Some of the effects are not observed until adulthood, demonstrating the latent developmental effects of exposure to this potent estrogen." For men, the DES sons, research results on the subject of fertility impairment have been inconsistent, but some abnormalities seen include hypospadias, testicular non-descent, and epididymal cysts.

There is an equally notorious European example with the drug thalidomide, which George Annas of Boston University has called a "tragedy" that "stands for all of the 'monsters' that can be inadvertently or negligently created by modern medicine." It was prescribed as a sedative and antinausea medication. Although it is now resurfacing as a drug for various types of diseases, it has a haunted past. Between 1959 and 1962, babies were born with severe deformities and absent limbs. It caused severe deformities in 8,000 children in 46 countries. The drug, not approved in the US, had been primarily given to pregnant women as a tranquilizer. Prescribing doctors found that the drug did not cause deformities in all babies of mothers who had taken the drug. A decisive factor was the stage of pregnancy during which the drug was taken: a fetus undergoes limb development somewhere between the fifth and eighth week of pregnancy. The drug interferes with this process, possibly, so one hypothesis goes, by cutting off circulation to the developing limbs. A small dose of the substance at that time had a devastating effect, whereas if taken some weeks later it did not cause any damage.

Estrogen: Fiend or Friend?

Fiend or friend – estrogen and synthetic estrogens are neither, or both. There is scientific evidence that substances can be hormonally disruptive to the body's endocrine system. But as numerous studies point out, the exact ways that developmental disturbances might be mediated remain obscure.

Some of the studies involve looking more closely at the endocrine system as it develops in the womb. Frederick vom Saal, developmental biologist at the University of Missouri, does just that. And he found that depending on the hormonal environment in the womb, mice pups differed in their behaviors. Scientists agree that to evaluate the effect of synthetic oestrogen it is necessary to know more about the combined impact of hormones on prenatal development – in humans as well as animals.

There is a hypothesis that would explain the decrease in sperm quality. Niels Skakkebaek and Richard Sharpe point out that the Sertoli cells in the testes of unborn males are damaged when exposed to estrogen. Fewer Sertoli cells mean less sperm. In the aforementioned report by the Danish environmental agency its 19 authors express their concern that estrogen-like substances might be responsible because of this mechanism for the rising rate of testicular cancer and falling sperm count.

It takes a long time between exposure to a substance and the development of its effect which makes it very difficult to draw accurate conclusions. "Our growing awareness of the vulnerability to environmental factors of the male genital tract and ability to reproduce tells us to be far more cautious." According to D.M. de Kretser, director of the Department of Reproduction and Development at the Australian Monash University, research and legal regulations for these chemical substances are vital. "Any delay would jeopardize the fertility of future generations."

It seems that there are a variety of both natural and synthetic substances, endocrine disrupting compounds that either mimic or interfere with the way vertebrates reproduce and develop. As researchers at the University of Texas in Austin point out, the so-called "threshold assumption" will be found not to apply to these compounds because they mimic the actions of the body's own molecules, for example estrogen, that are critical in the development of an organism.

Some of these compounds are bioaccumulated in the body and can thus affect not only an adult and the offspring of that adult but also the reproductive physiology of the offspring upon reaching adulthood. In Louis Guillette's view, the documented effects on the reproductive, endocrine and immune systems lead to concerns that wildlife around the world are being adversely affected by hormonally active agents. And as far as he and many other researchers are concerned, these effects carry a powerful message. "Wildlife serve as important sentinels of ecosystem health, including human public health." Studying them and the effects of contaminants on them will tell us more about them, and more about us. "The endocrine system exhibits an organizing effect on the developing embryo," writes Guillette. Thus a disruption of the normal hormonal signals can permanently modify the organization and future function of the reproductive system.

Critics

"The whole thing is a hypothesis dressed up as a fact," says toxicologist Michael Gallo of the Robert Wood Johnson Medical School. Bruce Ames of the University of California at Berkeley is equally reserved. "The whole thing is a political movement based on bad scientific research."

In 1951, a study documented reproductive disorders in sheep after their consumption of red clover. The effect is due to genistein, a naturally occurring phytoestrogen, a hormonally active agent. It is not exactly clear why plants have estrogenic compounds. Some researchers suggest that they may be part of the plant's defense strategy.

The active substances in these compounds are called isoflavones and when rams eat clover rich in isoflavones, their sperm count suffers. The family of flavenoids are found in fruit and vegetables and soy products.

The overall family of plant compounds that have estrogenic or anti-estrogenic activities are phytoestrogens. They are found in all things vegetarian such as beans, sprouts, cabbage, spinach, soybean, grains and hops. We eat about 1 gram of flavenoids a day. Soy-based infant formula has been shown to lead to higher concentrations of phytoestrogens in childrens' blood. High rates of phytoestrogen consumption have been shown to correlate with lower rates of various cancers. According to a report by the Institute for Environment and Health of the University of Leicester, men do not show reduced testosterone after consuming phytoestrogens.

Unlike synthetic estrogens, these compounds do not accumulate in the body. Because there are natural estrogens in many plants, it becomes difficult to establish what is called a baseline for exposure for these substances. After all, how can you be sure about the influence of external estrogens if you do not know the normal exposure to these substances? As the report of the National Academy of Sciences points out, "little research, particularly on phytoestrogen exposure" has been done. Monitoring efforts, the report states, should include sub-populations known to have high exposures, including infants on soy-based formulas, and vegetarians.

Environmental chemicals as endocrine disruptors have, in the words of Stephen Safe, toxicologist at Texas A&M University, "generated unbelievable press … but it was never a fact." Yes, exposure to high levels of these chemicals can be harmful. Linking low-level exposure to a clear toxic effect requires proof that has yet to be delivered, in his view. "You can correlate DDT levels going down with divorce rates going up, so you need more than correlation," he says. In his view lower-level exposure requires correlations as well as biological plausibility from animal studies or evidence from high-level exposure in humans. According to his analysis, many of the male and female reproductive tract problems linked to the endocrine-disruptor hypothesis are actually not correlated with synthetic industrial contaminants. In his view it may not be possible to completely eliminate suspect compounds from the environment, since there are also natural sources of chemicals like dioxin which can stem from forest fires and volcanic eruptions.

The Chemical Manufacturers Association is not exactly tone deaf with respect to endocrine disruptors. In one document a passage reads, "Industry continues to sponsor considerable scientific research to develop and contribute new information that will help address uncertainties and improve public understanding of the science relative to the endocrine issue." More research is needed, in their view. Few scientists, even those most critical of the chemical industry, will disagree with that. However the association says, "There is little scientific evidence that low levels of chemicals in the environment pose a risk to human health via endocrine disruption." Their take on the subject is clear.

Is there really such a thing as "eco-castration"? Without doubt there are certain worrying developments. Researchers cannot for certain answer what exactly is amiss. In many countries research programs are underway with various strategies to expand knowledge on the ecological and physiological effects of endocrine disruption. These studies involve both natural products as well as pharmaceuticals and industrial products that are hormonally active. Epidemiological studies are needed to look at the effects on humans more closely.

One of the challenges is to develop the right kinds of tests or assays to ascertain the effects of various substances in the lab. As Niels Skakkebaek and his colleagues recently pointed out in a study, screening programs need to have tests in place to discover endocrine-disrupting properties of a compound on a genetic level. His team also points to exposure to estrogens in food. Animals treated with sex steroids that promote their growth retain hormone residues in their meat. The Danish researchers have their doubts on whether the safety levels as determined by the Joint Food and Agricultural Organization/World Health Organization and the US Food and Drug Administration are adequate, particularly as they relate to pre-pubertal children.

The report by the National Research Council explains that there were some differences among their panel of experts, pertaining to the subject of endocrine disruption. "The differences are not confined to this committee but are reflected in the scientific community at large," they write. The views differ, for example, because the evidence from studies is weighed differently; some researchers find the extrapolation from one organism to another questionable. In general, the mechanism of action of hormonally active agents in the environment is, as the panel states, "not well understood." There is obviously work to be done. The recommendations of the committee are all-encompassing, including wildlife monitoring, long-term studies on populations exposed to hormonally active agents, and studies that look at carcinogenic, immunologic, neurologic, developmental and reproductive effects. Studies are ongoing.

7 The Future is Present

By coincidence I found out that a friend of mine had chosen to become a father in a rather unusual fashion. Jay, 32, smiled broadly as he told me the story – he was obviously a happy and proud dad. A week earlier a baby had been born. His. His parents didn't know. Actually he does not even live with the mother nor is he intimate with her. Actually, he never slept with her. But he is the father. Jay's sister is friends with two lesbian women who had been a couple for years and wanted a baby. They did not fancy the idea of a sperm bank, so they looked high and low for a father – until John's sister suggested her brother, whom they both knew. She described his attributes in detail: his physique, his personality, his mental abilities. The women decided he would be the ideal donor. "I thought about it, extensively," Jay says. "I realized that I believed in the equality of heterosexual and homosexual marriages and that if I could, I would express my views this way." He agreed to be their sperm donor. With Jay being a busy man, it turned out to be quite a challenge to get him to deliver semen at the right time. The bottom line is, it worked and a baby was born.

Once there was a woman who fell in love with a man who was allegedly infertile. But she desperately wanted his child. During one lovemaking session she requested he use a condom and mumbled something about a yeast infection. After his ejaculation, she slipped away into the bathroom with the condom. Unbeknownst to him, she kept his semen and later retrieved the sperm and used the "sample" for artificial insemination. She became pregnant with his child.

The first story is true. The second one is part of the plot of a novel by the inventor of the contraceptive pill, Carl Djerassi, entitled *Menachem's Seed*. Fiction and reality are not light years away from each other. For those who choose contraception, sex is possible without reproductive outcome. The newer developments are removing another facet of the intimate act – you do not even need to have both partners present; they do not need to know each other. The expression "having a child together" is getting an almost old-fashioned twang to it.

As author Gena Corea explains, the early applications of artificial insemination created court cases in the UK, Canada and the US. The children thus conceived were considered illegitimate, the procedure itself a form of adultery which was ground for divorce and even criminal prosecution. In the 1960s the British Medical Association found artificial insemination to be an "offence against society." In 1972, a British fertility clinic director wrote that he would refuse artificial insemination "to a spinster, or a couple of mixed colour or even of mixed religious denomination." In the 1970s, court cases surfaced in which, for example, a sperm donor sued for visitation rights to the child he fathered, although he and the mother were no longer dating.

As far as the social and political context of this technology goes, Corea sees this technology as "something created in the interests of the patriarchy, reducing women to Matter." Whether or not one agrees with her feminist analysis, it seems true that the new technologies are fundamentally changing how we reproduce, turning, in a certain sense, eggs and sperm into commodities.

"Human progress has been a series of triumphs over natural forces," wrote Edwin Embree, president of the Julius Rosenwald Fund in Chicago. He explains how man, in his words, has successfully bent the rules of the world "to the service of his ends": by mining coal which, in its normal state, is underground and turning it into a product that heats the human habitat; by finding a way by which cows can deliver milk long past the time in which the need of their calves for this liquid is there, so that milk may be available to him for nourishment. Man changes natural processes when he gives drugs to dull pain. "The whole history of medicine is a history of triumphs over natural forces," he wrote. Undoubtedly, medical advances have dramatically increased our lifespans, and have decreased suffering. When it comes to reproductive medicine, the idea of bending the world to the service of our ends becomes more complex to analyze.

And then there are the political sides to a technique. Eugenics, the idea that science could be applied to better the human race, is one of those scientific ideas that is often treated like an institutionalized relative: an ever-present yet embarrassing issue that is preferably rarely mentioned. Popularized and perverted by the Nazis in Germany, eugenics was not exactly viewed disfavorably in many scientific societies before World War II. In the US approximately 40,000 people classified as "feebleminded" had been sterilized by the mid-1940s based on eugenics laws passed in most states. The term originally coined by Francis Galton in the 1890s became a broad social and scientific movement. The American Eugenics Society favored research aimed at promoting some to reproduce and discouraging others who were thought to be "defective for society."

While scientific societies do not espouse these views anymore, it is interesting to read what they wrote. Society is experiencing, an "ever-increasing burden of the bungled and botched, of paupers, feebleminded and insane, of bums, thugs and criminals," explained Edwin Grant Conklin from Princeton University. In America and in other nations, the human race "stands in the utmost need of improvement." He explained in an essay that civilized society is presently organized such that the most intellectual, progressive and ambitious members of society are most heavily handicapped in reproduction. "The long period of education, intensive application to preparation for a career, luxurious ideals of family life and unwillingness to be burdened with children have greatly reduced their fertility have completely sterilized some of the best human stocks." In his words, "If the heredity of the race is to be improved such dysgenic social customs" need to be changed as they contribute to "race degeneration." A "premium" needs to be placed upon the reproduction of the most fit.

As Gena Corea writes, in 1935, Hermann Muller, a Nobel Prize-winning geneticist, thought up a program of so-called "positive selection" using artificial insemination to have "as well-endowed children as possible." The idea was to have women give birth to children fathered by estimable men, whose superior sperm would be collected in a special sperm bank. After his death, a man was to be assessed: "If his life work and his children were judged superior, his sperm would be used; if not, discarded," writes Corea. The banks would be intended for men wishing to bank sperm before vasectomy or for men wishing to protect their germ cells from the growing radiation hazards of industry, commerce, war, space flight and "the as yet unassessed hazards of the chemical mutagens of modern life." The eminent British biologist Sir Julian Huxley also believed in the use of "superior sperm" to be used in a program called "E.I.D. – eugenic insemination by deliberately preferred doctors." In his view the idea of anonymous donors should be abolished and instead details of the donor's family revealed. A businessman established, in 1976, The Hermann J. Muller Repository for Germinal Choice – purportedly a collection of sperm from Nobel Prize-winning men. Muller, originally in favor of the project, became disenchanted with the political slant taken and withdrew his name from the project. Nobel Prize winner William Shockley donated sperm to the bank. He also admitted, though, according to Corea, that his children had turned out decidedly less brilliant than he had hoped, and that actually they "represent a very significant regression". But he said the blame lay with the eggs of his first wife and their mother, who "had not as high an academic-achievement as I had." So-called genius and high achiever sperm banks which purport to select sperm donors mainly based on scientific achievements, mathematical and scientific aptitude, artistic and athletic ability do exist although this particular one, the Repository for Germinal Choice has, as one eugenics Website puts it, "regrettably" closed.

In her book *Mother Machine*, Gena Corea points to the dangers she sees in such developments. She states that most men greeted the possibilities of artificial insemination "with alarm, for it threatened the very basis of patriarchal descent." While they eagerly used artificial insemination in animals, they were in no rush to set up banks for *human* sperm," except for the men who saw the eugenic potential and "enthusiastically endorsed such use." She points out that physicians and medical students made up a majority of sperm donors and quotes a brochure published by the American Fertility Society in 1980 that

explains this fact by stating they and the younger medical personnel "are traditional donors and preferred because of their understanding of the biologic need
of the program, accessibility and selection with regard to health and intelligence." George Annas of the Boston University School of Public Health
pointed out acerbically that "they have chosen to reproduce themselves," thus
making eugenic decisions about what they consider superior genes for artificial
insemination.

Aside from various cults and medical researchers led astray, eugenic ideas
do not appear to be mainstream thinking in the twenty-first century. Given the
challenges that reproductive medicine poses, it seems simply a good idea to
keep some historical developments in mind. Some couples in infertility clinics
have told me that they feel pressured to have perfect children, without any
type of disability because "society" discouraged that and they would not be
able to handle the financial burden. It was not immediately apparent to me
where the pressure on these couples was coming from but this issue cropped
up in many conversations in different countries.

Ethical Grey Zones

Neither sperm nor semen are strangers to theological libraries of any denomination. There is a long tradition of analyzing and debating reproduction and
medicine in religious contexts. And that includes talking about sperm and
semen. Given the enormous demand for help to conceive and the difficult
questions fertility issues in general raise, it seems to be unwise for any religion
not to ponder the newer developments. According to some religions, assisted
reproductive technologies are permissible. The Catholic Church has a clear
stance against assisted reproduction techniques, because they are barriers
between the will to procreate and the expression of marital love. There are
many treatises on the subject and religious couples may wish to consult an
adviser of their choice to make medical decisions on these complex issues in
accordance with their beliefs.

Reproductive medicine, on almost a daily basis, is redefining the way
humans can reproduce. Eggs, sperm and embryos can be frozen. Determining
the legal status of an embryo kept in a tank of liquid nitrogen at a clinic but
belonging to a, now, divorced couple is not a trivial matter. Does a child
conceived through in-vitro fertilization have a right to know how he or she was
conceived? Who is the father if testicular tissue is transplanted to another man?
A Californian couple died in a plane crash in Australia without having defined
what to do with their frozen embryos. A court battle followed and in the end the
rights to the embryos were transferred to the couple's estate. In other cases,
clinics say that if couples do not retrieve the embryos after a certain amount of
time, they become the property of the research institute or hospital.

Difficult issues on which there are many opinions. Ultimately every couple
has to resolve some of these questions themselves. In conversation, one couple
who had conceived via in-vitro fertilization said that the choices, the options

and decisions were "absolutely overwhelming." Ian Wilmut, whose lab is responsible for cloning Dolly the sheep, reports that many couples approach him about cloning a child who has an incurable disease. He has always declined. Other scientists are apparently finding different answers to the requests, although the scientific community criticizes such views.

Sperm Banks

"Somehow I like the idea of having several children even though I will never meet them." The American medical student sitting next to me on the plane had told me that he had deposited sperm with a sperm bank. "For the sake of the next generation," he said. One of his professors had suggested the possibility. He said – to the glee of the students – that if you met the criteria of the sperm bank you could contribute to scientific research and help childless couples "in one shot." Aside from the small payment, the whole ordeal would actually be fun. The 23-year-old went on to say, "I want children of my own later, and I would like to father them in the normal way. My sister wants children, but her husband is having fertility problems. He is being treated but it looks like they are going to have to resort to a sperm bank soon." A sperm bank seems to be a practical and technical solution to a human biological problem.

Some people measure success in terms of achievements in sports, in the arts or in accumulating wealth. But there is another way to leave your mark: store a semen sample. Semen lasts pretty much indefinitely if kept in liquid nitrogen in sterile containers. Just in case you think this is an appealing idea and you are reaching for your car keys, perhaps it might be of interest that this is not a quickie kind of errand.

First of all, acceptance. "Our sperm bank does not accept just anybody. Our donors are all intelligent, people you would like to have as a friend, as a neighbor or as a colleague," states a brochure from a US sperm bank. A high percentage of donors are rejected. There is an extensive questionnaire to be filled out regarding a man's medical history and that of his family; extending even beyond mother and father. The questions cover the incidence of alcoholism in his family, heart attacks, cancer, diabetes, mental health problems. If any of these factors represents a danger for the potential offspring, the donor is rejected. In interviews physicians will wish to establish the reasons why the person wants to donate sperm. The tests proceed over a period of several months and about ten samples are analyzed. Apart from the interviews and a thorough medical check-up of the donor, the sperm is frozen, defrosted and again analyzed in a test run. A donor needs hardy sperm.

The sperm sample must meet very strict criteria in order to be accepted. Of course it is also checked for HIV, hepatitis B and C, herpes, syphilis and other infectious agents. Often the bank lab will screen for certain genetic conditions. In addition the donor will be asked about familial disease known to have a genetic component, such as congenital heart malformation, certain types of asthma or diabetes. The donor's family medical history should not show disorders such as Huntington's disease. And the list goes on. Semen donors will be screened for chromosomal abnormalities. The sample will be quarantined and re-tested. Donors should usually be under 40 years of age.

Sperm banks in general seem to adhere to the idea of clinical atmosphere and decor. Some locations try a bit harder than others. For example, The Sperm Bank of California also caters for single women or lesbian couples and the donors are treated to a more homey environment.

Once accepted, the sperm donor is included in the catalogue, anonymously. His blood group, his eye and hair color and his weight are listed. In addition many sperm banks offer more information about the donor: education, occupation, the condition of his teeth, religious beliefs, favourite subjects in school, ethnic background, leisure activities and talents. Is he creative? How many languages does he speak? What are his goals in life – travelling, career, marriage and children, happiness, politics or financial security? How does he describe himself – as funny, extroverted, thoughtful or energetic? Apart from that a catalog might list other physical characteristics such as the distance between his eyes and his head shape, as well as the shape of his nose, lips and earlobes. The Fairfax Cryobank in Virginia, for example, offers medical and genetic information about the donor as well as extensive personal profiles and even donor audio interviews and essays with short answers to such questions as "What is your most memorable childhood experience?" "When and if you ever have children, what would you like to pass to them?" They also offer a service called "photo matching" which helps patients to select a donor based on criteria they find important. Semen can be shipped to physicians or a health care provider anywhere in the world.

Some donors may be "identity-release" donors who, at the time at which they deposited their sample, will allow the sperm bank to divulge their identity to the child upon reaching 18 years of age. As the Sperm Bank of California states, even if it is an anonymous donor, a child may petition the sperm bank to contact him. "If, at the time of the contact, the donor agrees to be identified by the child, then we will obtain his written permission to do so." This sperm bank was the first to set up a service to match donors with children in this fashion.

The director of one sperm bank said: "Most people have quite definite ideas on what they are seeking in a sperm donor. Future parents are mainly concerned about the health of their child but they also would like to determine the physical characteristics and personality of their baby as much as possible," he explained. "I don't know what religion has to do with any of this, but some people just want to know."

Sperm banks are novel types of service centers and not exactly legal in many countries. In the US, there are around 200 sperm banks and an estimated 30,000–40,000 babies are born using donor sperm each year. The American Association of Tissue Banks sets guidelines for them and as a patient you will wish to make sure they adhere to these and are both accredited and licensed for operation. Perhaps the marketing of human eggs has been noted more frequently, for example due to the announcement by a group of supermodels that they planned to auction off some of their eggs. Or perhaps due to the idea of surrogacy and having someone else other than father or mother carry a child to term and then, with the assistance of a contractual agreement, "give" the child back. In the UK there are about 40 centers which actively recruit sperm donors, two-thirds of which are affiliated to the National Health Service while the others are private. The Human Fertilisation and Embryology Authority, HFEA, oversees the operation of all IVF clinics. A decision was made to stop all payments to semen donors. The British Fertility Society has protested, pointing out that the literature shows that paying semen donors is very important. In a study of 97 donors, 79% stated they would not donate if they were not paid. Even without payment, semen and sperm are sought-after commodities.

Critics of modern reproductive medicine techniques say that the sperm banks, along with infertility clinics, are bowing to the dangerous pressure of creating perfect children. As Ulla, 35, and a mother of three children conceived the usual way says, "I wonder if there is not too much pressure on the child and the parents to live up to an ideal which is unattainable." Aside from the complicated moral implications of those expectations, other sensitive and more practical issues come up. An andrologist at a fertility clinic told me about a lesbian couple who came in to the clinic with a long list of criteria for their future child: the man should be of athletic build, intelligent, wealthy and healthy. "I brought them file after file, they rejected them all." Sperm are being marketed to the often choosy customers. The goods have to be quite diverse. An American sperm bank on the East Coast was treating a childless couple from Laos but did not have any donors of the same ethnic background on their list. They offered sperm from a Chinese man. The couple were very offended as they found it politically completely unacceptable to have a Chinese child. And then there are other types of political correctness challenges. "There was a black woman," a doctor at a Californian sperm bank remembers, "who wanted a white donor, as she wanted her child to be as fair-skinned as possible." Obviously, it is not up to the physicians to tell her what to do or not to do, but sperm banks offer in their very existence a biological as well as an economic and political service.

No sperm bank will give any guarantees for the conceived children; the contracts state clearly that it is always possible for the children to differ greatly from both mother and sperm donor. There is no assured customer satisfaction or money-back guarantee. The donor will remain anonymous unless he has agreed otherwise. Obviously all of this entails a whole barrage of legal issues, from paternal child support payments in times of need to the child's quest for his or her own identity.

In Britain, the case of Diane Blood caused great controversy when she requested that she be inseminated with the sperm of her husband, who was in a terminal coma. She took her case to the courts and defended it by stating that she already had a say on whether her husband's body organs, such as his cornea or kidneys, could be used for medical purposes since she was the next of kin. Critics argue that sperm is not comparable to other body tissue. Other such cases have followed in other countries. Ethicists mention that grief may be such an overpowering emotion that it can cloud a person's judgment. And then there is the issue of the man's consent to the whole procedure and his post-mortem fatherhood. It is doubtful whether courts will be able to keep people from pursuing these types of options in reproductive medicine.

The fact that sperm can be frozen, then thawed and still be motile was discovered by Lazzaro Spallanzani, an Italian Catholic priest and biologist in 1776. Around this time the first experiments of artificial insemination in animals were carried out, but it was not until the nineteenth century that sperm banks for cattle were set up. And that was when the idea of freezing the sperm of soldiers going off to battle in order to inseminate their wives was also debated. But it took quite some time before the cryopreservation of sperm was mastered. In 1949, scientist A.S. Parkes experimented with added glycerol to protect the sperm from damage due to freezing. Other researchers such as Jerome K. Herman proved for the first time that frozen and defrosted sperm were capable of fertilizing an egg. Sperm banks developed rather slowly. Nowadays nearly every scientific institution dealing with modern reproduction techniques has its own sperm bank or is affiliated to one.

Before it is stored, the ejaculate is analyzed according to the WHO guidelines. Then comes the deep freeze with plenty of challenges inherent to the process. Masturbating and placing a sample in your freezer will not do. Sperm need special treatment otherwise they will not survive the procedure. For example, sperm are exposed to extreme temperature changes that may change their shape and function. Ice crystals which form on the outside and the inside of the cell membrane can disrupt the sperm membrane, dehydration may also cause cellular damage. In order to avoid that, protective agents are added, and it seems that many clinics and sperm banks have their own, rather secret, concoctions for this purpose. They usually contain glycerol and sorbitol, or agents based on egg yolk that protect the cell membrane, as well as antioxidants or other substances.

The ejaculate is mixed with the protective medium and filled into straws, thin tubes that are placed together in sets of cryocassettes. Freezing and thawing needs to follow some established velocities and procedures, otherwise all the preparation will have been for naught. The key then is to keep the temperature constant at -196 degrees Centigrade. One cryopreservation expert described the tanks as a special kind of pressure cooker in which the amount of liquid nitrogen remains constant. As one infertility physician told me in an interview, "It would be better to keep my sperm samples in my practice. But what if one of the tanks develops a leak while I am away on vacation?" And he added, "That is why I prefer to use the services of professional storage facilities."

Security is a prime issue in these facilities and this does not only mean security in an engineering sense. Basically no one except the donor himself may give permission for the sample to be removed or thawed. Even the man's wife cannot request that the sample be released. Which of course leads to many conundrums – for example, what happens if a man is ill, incapacitated or perhaps has even passed away? Is it a criminal act when a woman wishes to achieve a pregnancy using her dead husband's sperm?

Maybe these are not questions only doctors can solve. Some physicians and researchers reported feeling a bit overwhelmed by needing to make all the decisions on such questions. "What is needed is a wider public discussion," said one doctor when asked about such questions as whether he would artifi-cially inseminate the wife of a terminally ill man. On such topics so close to everyday life and decisions, public discussion about these issues seems prefer-able to treating the subject as an unspeakable taboo or settling it only in the courts. What if a man decides to use his donated sperm to inseminate a woman who is not his wife? What if a wife gains access to her ex-husband's sperm and inseminates herself? A friend? Who has legal custody of a child if one is born from stolen sperm? Who is the true mother and the true father? There have been scandals over mixed-up sperm samples and lack of hygiene in sperm banks. The first test-tube baby was born in 1978, so this is still a rather new business. Even if it is not the most attractive route, reproductive medicine is sure to deliver enough court battles to keep many lawyers quite busy.

Studies on the long-term effects of the life on ice on sperm's vitality and fertilization capacity have really not yielded any conclusive results. It appears that sperm, while not as good as new after a deep freeze, are not seriously impaired. They do lose a good deal of their motility in cryopreservation. But studies are lacking on whether they sustain genetic flaws. Setting some of the flashier controversies aside, the cryopreservation of sperm is for some men an important medical option. If testicular cancer is diagnosed, and a man still has a desire to father a child, a physician will recommend that he store a sample.

Patients with testicular cancer often have to face aggressive chemotherapy and radiotherapy as part of their treatment regimen. In a study of 195 patients with an average age of 28, 30% were already married and 10% had one child. Although many couples may not start a family until their thirties, these patients were advised to bank sperm. Doctors know how difficult it is to face a diagnosis of testicular cancer. The prospect of infertility almost takes a back seat in those moments since a patient may just be focusing on survival. Testicular cancer is treatable when it is caught early or even later, as cyclist Lance Armstrong has lived to tell. But it is hard to decide on sperm banking when there are many other decisions to be made. Jon Pryor at the University of Minnesota and his colleagues discovered that only about 27% of male cancer patients use sperm cryopreservation. His survey among oncologists revealed that this fact is mainly due to a lack of awareness among physicians about some newer developments in assisted reproductive technology. The procedure through which a sperm can be injected into an egg was known to only 26% of the oncologists who responded to the survey. Being an informed patient seems to be important in these cases.

Chemotherapy negatively affects sperm production, and it can damage the DNA in sperm. Some men with testicular cancer show poor sperm quality at the time of their diagnosis. This presents a problem for sperm banking for use at a later date. As one textbook puts it, "The better the prefreeze motility is, the better postthaw motility tends to be." And if motility is poor, a physician will propose applying ICSI (intracytoplasmic sperm injection) to conceive a child.

Men who are having a vasectomy may also choose to cryopreserve a semen sample in case they decide to have a child at a later date and do not wish to attempt to reverse their sterilization operatively.

Semen and Sperm in the Modern Infertility Clinic
"It is Not Working"

Asking around in my circle of friends and acquaintances, it struck me how many people were trying to have a baby and the "normal" route to conception was not working. Some couples report that when they first go see a doctor, their husbands or partners are basically sent home. Even though the problem could be with the man, there is a tendency to treat the woman first.

"In 95–98% of all cases the women are the first to have tests performed," said German andrologist Walter Krause from the University of Marburg. Men should be involved in these first steps but it really seems to be a woman's issue. Yatsushita Yamamoto, a researcher at the Japanese Tottori University, told me at a conference that women in Japan have a lower status than men. In the case of involuntary childlessness the woman's mother or father tells the woman to go to the doctor. Nobody would consider the man as being the possible source of the problem, he said. "This attitude should change," he said, and conceded that it would take time.

Physicians treating a couple need to think of many possible causes for their infertility. At a conference, Rebecca Sokol, an andrologist at the University of Southern California School of Medicine, described how she was sought out by a couple. The wife had undergone four cycles of IVF. For over a year they had tried everything and the woman had invested much time, energy and money in her attempts to get pregnant. When the man was finally examined it was found that he had tumors in both testicles that were suppressing sperm production.There was no way she could have become pregnant by him. He was subsequently treated for testicular cancer. Sometimes medical procedures or complicated processes are unnecessary; sometimes counseling is enough. Another couple was desperate when they came to Rebecca Sokol having tried everything. It turned out that neither the man nor his semen had ever been examined at all. She asked the man what his occupation was. "Glassblower," he replied. And Dr. Sokol reported having a hunch. Semen analysis revealed his semen did not contain a single sperm. She asked him to take an extended leave of absence. "Six months later the wife was pregnant," she said triumphantly. Apart from that simple recommendation, no other treatment was necessary. Presumably the high temperatures at his workplace had completely, but temporarily, suppressed sperm production in his testes.

John Pryor, an andrologist at the University of Minnesota, says, "Men are afraid to talk to a doctor about infertility and potency. They are too macho for that." We are sitting in a corner of a plush hotel lobby where he is attending a conference. He puts his hand in front of his genitals as if to hold his testes. "Do you have balls?" he said. "That is like asking: are you a man? Men suffer from lowered self-esteem when confronted with infertility or any kind of problem with their testicles or penis," said Pryor. "I try to be as sensitive as possible with my patients because I realize how difficult it is for them."

Doctors need to be able to hear a patient out and the options in fertility treatment require detailed discussion. "I wish people were more knowledgeable," said one gynecologist. "Sometimes the women are up to their eyeballs in hormones, suffering from bad side-effects and depression. There are too many quacks in this field, even in university hospitals." Doctor–patient communication challenges, an evergreen in medicine, are particularly present in reproductive medicine, it seems. As Gerald Schatten of Oregon Health Sciences University says, "When you go to the doctor you ask about issues and the doctor will say 'We have therapy.' What you, the patient, will hear is 'well-tested, beneficial.' In the case of assisted reproduction that is not really the case for all the techniques that are offered." These days, often to the chagrin of physicians or health insurance companies, it pays to be an informed patient. At the same time it is better to have another set of ears listening in to be able to cross-check which messages did get across and which did not.

Testing Together

When a couple comes to the doctor with the complaint that "it doesn't work", the ensuing treatment can be a lengthy affair. At the same time, the first consultation can be a bit of a cold shower when they hear that they have about a 20–30% chance of pregnancy from regular unprotected sex. Spontaneous termination of the pregnancy, at different developmental stages, is not rare. For some unknown reason an embryo does not settle in the uterus and pregnancy is not taken to term.

A committed doctor will want to speak thoroughly with a couple about many aspects of treatment. "They should get the feeling that they can come to this doctor with all their questions and worries, their problems and thoughts," said Gerd Leydendecker, gynecologist in the city hospital of Darmstadt in Germany.

Pressure and Stress

You will come across ads or brochures saying the success rate of a particular institution or a particular technique is 45 or 50%. Don't believe it. IVF doctors quote that the range may be closer to 20–25%. Self-help groups think it may be as low as 15%. As Pamela Madsen, executive Director of the American Infertility Association, points out, "For instance, depending upon a patient's age, success rates can vary greatly from center to center. Simple statistics cannot tell the whole story." The rate of miscarriages after assisted reproduction is about the same as in normal pregnancies, about 10–14%. When shopping around for a clinic, it is hard to compare the touted success rates. In many cases, patients with relatively low chances of achieving success are simply taken out of the reported statistics.

Couples involved in assisted reproduction say that they feel under pressure to agree to complex treatments and to keep going even after a number of cycles fail. Physicians I asked at conferences say they are the ones who feel pressure from the couples who demand immediate treatment and quick success. "This is sometimes difficult for the younger staff in the clinics who feel the pressure by patients who put all their hope into the technical procedures. Sometimes I would rather send the couple home to try to conceive the normal way," a gynecologist stated. Psychological problems can suppress ovulation or decrease a man's sperm quality, but most couples don't want to hear that.

Sperm quality will vary depending on many factors, even the season. Most doctors want to talk to the man and the woman. "There shouldn't be any secrets between them," said one gynecologist. Roman Pyrzak, andrologist at the Fertility Institute in New Orleans opposed this view and gives an example. Some men answered "no" to the question "Have you fathered any children prior to your marriage?" when their wife was present, but admitted in a one-to-one talk to have been responsible for a pregnancy when they were younger. Some men don't want their wife to know. Generally, men are not as ready to talk about their intimate sphere as their partners may be. In the course of fertility treatment, it seems that a couple will also learn quite a bit about each other. Yakov Epstein, a psychologist at Rutgers University and board member of INCIID, the International Council on Infertility Information Dissemination, discovered in a survey that 32% of women undergoing fertility treatment "learn that men have a different way of dealing with their feelings", and 40% say that in the course of the treatment they "learn that each partner deals with infertility in his/her own way."

The Diagnosis

Before any kind of treatment can start, diagnosis is essential. First, it is usually the woman who will undergo a routine infertility work-up that involves answering questions about her medical history. There will be a physical exam and various blood tests to check hormone levels. Other exams include a cervical mucus test. This involves, for example, a post-coital test right before ovulation. A physician will want to see how well sperm can penetrate and survive in the cervical mucus. They pick the time right around ovulation when vaginal mucus is most conducive for sperm passage. Other tests will involve assessing the uterine lining as well as the uterus and ovaries in general, using ultrasound. Other tests may be the examination of the fallopian tubes. A hysterosalpingogram involves injecting a dye into the uterus and fallopian tubes. In an X-ray, the dye will appear white and thus a physican can see if the tubes are blocked. For men, a work-up includes questions about medical history, a physical exam and a semen analysis. (See Chapters 2 and 6.)

If the physician chooses to get sperm and egg together in the artificial surroundings of a lab, egg retrieval and a semen sample are needed. A woman will be prescribed ovulation-inducing drugs which stimulate multiple eggs in her ovaries. This process, called superovulation, is different from the normal menstrual cycle during which usually only one egg ripens fully. Not all women respond in the same way to the drugs prescribed for superovulation and a regimen usually has to be individually adjusted. The next step is egg retrieval.

The hormonal prerequisite for that is a so-called LH surge, a surge in luteinizing hormone that causes the release of the eggs from the ovary. For example, a woman will receive an HCG (human chorionic gonadotrophin) injection, and about a day and a half later eggs will be retrieved.

Yes, egg retrieval can hurt. Which is why anesthesia is sometimes used, or sedation, because the procedure is actually invasive. A probe is used to guide a needle into the woman's vagina and then to the ovaries. In other words, instead of following the path sperm would take, the needle goes through the vaginal wall and then punctures the ovary. The procedure is called ultrasound-guided transvaginal puncture of the follicles. Some centers allow husbands to be with their wives during this procedure. The eggs are then removed, immediately placed in nutritive fluid and placed in an incubator.

If the man is responsible for the involuntary childlessness, doctors have several options. Sometimes it is psychotherapy for the man or for the couple; it might also be an appropriate drug or a surgical procedure. These options are described in Chapter 6. Basically at this stage, the clinic will need a semen sample to analyze sperm motility and shape. "Sometimes I am really horrified how ignorant men are concerning their own body, regardless of their occupation. Men don't know anything. The worst are the lawyers – they want to know all the ifs and buts – and every second sentence they begin with the words: 'When you say that, do you mean …?' and interpret everything in the wrong way," said an andrologist at one clinic. No matter how much scientists argue about the influence of stress on sperm, at infertility clinics specialists see the evidence every day. Stressed men have reduced semen quality.

"I am going to abstain from sex for a long time so that my semen will turn out super," one man said to his physician. Unfortunately that does not help as sperm perish after two weeks to make room for new ones. Another man claimed that he normally had sex twice a week but under the microscope it was clear that he had fibbed and had probably not had sex for a while. The sperm head membranes were beginning to dissolve and there were a fair number of dead sperm in his semen. When the doctor told the man and asked him whether he really ejaculated twice a week, the man was surprised. "How do you know?" The doctor explained that he could tell from the way the sperm looked. Sperm tell a more true tale than the donor in some cases. And if a man does not stick to the prescribed period of abstinence, that will be clear to the andrologist as well.

While researchers tend to have their doubts about whether semen quality has dropped in recent years, physicians in infertility clinics answer this question with a prompt "yes." If a man is a smoker, he can count on his andrologist to tell him to stop before treatment begins. Couples will be asked if they have just recovered from any kind of illness. Even a fever, for example, can impact sperm production. A doctor will also ask about the couple's sex lives, including the frequency of intercourse. Questions will revolve around whether the couple are feeling stressed.

If a man is diagnosed as having reduced fertility, he might have to undergo further treatment. Sperm quality cannot be raised quickly, so a variety of options will be explored. In some cases, if the sperm cannot get to the egg, the egg will come to the sperm.

One main prerequisite a physician will be looking for is to make sure the testes are indeed producing sperm that are at least theoretically capable of fertilizing an egg. The first test-tube baby was born in 1978. The techniques available in modern reproductive medicine have developed quite a bit since then. And so have the acronyms with which patients are bombarded. IVF is perhaps one of the most well known. In-vitro fertilization implies that fertilization is taking part outside the body.

Sperm Without Ejaculation

If the ejaculate does not contain any sperm, due perhaps to a blockage of some sort in the male reproductive tract, sperm can be collected from elsewhere. This technique can also be applied with men who have had a vasectomy and decide to father a child after all. One place to harvest sperm is the epididymis. A tiny tube is inserted into this organ where the sperm are maturing much as wine in a cask.

The procedure, termed MESA (microsurgical epididymal sperm aspiration), is delicate and time-consuming. In some cases IVF treatment may fail with sperm harvested through MESA, because of maturity issues. What some believe to be true for the penis – the longer the better – is certainly true for the epididymides: the longer the better. The longer the epididymides, the better the chance of finding sperm ready to fertilize.

In other cases, TESE (testicular sperm extraction) is the preferred procedure, or PESA (percutaneous epididymal sperm aspiration). According to a German physician who runs an infertility clinic, some specialists who haven't mastered these techniques do not tell their patients and advise them to use donor sperm. "That is a shame," he said. "If men desire children, an attempt should be made to help them use their own sperm."

If a man suffers from retrograde ejaculation, for example if he is diabetic, and the sperm ends up in the bladder, sperm can be harvested from there. A man will be asked to empty his bladder before ejaculation and it will be rinsed with a particular medium that protects the sperm. When the man ejaculates, the sperm will be obtained through a catheter.

While waiting to interview a physician who performs assisted reproduction procedures, a man and his wife were also in the waiting room. The couple had two children, one of whom was climbing onto her father's wheelchair and into his lap and he read to her. I wondered how they had "done it" but refrained from asking. The gynecologist told me later that IVF had been applied and he had harvested the man's sperm through electroejaculation, or a vibrating instrument that is inserted into the rectum.

Sperm, once harvested, are not immediately ready for the assisted fertilization. They are washed and filtered. Bacteria, which may be present in the semen, need to be eliminated to avoid infecting the female partner. Prostaglandins may cause the uterus to contract. Although this may help the sperm to propel their way through the female reproductive tract after intercourse, in assisted reproduction these contractions are not what the doctor ordered.

Sperm are centrifuged which allows white blood cells and dead spermatozoa to be separated from the more active sperm. Sperm will then be exposed to the swim-up test so that the most motile sperm can be collected. Then clinics might choose to keep the sperm in a specific nurturing medium that might also contain pentoxyphyllin or caffeine, both of which are known to stimulate sperm motility.

Not all techniques of assisted reproduction involve egg retrieval. One of the earlier assisted reproduction techniques was to deposit semen into the vagina or cervical canal of a woman, but IUI (intrauterine insemination) is now preferred during which sperm are injected directly into the uterine cavity and the fallopian tubes. It is all a matter of timing. Once it is established that the woman is ovulating – either by ultrasound or hormonal tests – the sperm are taken at the right time to the right place. Another method of this type is GIFT (gamete intra-fallopian transfer). Sperm and egg are brought together in a test-tube and then transferred into the woman's body. In these methods fertilization still takes place inside the woman's body. Other methods involve bringing egg and sperm together artificially in the lab, which is termed in-vitro fertilization, and then transferring the embryo to the woman's body.

If sperm are not entering the egg in the test tube, methods of so-called microassisted fertilization can be applied. For example, there is a technique called zona drilling in which a hole is drilled in the zona pellucida of the egg. The sperm now can slip through the hole. A larger hole may be drilled, as part of a procedure called PZD (partial zona dissection). This method is not viewed very favorably because of the risk of polyspermy, that is, several sperm attempting to fertilize the egg at the same time rendering the embryo unviable.

Using SUZI (sub-zonal sperm injection), a sperm is injected directly into the so-called perivitelline space, between the zona pellucida and the egg membrane.

The method which has attracted the most attention is one in which all hurdles to the egg are bypassed: ICSI (intracytoplasmic sperm injection), in which the sperm is injected directly into the egg. Sperm need not be motile, nor do they have to penetrate any part of the egg by their own propulsion or acrosome reaction. A needle pushes it in.

Sperm Preparation

Preparing sperm for these techniques involves a lab preselection of sperm. Usually, the so-called swim-up test will be used to pick the most motile sperm.

ICSI was pioneered in Belgium by Andre Van Steirtegheim and his colleagues at the Center for Reproductive Medicine at Dutch-Speaking Brussels Free University. It is a novel kind of procedure in that it was used first in humans rather than animals.

It has been shown to be highly efficient, particularly in treating couples in which the male partner suffers from some form of fertility problem. ICSI is considered to be a milestone in infertility treatment, a kind of quantum leap. Immature sperm or sperm that are immotile can be used in this procedure. Rather than needing to resort to donor sperm, a physician can use the husband's sperm which, for many couples, is a wonderful bonus of this technique. Worldwide, approximately 20,000 babies have been born using this technique.

Only a few years after its introduction ICSI has become one of the most successful therapies in reproductive medicine. The American gynecologist Alan DeCherney said at a conference, "This is fantastic – quick, cheap and successful. Even gynecologists can master the technique with a bit of practice." His co-panelist, Rebecca Sokol, expressed her doubts, saying it involved no diagnosis and was only treating the sperm and not the patient. DeCherney felt it was a more financially efficient method than extensive diagnostic tests. ICSI is used widely. But even proponents are pointing out that there are still plenty of unknowns when it comes to this procedure. Van Steirtegheim and his colleagues pointed out in 1998 that parents need to be informed of the risk. After ICSI, some studies have found a higher incidence of chromosomal anomalies in the children. "At this point, we think that patients should be informed and counselled before any treatment on the basis of the available data as to the higher risk of transmitted chromosomal aberrations, the risk of *de novo*, mainly sex chromosomal aberrations and the risk of transmitting fertility problems to the offspring and that a free choice of prenatal diagnosis should be available in all ICSI settings," they wrote in a study. Since then a number of researchers have been looking closely at the issues surrounding assisted reproduction and the sex chromosomes. More about that later on in this chapter. The risks associated with ICSI have been the topic of many studies. A study at the Swedish Sahlgrenska University Hospital showed that babies born after ICSI did show an increased risk of abnormalities such as hypospadias, but this risk seemed correlated with their premature or multiple births.

Assisted reproduction researchers say they still have some way to go to optimize the procedures for patients. The hormonal treatment of women is demanding, as are the frequent exams. The desire for a child can be lost in the complicated and time-consuming process. Quicker and safer methods, drugs with less side effects, fewer multiple pregnancies, fewer spontaneous terminations of pregnancies, more insight into the genetics of the method, higher overall success rates, are all facets that reproductive medical specialists would like to improve.

The methods are helping couples to conceive. But often, perhaps in 70% of all cases or even higher, the process does not work. Counselors advise that at some point many couples have to come to terms with childlessness, when everything that modern medicine has to offer has been tried.

One woman told German counselor Uschi Radermacher that she had asked her doctor to suspend the treatment for one cycle, to which he had responded: "Why? Everything is going fine." Such reactions make women uneasy and they only rarely mention their inner fears and anxieties to the doctor because the treatment might be withheld. "Many women say that the most important thing in their life is to have a baby." Studies on how assisted reproduction affects men and how it affects them when it does not assist in their reproduction are rare.

Some researchers say that men are under less pressure in general and are not asked as frequently as women whether they have children. Men experience shock, anger, grief and disappointment when diagnosed as infertile; younger men more so than older ones. "I feel less of a man," said Tom, 26. "A friend of mine had just made his wife pregnant and boasted about it. I asked myself what he would say if I told him that my sperm were not good enough. I didn't tell him as I felt ashamed." Jack, 34, spoke of his crisis of confidence in regard to his life and career. He felt all his achievements had been in vain as his motivation had been his desire to support a wife and children. Feelings of guilt, depression and anxiety are common with men in that situation and after only a little counseling they very often withdraw. "Then I always feel quite helpless," said Uschi Radermacher. "How can you help someone who doesn't want to talk? We need self-help groups for men as we have for women."

It is one thing to have counseling as a couple, but there are perhaps issues that might also be discussed separately. Physician, Werner Gehring said: "In my experience men need more attention than women. They don't like admitting to weaknesses. They want to be courageous and strong." It is wrong to treat men without regard for their feelings. "Men often believe that having bad sperm quality makes them inferior."

"Men and emotions – there is lot to say about that issue. Boys don't cry. They have deeply internalized that. I often don't know what to offer men," said

Uschi Radermacher. She is very proud of one of her clients who had come to terms with his infertility. During a training seminar at work, totally unrelated to fertility and fathering, all participants had to introduce themselves and say a few words about themselves. When it was his turn, he said that he was married but that he didn't have children because he was infertile. Some participants reacted with embarrassment, averted their eyes, there was silence in the room. During the break one man came to him and said that he had the same problem.

Legal and Financial Aspects of Assisted Reproduction

Doctors are obliged to treat their patients according to the Hippocratic oath: use their ability and judgment to find a regimen to benefit their patients and abstain from whatever is deleterious or mischievous. Every treatment the doctor decides on has to be medically justified, legal and in concordance with current standards of good practice. After the patients have been given all the relevant information regarding the treatment they will be asked to sign a consent form.

When couples try to have a child in the natural way but are unable to do so, assisted reproduction may help them. In the 1970s a researcher at Vanderbilt University attempted to fertilize a human egg in the test tube. Because of doubts about the procedure, the National Institutes of Health stated that it would only fund the procedure after revision by an ethics board. As Barbara Menning, founder of Resolve, points out, the researcher Dr. Pierre Soupart died in 1981 without having received a grant for his work or having seen these techniques advance in the US. By then the first test-tube baby had already been born in the UK. In the US, states Menning, "with the lack of federal support and federal funding, the private sector was called on to pioneer the first efforts in this country, and indeed it did." Assisted reproduction has turned into quite an industry.

The legal questions this industry raises are complex. Do children have a right to know how they were conceived? A self-help group in the US reports that being a test-tube baby is a form of abuse. Is there a risk of incest, especially in rural areas, if half-siblings with the same donor father marry without knowing?

The insurance questions are resolved in some states, but not all. Health insurers first argued that they would not offer coverage since infertility is not a disease or an illness. Based on the work of advocacy groups this view has begun to change. Insurance issues will vary from one carrier to the next.

Sex Determination

Imagine a scenario in which all men on earth decided to pack up and leave to go and live on another planet, destroying all sperm banks before they leave and avoiding all unprotected intercourse with women nine months prior to their departure. Their destination, a place one could call Planet Blue, will be set up just as men desire, perhaps with plenty of TV sports channels and high-tech remote controls. On the women's planet, or Planet Pink, women would be left to their own devices. On both planets scientists would have to figure out how to manage reproduction if the inhabitants wanted to stay on their respective heavenly bodies. On both planets cloning would be an option. Rather than manufacturing identical individuals, though, it might be a better idea to allow genetic material to recombine as it did in the days when men and women lived together. So, on the pink planet, researchers would need to figure out how to fuse two eggs and their genetic material. In the course of a special kind of IVF treatment, an embryo might very well develop in a woman's womb. Fusing two sets of women's chromosomes means, however, that the embryo will, by necessity, be a girl, since women carry the XX sex chromosome combination. On Planet Blue, scientists might venture to explore fusing two sperm. That would lead to either an XX , XY or YY constellation. To date, that kind of fusion has not been performed and the YY chromosomal combination is not known to be viable. Men and women both have 23 sets of chromosomes, much like two sets of silverware. One particular set, the sex chromosomes, differs between genders. Women have two X-chromosomes; men have one X- and one Y-chromosome. Their sperm come in two versions, the X- and the Y-bearing sperm, with a set of chromosomes 1–22 and number 23 is either an X or a Y. So sperm are decision makers. Depending on whether the Y- or the X-sperm gets to the egg, that will determine the gender of the baby. If a Y-carrying sperm gets there first, the baby will be a boy; if the X-carrying sperm makes the race, the baby will be a girl.

"No, I do not do that," said one andrologist firmly who runs a large sperm bank in the US with years of experience and exposure to mothers- and fathers-to-be and their requests. "No, I do not predetermine the child's gender. People have to take it as it comes." Given the possibilities in reproductive medicine, one has to consciously make a decision not to do something. Other physicians at sperm banks and the clinics to which they are affiliated make different decisions. In some cases, couples may wish to predetermine gender because of a familial disorder that would be inherited by boys, but not girls. Other couples may have other reasons for their desire to have a boy rather than a girl, or vice versa. Although not permissible in some countries, it is not very complicated to predetermine a baby's gender when doing IVF. And that is all about sorting sperm.

The Genetics and IVF Institute in Fairfax Virginia offers sperm sorting, a method currently in clinical trial, to reduce the probability of sex-linked diseases and also for "family balancing." Their filtration methods have turned out to be fairly reliable. X-carrying chromosomes contain about 3% more genetic material than Y-chromosomes. So the X-chromosome is a bit heavier. In the lab, sperm can be marked with a fluorescent dye, and in a procedure called flow cytometry, sperm can be separated according to the amount of DNA they have. DNA analysis can then be used to see if the sorting is pure. This involves attaching probes to the X and/or Y that will emit a particular telltale color in another type of procedure called fluorescence in situ hybridization. In the process in Virginia, the MicroSort process, the probability of conceiving a girl with the enriched sample is an average of 90% and for the Y-chromosome it is 73%, with over 150 babies having been born so far using this procedure.

While the process of gender selection in this way is illegal in some countries, it is legal in the US. To sort sperm for the purpose of family balancing, the institute requires that the patients be a married couple with at least one child. And in addition this process can be essential if parents wish to avoid certain inheritable and gender-linked diseases. In the 1980s reports from China and India stated that prenatal tests such as amniocentesis were being used to selectively abort female fetuses. Preventing their abuse, and this is true for both the older and the newer gender selection techniques, appears difficult.

Sex determination is an old wish and history is replete with attempts to find the right method to produce a boy or a girl at will. The Greek philosopher Anaxagoras (500–428 BCE) assumed that the right testicle would create male babies, the left one female babies. He suggested quite a painful procedure as a method of gender determination in which the man should tie off the appropriate testicle for the desired result. Apparently this method was practised until the eighteenth century. A French aristocrat was reported to have had his left testicle completely removed to ensure he only fathered male offspring. Another predetermination method that is both painful and not recommended dates back to the eighteenth century. Prior to intercourse a man should pinch his left testicle to ensure that semen came only from his right testicle which would lead to a boy. This method is painful and unhealthy. In addition, it will never yield the desired result as both testes contain X- and Y-bearing sperm. According to other methods certain positions during intercourse favor the conception of one gender, none have which has been shown to work. A Kamasutra geared toward gender selection does not exist.

Austrian doctor Wilfried Feichtinger co-authored a book with dietician Gertrud Reiger about nutritional ways to determine your baby's gender. What they believe is that the mineral balance in your body supposedly influences the child's gender. It is based on the idea of potassium and sodium versus calcium and magnesium. If a couple wants a boy they should choose a diet with a higher potassium and sodium content; for a girl it is the calcium and magnesium that matters. The mother-to-be is instructed to follow the diet, but the authors state that for psychological reasons and to show his "solidarity" the father-to-be should also comply with the regimen, making it more fun to cook the same meals together.

Many of the recipes sound interesting: breakfast for the couple with a baby girl in mind consists of banana muesli, the boy-wishers should have fruit salad with sour cream and cinnamon. Lunch is, for the boy-favoring group, onion rings baked in tinfoil and the girl-group will need to bake fish with tomatoes, garlic and pepper. One nutritionist I interviewed declared this diet theory to be "complete and absolute nonsense" and actually a danger for people who, for example, have to watch their sodium intake.

In the 1930s, researchers tested baking soda-based vaginal douches to supposedly promote a boy. The more acidic approach, the vinegar douche was thought to be more likely to produce a girl. As it turned out there was never any experiment on that method because no patient purportedly felt strongly enough about having a girl. Research on this entire approach was abandoned because it was not showing any success.

Why Oh Y?

"If you have a Y-chromosome and a PhD you qualify," wrote biochemist and science journalist Karen Hopkin to scientists, looking for candidates for her particular project: the so-called "Studmuffin Calendar," a photo calendar of scientists with hunk physique. Setting the academic criteria aside, if a Y makes a hunk or even a male with lesser muscles and yet breathtaking charm, it seems intriguing to find out how the Y-chromosome manages its job. David Page, a Howard Hughes Medical Institute Investigator at MIT's Whitehead Institute in Cambridge, Massachusetts, and his team study the sex chromosomes. "In a sense," states Page, "the body is really a germ cell container." Our precious heritage is in our germ cells, our eggs and sperm respectively.

When the Y first caught his attention, as science journalist Carol Cruzan Morton puts it, "it had all the appeal of rapidly eroding beach-front property." The Y was originally even going to be left out of the gigantic effort to sequence the human genome. While names may not hurt as much as sticks and stones, the Y-chromosome is getting verbally pummeled. "Functional wasteland," "genetic junkyard," "degenerate," "copycat," "Rodney Dangerfield of chromosomes," "non-recombining desert", are on the name-calling list. "All those names are right," says Page. "I buy into the following idea: both the X and the Y have evolved from regular chromosomes, socalled autosomes. While the X has retained most of its genes, the Y has lost them. So in that sense, yes, the Y is a degenerate." The X-chromosome harbors around 3,000 genes, the Y somewhere around 20, many of which Page and his lab have identified. Once upon a time, the X and Y were equal partners, probably around 200 million years ago. But then they parted ways. And that has not turned out to be the best thing for the Y. Most of the genes on the Y are deteriorating.

"What is known about the Y chromosome? Half the population does not have one, and defects are generally compatible with viability. Genes on the Y chromosome have for seven million years of human evolution been exposed to the mutation-promoting environment of spermatogenesis within the testicle, whereas genes on the X chromosome and the autosomes have spent half of this time within the relatively inert environment of the ovum," writes urologist T.B. Hargreave of the University of Edinburgh. The Y does not live in a safe neighborhood, say some. For a long time scientists have thought that the male germ line, with its much higher number of cell divisions, has a dramatically high mutation rate compared to the female germ line. As Page and his colleagues recently found, actually this rate has been "only modestly higher in males than in females" during the last 3–4 million years of human evolution.

David Page drinks his coffee out of a teal-colored mug that reads, "Save the Males." So the situation seems to be serious. "I like to state the pejorative, like 'degenerate' to prepare people to hear the other side of the Y story," explains Page. In sexually reproducing species, chromosomes and the genes they contain go through a mix-and-match game. One complete set comes from each parent and meet when sperm meets egg.

The mixing and matching may involve having pieces of chromosome 3 recombine by using bits from the partner of chromosome 3. Other chromosomes may do likewise. This combinatorial trick explains why a child may look like his or her parents but is not a clone. And this explains why sex is a good thing, because during this activity, genetic copying mistakes – which occur all in a day's work of a chromosome – are edited out and fixed. While the chromosomes are doing this dance, however, there is one wallflower. The Y-chromosome.

In the cells that produce sperm, and also as eggs are produced, chromosomes become paired and when they separate, each sperm and egg receives a single set of chromosomes. As sperm are formed, for example, the X- and Y-chromosomes line up and exchange a teeny bit of information in which one small region of the Y-chromosome is involved. The rest of the Y-chromosome does not participate in this important element of sex, the genetic exchange. By avoiding this editing process, mistakes are accumulated on this chromosome. They become no longer functional and over time they are eliminated completely. The Y becomes a shadow of its ancestral self.

The good news is that what the Y is doing is becoming a specialist, says Page. Half of its genes are involved in spermatogenesis. One decision-maker of a gene on the Y was identified by British researcher Peter Goodfellow and his colleagues. It is called sex-determining region Y, or SRY. If you have it, you get testes. Without it, an embryo develops ovaries. So while the Y is poor in genes it is rich in influence. But the influence is a quick-fix. SRY acts on the developing embryo for about a day or two and the rest of male development is regulated by genes elsewhere in the genome. Late on in the boy's life, the Y is then actively involved in sperm production. At least half of the genes on the Y-chromosome appear to tend to this job of sperm production. Which is why the Y is of particular interest for male fertility issues.

A region of the Y was implicated in male infertility in 1976 by Italian researchers. They called it AZF (azoospermia factor), for the condition in which a man's semen contains no sperm. Page and his co-workers zeroed in on AZF and discovered quite a bit about its link to fertility. Together with Renee Reijo Pera, now a professor at the University of California at San Francisco, they located a gene family they termed DAZ ("deleted in azoospermia"). Apparently the region encodes proteins required for normal fertility in men and actually all tailless primates. When deleted, azoospermia results.

Then, in 1999 Page and other members of his lab identified a change within the AZF region called AZFc. In particular he was looking at this region of the Y in men undergoing ICSI. And he found particular genetic deletions were being transmitted via ICSI to the sons of these men. "Our observations provide a concrete foundation for alerting couples to the likelihood of transmitting infertility-causing Y deletions by ICSI," Page and his colleagues write in their scientific paper. So why should couples think about the Y? An azoospermic man has no sperm. In ICSI, sperm can be retrieved from the testes or epididymis. What Page and his colleagues were showing was that in all likelihood ICSI was passing on Y deletions. If this deletion pertains to a gene involved in fertility, then it is not unlikely that the conceived sons will be infertile and they too would need to resort to ICSI. This study is not exactly encouraging to those researchers who wonder about possible troublesome implications of ICSI.

"Perhaps the unpaired segment of the Y chromosome has become like a fuse, a fuse that will be the first point to 'blow' if the circuit becomes overloaded by mutations. Come to think of it, the scrotum makes a pretty good fuse box. By blowing a fuse – causing a mutation in one of the Y-linked genes controlling spermatogenesis – Nature ensures that these mutations are not transmitted to succeeding generations. Is there a message here about ICSI?," writes Roger Short of the University of Melbourne. ICSI is a successful technique, a godsend to some couples in which the man has fertility problems that only ICSI can help to circumvent. However, the question crops up about what kind of Y is being transmitted in this process. In order to know that for certain, many other facets of the Y must be understood.

Throughout evolution, the Y-chromosome has been acquiring genes. "The story of the Y is not entirely one of being just the rotting X chromosome," says Page. "It is different from all other chromosomes because of subtle biases it has integrated over hundreds of millions of years." While the integration has gone on, the Y has also chosen to be celibate, not exchanging genetic material with a partner.

As Laurence Hurst, evolutionary biologist of the University of Bath, and Linda Partridge of University College in London explain, sexual reproduction increases the likelihood of evolutionary conflict. "Sex-specific selection has been important in the evolution of the sex chromosomes." They point out that there will be selection for "the suppression of recombination between the sex-determination region and the male-advantage/female disadvantage-genes linked to it, because then they will not be transmitted to daughters."

So by being a specialist, the Y is also keeping characteristics to itself that are to its advantage. But by sticking to life as a virgin, however, it is going down a genetically risky path since the chromosome clocks up more genetic errors than other chromosomes. And that leads to its decay. So far only a few virginal life forms are known that have escaped rapid extinction. So the future of the Y is not bright.

As Page points out, all other chromosomes outside the Y are evolutionary compromises between the interests of males and females. "The Y is uncompromisingly male-beneficial," says Page. As we study the evolution of the Y-chromosome and its molecular biology, he says, the adaptive pressures acting on it, the Y begins to make sense. "It is almost as if the Y has chosen to be male-specific real estate and to personally tend to one cell type, the male germ cells," says Page. "We do not know why it has chosen to do this."

The man, the Y, his sperm and his semen: a fascinating puzzle.

Questions, Facts and Figures

Questions, Questions

If I masturbate or have sex frequently, will I run out of semen?
In contrast to all other natural resources on this planet, such as water or oil, semen is not a limited resource. Men do not receive a certain amount at birth and have to economize. From puberty to death, the testes produce sperm and glands produce semen. An injury or an illness, however, may bring sperm and semen production to a halt, as may certain types of surgery.

Does the amount of semen decrease with age?
Seminal fluid is a cocktail with components arising in various glands of the male reproductive tract. The prostate gland, the seminal vesicles, the epididymides are among the contributors. Semen production begins at puberty and stays true for a man's entire lifetime. The amount of semen as well as the number of sperm it contains can decrease slightly with age, but the difference is hardly noticeable.

Is it possible to increase the amount of ejaculate?
Semen volume varies from one ejaculation to the next. Consciously influencing the amount of semen expelled is not possible. It depends on such factors as hormones, frequency of ejaculation, length of stimulation and the function of the participating muscles.

Should a man ejaculate regularly to prevent sperm from going stale?
Sperm take care of themselves. And they do not live forever. They are stored in the epididymides for about two to three weeks after which they perish and are reabsorbed by the body. Less frequent ejaculation does mean that the number of dead sperm in the ejaculate rises.

What effect does an enlarged prostate gland have on semen?
Urine as well as semen leaves the body through the urethra. The prostate gland is situated in the upper part of the urethra, nearly at the neck of the bladder. A benign enlargement of the prostate gland is quite common in men over 50 who should always consult their physician when they notice bodily changes. Generally an enlarged prostate has no impact on sperm production and the

amount of seminal fluid remains the same. Many men with an enlarged prostate experience a more frequent urge to urinate and some suffer from a loss of libido or erectile dysfunction.

Can you see sperm in the seminal fluid with your naked eye?
No. Sperm are very small and can only be seen under the microscope. They are approximately 0.05 millimeters long.

How many calories are there in one ejaculate?
If swallowed, one ejaculate contains approximately 5 calories.

Can you have an orgasm without ejaculating?
Before puberty, the body does not produce semen or sperm. So when a young boy masturbates he can have dry orgasms. After extended sessions of love-making that involve several ejaculations, orgasms may run dry as well. There can be medical reasons that cause a man to reach orgasm without ejaculating. And if the situation persists, it is best to contact a doctor.

Some men say they have a "semen leak" – what is that?
Bowel movements can exert pressure on the prostate gland which delivers around 10–30% of semen. This pressure can cause some of the prostatic secretion to be pushed out via the urethra. This is nothing to be worried about. However, if you feel that liquid is oozing out of your penis when you are standing up or lying down, then you should contact a physician. The discharge is not necessarily semen. Certain venereal diseases cause pus or other discharge from the urethra. In that case self-medication using antibiotics left over from last year's winter flu is not a good idea. It may not be the right treatment and the infection you have might get worse. To prevent venereal disease, use a condom.

What effect does sterilization have on semen?
After a vasectomy, ejaculation will still involve semen, but it will be void of sperm, although not immediately after the procedure is done. Sperm only make up 1% of the semen volume so you will hardly detect a lessened semen quantity.

Is it advisable to always go all the way to orgasm when masturbating?
There is no right or wrong way to masturbate, it is a question of individual preference. Some men feel pressure in the testes if they interrupt their masturbating. In slang this is called blue balls and is no cause for alarm. As sexual excitement ebbs off so does the feeling in the testes. Some men experience pain in the testes after frequent ejaculations. When in doubt, speak to your doctor about these issues.

How can paternity be determined?
In court cases involving paternity when the purported father denies that he is the biological father, a test may be performed to determine the truth. Either he must prove that he is incapable of intercourse for medical reasons or he must provide a sample. This need not be a semen sample, since any blood cell will deliver the DNA needed for analysis, such as cheek cells. Some controversy has erupted over the practice of some fathers having their children's DNA analyzed to ascertain if they are the true fathers.

What questions will I have to face when I am involved in a fertility work-up?
Every doctor has his or her own set of questions. I spoke to a number of physicians in different countries and pulled together a number of questions. You might hear all or some of the follow questions:

- Do you suffer from one of the following diseases: diabetes, high blood pressure, tuberculosis, cancer, infections?
- Do you have high cholesterol?
- Do you have any allergies?
- Have you had a heart attack? A stroke? Other illnesses?
- Have you had any illnesses or infections that affected your genitalia or your reproductive glands? Orchitis, mumps, epididymiditis, varicoceles, hydroceles, testicular tumours, testicular injuries, hernia, testicular torsion, testicular maldescent, prostatitis, urethritis, gonorrhoea, phimosis, or other?
- Have you ever had a venereal disease?
- Have you had any operations?
- Have you had any injuries? In the pelvis, spinal cord, skull/brain?
- Have you ever been treated with hormones?
- Are you taking any kind of medication?
- Do you smoke? When did you start? How long ago did you stop? How many cigarettes a day did you or do you smoke?
- How much alcohol do you drink daily?
- Do you take recreational drugs?
- Do you work out?
- Do you take steroids?
- How much coffee and tea do you drink?
- Do you go to the sauna regularly?
- Do you have a partner or wife?
- How long have you been in that relationship?
- Have you been married before?
- Do you have children?
- Do you want children?
- Have you ever fathered a child? (For example, a woman you were seeing had a miscarriage or an abortion)

- What kind of contraception do you use? Rhythm method, pill, coil, condom, coitus interruptus, others?
- Do you have any problems with potency? What kind?
- Any ejaculation problems? Since when?
- Any erection problems? Since when?
- Any lack of libido? Since when?
- How often do you have intercourse per month?
- How often do you masturbate per month?
- When was your last ejaculation?
- When do you normally have intercourse? In the morning, in the evening, irregularly?
- Do you have intercourse regularly? (For example, only at weekends, not on certain days etc.)
- Have you ever had a semen analysis?
- Have you ever had fertility treatment?
- How many hours a day do you work?
- Do you have regular working hours?
- Is your job stressful?
- Do you work shifts?
- Are you exposed to excessive heat or hazardous substances at work?

A physician who is also a sex therapist might add such questions as these:

- Do you have a sexual preference?
- Are you bisexual or homosexual?
- How would you describe your male self-image?
- Did you have serious conflicts during puberty?
- Was your upbringing anti-sexual in any way?
- Was your sexuality ignored?
- Were you abused or molested?
- Does pornography play a role in your sex life?
- Do you frequently change sex partners?
- Do you masturbate? How often?
- Do you go to prostitutes?
- Do you have a good friend with whom you can talk about sexual matters?

Is there such a thing as optimal semen?
No. Sperm and semen differ slightly from man to man. Experts have some standards to ascertain whether semen is more or less fertile but not every researcher agrees on this subject. The following standards have been set up by the World Health Organization and are useful to compare results from different labs. If you go to an andrologist and are given a semen analysis chart, the following information may be helpful.

Normal semen parameters according to WHO:

Volume	2.0 milliliters or more
pH	7.2–8.0
Scent	chestnut blossom-like
Color	grey-white, yellowish
Consistency	viscous, liquifies after about 30 minutes
Sperm concentration	upwards of 20 million per milliliter of ejaculate
Sperm count	upwards of 40 million per milliliter of ejaculate
Mobility	at least 50% of all sperm with forward progression (either rapid progression or slow progression), at least 25% of all sperm with rapid forward progression
Morphology	at least 30% of all sperm have a normal shape
Percentage of live sperm	75% of all sperm are live
Leukocytes	less than 1 million per milliliter of ejaculate
Alpha-glucodisase	more than 11 mU/ejaculate
Zinc	more than 2.4 mmol/ejaculate
Fructose	more than 13 mmol/ejaculate

Various kinds of semen have been given different names according to WHO classification

Normospermia	normal ejaculate (see above)
Oligospermia	sperm concentration under 20 million sperm per milliliter of ejaculate
Asthenospermia	less than 50% of the sperm are progressively motile, either fast or slow, or less than 25% are progressive and rapid
Teratozoospermia	less than 30% of the sperm have normal shapes
Oligoasthenoteratozoo-spermia (OAT)	Combination of all three defects
Azoospermia	no sperm in the ejaculate
Parvispermia	ejaculate under 2 milliliters in volume
Aspermia	no ejaculate

Facts and Figures

The penis
At night, men might experience three to five nocturnal erections during the REM phases of their sleep. During erection the blood volume is six to ten times the normal amount in the penis.

Testes

The tubules in the testes where the sperm are produced are tightly coiled – unravelled they would be 300 meters long.There have been studies on testicular volume and their variations among ethnic groups.

Sperm

During ejaculation the sperm are subjected to enormous shearing forces. It is estimated that the ejaculate leaves the male body at a speed of 17 kilometers per hour.

The ejaculate contains approximately 5 calories.

Sperm production and maturation is perhaps one of the most complex processes in the body and lasts about 90 days.

Per testicle, the body produces about 1,000 sperm per second.

Sperm swim approximately 4 millimeters per minute.

To cover 1 centimetre, an individual sperm has to swish its tail 800 times.

After ejaculation in the female vagina, some sperm reach the fallopian tubes in 30–60 minutes.

Often, sperm get there faster due to strong muscular contractions of the uterus that propel the sperm upwards.

In the acidic environment of the vagina sperm can only survive for a few hours; once they reach the vicinity of the cervix, their survival rate is extended to several days.

Further Information and Useful Addresses

Here is a list of books, brochures and Websites that you may wish to consult. At http://www.semenbook.com I am posting this type of information as well. This list is certainly not comprehensive.

TESTICULAR SELF EXAM

Descriptions of how to do it and why can be found at various sites such as:

Eisenhower Army Medical Center
Website:
http://www.ddeamc.amedd.army.mil/info_pat/takingcare/health_info/testicular.htm

MenWeb
Website: http://www.vix.com/menmag/testican.htm

SEX EDUCATION
US

The Sex Education Coalition
PO Box 341 751, Bethesda, MD 20827-1751
E-mail: Webmaster@SexEdCoalition.org
Web: http://www.sexedcoalition.org
An organization of educators, health care professionals, trainers and legislators "dedicated to providing information and supporting informed discussion concerning sexualty education."

Scarleteen
A detailed Website targeted at teens, although it may seem to have more information for girls than boys, certainly informative for both.
Web: http://www.scarleteen.com

UK

Sex Education Forum
National Children's Bureau, 8 Wakley Street, London EC1V 7QE, UK
Phone: 020 7843 6052/6056

E-mail: sexedforum@ncb.org.uk
Web: http://www.ncb.org.uk/sexed.htm

Brook Centres
Phone: 020 7284 6070
Web: http://www.brook.org.uk
E-Mail: information@brookcentres.org.uk

CONTRACEPTION
US

EngenderHealth
440 Ninth Avenue, New York, New York 10001, 212-561-8067
Web: http://www.engenderhealth.org
Formerly called the Association for Voluntary Surgical Contraception, this non-profit organization is dedicated to reproductive health around the world and in the US. The number 1-888-VASEC-4-U, with information in English and Spanish, is a vasectomy information line, toll-free, 24-hour, confidential giving you prerecorded information on vasectomy, and the Vasectomy Information Line can connect you with a provider at a health facility near you.

The World Health Organization has a booklet online called *Vasectomy: What Health Workers Need to Know*
http://www.who.int/rht/documents/FPP94-3/fpp943.htm
They also offer a film called *No Scalpel Vasectomy* for $10.

JAMA Women's Health
Contraception Information Center
Web: www.ama-assn.org/special/contra/support/ppfa/vasecto4.htm
Although the name seems to imply it is just for women, this site contains information of interest to men as well.

UK

International Planned Parenthood Federation
Regent College, Regent's Park, London NW1 4NS, UK
Phone: 020 7486 0741

AIDS
US

Centers for Disease Control
Division of HIV/AIDS Prevention
Web: http://www.cdc.gov/hiv/dhap.htm

CDC National AIDS hotline
Phone: 1-800-342-2437 (English) 1-800 344-7432 (Spanish)

Stop AIDS Project
2128 15th Street, San Francisco, CA 94114
Aids hotline 1-800-367-2437
Web: http://www.stopaids.org

UK

National AIDS Helpline
Phone: 0800 567 123

Terrence Higgins Trust
52–54 Grays Inn Road, London WC1X 8JU
Phone: National Helpline: 020 7242 1010: Counselling: 020 7835 1495
Aids Treatment Phoneline: 0845 947 0047
E-mail: info@tht.org.uk
Web: http://www.tht.org.uk

British Medical Association
Foundation for AIDS
Web: http://www.bmaids.demon.co.uk

UK National AIDS Trust
New City Cloisters, 188/196 Old Street, London, England, EC1V 9FR
Phone: 020 7814 6767
E-mail: info@nat.org.uk
Web: http://www.nat.org.uk

FERTILITY, INFERTILITY

The American Society for Reproductive Medicine
1209 Montgomery Highway, Birmingham, Alabama 35216-2809
Phone: 205-978-5000
Fax: 205-978-5005
E-mail: asrm@asrm.org
Web: http://www.asrm.org
The professional society devoted to reproductive medicine offers on their
Website the possibiity of finding a doctor, such as a reproductive endocrinol-
ogist, a reproductive surgeon or an assisted reproductive technology clinic.
The patients' homepage offers fact sheets on techniques as well as a state-
by-state run-down of the infertility insurance laws.

Resolve
The National Infertility Association
1310 Broadway, Somerville, MA 02144
E-mail: resolveinc.@aol.com
Web: http://www.resolve.org

HelpLine for infertility information 617-623-0744
Monday through Friday 9am to noon and 1pm–4pm Eastern time
Monday evenings from 5pm–9pm
Medical Call-in for members Wednesdays from 1pm–4pm 617-623-0744
Offers support groups to share experiences and information about medical treatments, dealing with family, friends, adoption, etc. Some are led by a mental health professional. In addition many regional chapters of RESOLVE offer meetings by members who wish to talk to each other. They are free for members and arranged informally as drop-in sessions. Has a quarterly newsletter for members.

InterNational Council on Infertility Information Dissemination (INCIID)
PO Box 6386, Arlington, Virginia 22206
Phone: 703-379-9178
Fax: 703.379-1593
E-mail: INCIIDinfo@inciid.org
Web: http://www.inciid.org
Informative website with links to lists of professionals, a detailed glossary of infertility terms and acronyms and a number of fact sheets. The site also offers bulletin boards moderated by a physician. Also has a table of the normal ranges for a semen analyis. http://www.inciid.org/semenanalysis.html

The American Infertility Association
666 Fifth Avenue, Suite 278, New York, NY 10103
Phone: 718-621-5083
E-mail: 718-621-5083
Web: http://www.americaninfertility.org
Offers a newsletter, a message board, links to treatment centers and physicians. A national non-profit organization dedicated to helping men and women make decisions on family building and reproductive health. They sponsor conferences and meetings on various subjects of interest to couples trying to conceive.

http://www.infertility-info.com
A Website with info about in-vitro fertilization. Sponsored by Zander Medical Supplies which provides instruments to clinics involved in assisted reproduction.

Ferti.Net
http://www.ferti.net
A Website funded by a grant from pharmaceutical company Serono offers general and specific information on many fertility issues, although it is not targeted in particular toward men.
Offers a list of patient associations and fertility centers throughout the world.

International Federation of Infertility Patient Associations
Charter House, Suite 8, 43 St. Leonards Road, Bexhill-on-Sea
East Sussex, TN40 1JA, UK
Phone: 01424 732361
Fax: 01424 7311858
E-mail: office@child.org.uk
Web: http://www.repromed.org.uk
An organization that offers international perspectives about infertility.

The National Fertility Association (ISSUE)
114 Lichfield Street, Walsall WS1 1SZ, UK
Phone: 01922 722 888
Web: http://www.issue.co.uk
E-mail: info@issue.co.uk
An organization that works "to improve comprehensively the quality and
delivery of infertility care." In addition to counselling on the phone and fact
sheets they also have a regular magazine and sponsor various events geared
toward involuntarily childless couples. Online they have a map through which
you can obtain services offered in your county of the UK.

National Infertility Support and Information Group
P.O. Box 131, Eglinton Street, Cork, Republic of Ireland
E-Mail: nisig@indigo.ie
A group of infertile couples who came together in 1996 offering information
to infertile couples.

Environmental Endocrine Hypothesis
Web: http://www.epa.gov/endocrine

International Program on Chemical Safety (WHO/UNEP/ILO)
Global State of the Science Assessment of endocrine disruptors
Web: http://endocrine.ei.jrc.it/gaed.html

Rachel's Environment & Health Weekly
An environmental weekly that focuses on the influence of toxic substances on
human health and the environment
Web: http://www.rachel.org/bulletin
Published by
Environmental Research Foundation, P.O. Box 5036, Annapolis, MD 21403
Fax: 410-263-8944
E-mail: info@rachel.org

OCCUPATIONAL HEALTH
US

National Institute for Occupational Safety and Health
The Effects of Workplace Hazards on Male Reproductive Health
A list of some substances which are known to damage male reproductive
health and a short explanation of the effects.
Web: www.cdc.gov/niosh/homepage.html
NIOSH Publication No. 96-132
Phone: 1-800-356 4674

UK

Directory of Sites in Occupational and Environmental Health
Web: http://www.agius.com/hew/links

British Occupational Health Strategy
Securing Health Together: An Occupational Health Strategy for England,
Scotland and Wales
Web: http://www.ohstrategy.net/strategy/strat_intro.htm

PROSTATE HEALTH AND DISEASE
US

American Cancer Society
Web: http://www.cancer.org
An information and resource-packed packed site run by the American Cancer
Society. In their cancer resource center, you can, for example, pick "prostate
cancer." There is information, and a free brochure about "Man to Man" an
education and support program dealing with prostate cancer for men and their
families which you can order online. Other brochures are: *Should I be Tested
for Prostate Cancer, Prostate Cancer Treatment Guidelines for Patients* and
Cancer de la Postrata Guias de tratamiento para los pacientes.
Phone number for general information: 1-800-ACS-2345. You can also place
inquiries via e-mail from their site.

Centers for Disease Control and Prevention (CDC)
Cancer Prevention and Control
4770 Buford Hwy., NE MS K64, Atlanta, GA 30341
Phone: 1-888-842-6355
Web: http://www.cdc.gov
E-mail: cancerinfo@cdc.gov
This governmental agency offers a PDF file on their website called: *Prostate
Cancer: Can We Reduce Deaths and Preserve Quality of Life?*

National Cancer Institute
Web: http://cancernet.nci.nih.gov/Cancer_Types/Prostrate_Cancer.shtml

A detailed brochure about prostate cancer, treatment options, support with links to other information offered by the National Cancer Institute.
Phone: 1-800-4-CANCER

MedlinePlus
Web: http://www.nlm.nih.gov/medlineplus/prostatecancer.html
This service of the National Library of Medicine has a Website listing news from various publications – popular press and governmental agencies – on prostate cancer.

http://www.prostate.com
A site dedicated to prostate cancer, with special sections about treatment options, and a "what to ask your doctor" section. Affiliated with pharmaceutical company TAP, the company that produces a drug used in the treatment of advanced prostate cancer.

http://www.prostatehealth.com
Informative site with general and specific information, about the prostate in general and about infections and diseases and their treatment.

UK

CancerBACUP
Web: http://cancerbacup.org.uk/info/prostate.htm
An informative site with links to various resources. They have booklets on various aspects of treatment, as well as many aspects not mentioned elsewhere such as "talking to children" or "your feelings."

CancerHelp UK
Web: http://www.cancerhelp.org.uk
An information service about cancer from the University of Birmingham with a site on prostate cancer.

SOME ORGANIZATIONS OF INTEREST

CaP Cure (The Association for the Cure of Cancer of the Prostate)
1250 4th Street, Santa Monica, CA 90401
Phone: 1-800-757-CURE or 310-458-2873
Web: http://www.capcure.org

National Prostate Cancer Coalition
1156 15th Street, NW, Washington, DC 20005
Phone: 202-463-9455
Web: http://www.4npcc.org

BOOKS

Helping the Stork: The Choices and Challenges of Donor Insemination
(Carol Frost)
One of several books on this particular aspect of reproductive medicine.

The Couple's Guide to Fertility
(Garry Berger, Marc Goldstein, Mark Fuerst)
An overview of infertility diagnoses and treatment options. Explanations of the tests and all the phases of assisted reproduction.

How to be a Successful Fertility Patient
(Peggy Robin)
Some call this book a "beginner's guide" for couples starting on the road to infertility diagnosis and treatment.

How to get Pregnant with the New Technology
(Sherman Silber)

Select Bibliography

American Society of Andrology. 1995. *Handbook of Andrology*. Lawrence, Kansas: Allen Press.

Birkhead, Tim. 2000. *Promiscuity*. London: Faber and Faber.

Blackwelder, Richard and Benjamin Shepherd. 1981. *The Diversity of Animal Reproduction*. Boca Raton, Florida: CRC Press, Inc.

Colborn, Theo, Dianne Dumanoski and John Peterson Myers. 1996. *Our Stolen Future*. New York: Dutton.

Corea, Gena. 1985. *Mother Machine*. New York: Harper & Row Publishers.

Diamond, Jed. 1997. *Male Menopause*. Naperville, Illinois: Sourcebooks, Inc.

Eberhard, William G. 1985. *Sexual Selection and Animal Genitalia*. Cambridge, Mass. and London: Harvard University Press.

Fisher, Helen. 1982. *The Sex Contract*. London: Palladin/Granada Books.

Gould, James L. and Carol Grant Gould. 1989. *Sexual Selection*. New York and Oxford: Scientific American Library, W.H. Freeman and Company.

Hargreave, T.B.. 1994. *Male Infertility*. New York: Heidelberg; Berlin: Springer-Verlag.

Hite, Shere. 1981. *The Hite Report on Male Sexuality*. New York: Ballantine Books.

Johnson, Martin and Barry Everitt. 1988. *Essential Reproduction*. Oxford: Blackwell Scientific Publications.

Knobil, Ernst and Jimmy D. Neill (eds). 1994. *The Physiology of Reproduction*. Vols 1 and 2. New York: Raven Press.

Laqueur, Thomas. 1990. *Making Sex. Body and Gender from the Greeks to Freud*. Cambridge, Mass. and London: Harvard University Press.

Morgentaler, Abraham. 1993. *The Male Body*. New York: Simon and Schuster.

National Research Council. 1999. *Report on Hormonally Active Agents in the Environment*. Washington, DC: National Academy Press,.

Nieschlag, E. and H.M. Behre (eds). 1997. *Andrology. Male Reproductive Health and Dysfunction*. New York, Heidelberg, Berlin: Springer-Verlag.

Pinto-Correia, Clara. 1997. *The Ovary of Eve*. Chicago: University of Chicago Press.

The RESOLVE Staff. 1999. *Resolving Infertility*. New York: HarperCollins.

Sirosky, Mike and Robert Krane (eds). 1990. *Manual of Urology*. Boston, London, Toronto: Little, Brown and Company.

Spallanzani, Lazarro. 1803. *Tracts on the Natural History of Animals and Vegetables*. Edinburgh. Printed for William Crech and Archd. Edinburgh: Constable.

Toppari, Jorma et al. 1995. *Miljoprojekt 290: Male Reproductive Health and Environmental Chemicals with Estrogenic Effects*. Ministry of Environment and Energy, Denmark, Danish Environmental Protection Agency.

Wendt, Herbert. 1965. *The Sex Life of Animals*. New York: Simon and Schuster.

Zilbergeld, Bernie. 1992. *The New Male Sexuality*. New York: Bantam Books.

Index

Compiled by Sue Carlton

NIOSH (National Institute for
      Occupational Safety and Health)
      127–8, 132, 133
nitroglycerin 48
normospermia 177
nutrition
      and gender determination 168
      see also diet

occupational health 122–34
      regulations 132
      safety 132–4
oligoasthenoazoospermia 177
oligospermia 177
Olsen, Jörn 126
opioids 121
oral sex 51, 63–4, 81
orchidometer 32
orgasm 5–20
      see also ejaculation
Origines 98
ovulation 59, 64, 116
oysters 48

Page, David 169–71, 172
Paley, Maggie 35
Palmer, Craig T. 68
pangenesis theory 99
parasympathetic nerves 8
Parker, Geoff 92
Parmenides 100
parthenogenesis 90
Partridge, Linda 171
parvispermia 177
paternity 94, 95–6, 175
Paulsen, C. Alvin 122, 136, 138
PCBs (polychlorinated biphenyls)
      139, 143
PDE-5 (phosphodiesterase type 5) 37
Pechenik, Jan 90
Pedanius Discorides 46
Penetrak score 112, 115–16
penis 30–1, 35, 177
      animals 95
      duplication 30
      and erection 7–8
      evolution of 16
      and fashion 35–6

implants 40
and performance 35–7, 39, 40
rings 49
size 16, 31, 39–40, 88
pentoxiphyllin 120, 121, 163
perivitelline space 62, 164
PESA (percutaneous epididymal sperm
      aspiration) 162
pesticides 122–3, 124–5, 140, 142
Peterson, Richard 144
phentolamine 38
pheromones 22, 89
phimosis 104
phthalates 131, 144
phytoestrogens 146–7
pineal gland 141
Pinker, Steven 17
Pinto-Correia, Clara 97, 102, 103
pituitary 74, 141
plastic surgery 39, 40
Plato 99
pollution 136, 137, 143
      see also chemicals; pesticides
polyamines 27
Porath, Avi 123
porn movies 57
positive selection 151
Potashnik, Gad 123
potency 15, 35–57
Potts, Malcolm 31
      see also impotence; infertility
'pre-cum' 9, 64, 74, 80
priapism 14, 97
Price, David 86
promiscuity 17, 85, 92, 93
Propping, Dirk 110
prostaglandins 27, 115, 163
prostate gland 14–15, 27, 32–3, 115,
      120, 173–4
prostatic secretory proteins 27
prostitutes 81
Pryor, Jon 157, 159
psychological factors
      in erection 7–8, 37
      in fertility 116–19, 160
pubococcygeus muscles (PCs) 13,
      36
Pyrzak, Roman 40, 160